THE CRITICAL RESPONSE
TO TOM WOLFE

THE CRITICAL RESPONSE
TO TOM WOLFE

EDITED BY
DOUG SHOMETTE

Critical Responses in Arts and Letters, Number 3
Cameron Northouse, Series Editor

Greenwood Press
Westport, Connecticut • London

Library of Congress Cataloging-in-Publication Data

The Critical response to Tom Wolfe / edited by Doug Shomette.
      p. cm.—(Critical responses in arts and letters, ISSN
1057-0993 ; no. 3)
  Includes bibliographical references and index.
  ISBN 0-313-27784-2 (alk. paper)
  1. Wolfe, Tom—Criticism and interpretation.   I. Shomette, Doug.
II. Series.
PS3573.0526Z64 1992
813'.52—dc20   92-8639

British Library Cataloguing in Publication Data is available.

Library of Congress Catalog Card Number: 92-8639
ISBN: 0-313-27784-2
ISSN: 1057-0993

First published in 1992

Greenwood Press, 88 Post Road West, Westport, CT 06881
An imprint of Greenwood Publishing Group, Inc.

Printed in the United States of America

The paper used in this book complies with the
Permanent Paper Standard issued by the National
Information Standards Organization (Z39.48-1984).

10 9 8 7 6 5 4 3 2 1

Copyright Acknowledgments

The editor and publisher gratefully acknowledge permission for use of the following
material:

Excerpts from *The Bonfire of the Vanities* by Tom Wolfe. Copyright © 1987 by Tom
Wolfe. Reprinted by permission of Farrar, Straus & Giroux, Inc. Also used by
permission of Jonathan Cape Ltd.

Excerpts from *The Electric Kool-Aid Acid Test* by Tom Wolfe. Copyright © 1968 by
Tom Wolfe. Reprinted by permission of Farrar, Straus & Giroux, Inc.

Every reasonable effort has been made to trace the owners of copyright material in
this book, but in some instances this has proven impossible. The editor and publisher
will be glad to receive information leading to more complete acknowledgments in
subsequent printings of the book and in the meantime extend their apologies for any
omissions.

Contents

Contents

The Right Stuff

From Bauhaus to Our House

Contents

Series Foreword

Critical Responses in Arts and Letters is designed to present a documentary history of highlights in the critical reception to the body of work of writers and artists and to individual works that are generally considered to be of major importance. The focus of each volume in this series is basically historical. The introductions to each volume are themselves brief histories of the critical response an author, artist, or individual work has received. This response is then further illustrated by reprinting a strong representation of the major critical reviews and articles which collectively have produced the author's, artist's, or work's critical reputation.

The scope of *Critical Responses in Arts and Letters* knows no chronological or geographical boundaries. Volumes under preparation include studies of individuals from around the world and in both contemporary and historical periods.

Each volume is the work of an individual editor, who surveys the entire body of criticism on a single author, artist, or work. The editor then selects the best material to depict the critical response received by an author or artist over his/her entire career. Documents produced by the author or artist may also be included when the editor finds that they are necessary to a full understanding of the materials at hand. In circumstances where previous, isolated volumes of criticism on a particular individual or work exist, the editor carefully selects material that better reflects the nature and directions of the critical response over time.

In addition to the introduction and the documentary section, the editor of each volume is free to solicit new essays on areas that may not have been adequately dealt with in previous criticism. Also, for volumes on living writers and artists, new interviews may be included, again at the discretion of the volume's editor. The volumes also provide a supplementary bibliography and are fully indexed.

While each volume in *Critical Responses to Arts and Letters* is unique, it is also hoped that in combination they form a useful, documentary history of the critical response to the arts, and one that can be easily and profitably employed by students and scholars.

Cameron Northouse

Introduction

In 1965, Americans were thinking about the Berlin Wall, Castro, LBJ and "The Great Society," civil rights, and Viet Nam. The younger generation was driving "muscle cars," eating burgers at drive-in restaurants with live carhops, and worrying about Viet Nam.

The time was right for a bright young journalist who could write about all of these things with a new vocabulary that would make us laugh, provide information about almost everything, and do so with little interference from his own point of view on the topics. Tom Wolfe did just that.

After receiving his Ph.D. from Yale, Wolfe went to work at the *Springfield Union* for $55 a week. From 1959 to 1962, he was a reporter for the *Washington Post*, where he won an award for his Cuban reporting. From there he went to the *New York Herald Tribune* (1962) as a reporter. In 1966 and 1967, he worked at the *Tribune* as a magazine writer. He became a contributing editor to *New York Magazine* in 1968, and continued in that position until 1976.

The Kandy-Kolored Tangerine-Flake Streamline Baby (1965) includes twenty-two pieces written in the previous fifteen months, about subjects as diverse as LBJ's wardrobe, and young breasts that point upward like anti-aircraft batteries. Each of the articles was previously published in magazines or newspapers of considerable circulation, but when assembled, they presented possibly the largest collection of hyphenated words, superfluous punctuation (and often total lack of punctuation), and repetitious usage of current sounds available in print. As a bonus, there were eighteen caricature drawings included, which received somewhat less praise from the critics than the text itself.

As one might expect, the volume of criticism regarding Tom Wolfe's work grew with his reputation. At the time *Kandy-Kolored* was published Wolfe was best known for his April, 1965, two-part article in *New York Magazine* (not in this collection) which presented William Shawn (*New Yorker*) as a "museum keeper" in charge of the magazine's staff. A few weeks earlier he had written an article on Norman Mailer's *An American Dream*. Dwight Macdonald commented on the article in the *Sunday Tribune's* Book Week: ". . . the only way Wolfe could explicate his low estimation of the novel was to jeer at the author's private life and personality - or rather his persona . . . ." [1]

This collection begins with an assessment of *The Kandy-Kolored Tangerine-Flake Streamline Baby* by Kurt Vonnegut, Jr., and it ends with Luther Carpenter's judgment on *The Bonfire of the Vanities*. Wolfe published eight other books in this time period. The reviews of *The Electric Kool-Aid Acid Test* (1965) and *The Pump House Gang* (1965) are together in one section simply because the almost simultaneous publication of these two books generated joint reviews. There is no coverage of *In Our Time*, because very little was written about this book of caricatures. However, comments about Wolfe's drawings are noted in several reviews, since the drawings are found in some of the other texts. One will find thirteen reviews of *The Painted Word* (1975) and *From Bauhaus to Our House* (1981) because there was considerable controversy centering on Wolfe's qualifications to discuss modern art and architecture.

Tom Wolfe was thirty-three years old when *Kandy-Kolored Tangerine-Flake Streamline Baby* was published in 1965. The book went into its fourth printing in one month and had sold over ten thousand copies by August, 1965. That same year Wolfe held a one-man exhibition of his drawings at Maynard Walker Gallery in New York .

Kurt Vonnegut, Jr. (*New York Times Book Review*, 27 June 1965)* said of Wolfe, "He is no shrinking violet, neither is he a gentleman. He is a superb reporter. . . . He is a dandy and a reverse snob." Vonnegut said Wolfe knows "stuff nobody else knows," and adds that if Wolfe had headed the Warren Commission, we might have caught a glimpse of our nation. Vonnegut tags Wolfe, as others do later, as one who casts himself as a teenager, and is "annoyed by almost anything an American grownup not associated with automobiles may say or do." In the final analysis though, Vonnegut describes *Kandy-Kolored* as an "Excellent book by a genius who will do anything to get attention."

Wolfe's use of language as a weapon and punctuation as an attention-grabber was not new. But it was what reviewers talked about. *Newsweek* (28 June 1965) called him a "tall, flop-haired, dandified wordpecker" (more Wolfeisms), who had made the biggest impact of any journalist in years. It is interesting to note that the *Newsweek* staff writer described *Kandy-Kolored* as "a book that will be a sharp pleasure to reread years from now, when it will bring back like a falcon in the sky of memory, a whole world that is currently jazzing its way somewhere or other." Macdonald disagreed with *Newsweek*, predicting the subjects would "prove only of ephemeral interest." [2] Twenty-six years is a reasonably good test of time, and to read this book now causes one to pay attention to Wolfe's observations.

Joseph Epstein[3] described Wolfe's penchant for the "American freakshow: the teenage netherworld, lower-class sports, and the poor rich." He termed Tom Wolfe's prose style "shotgun baroque," occasionally becoming "machine-gun rococo." Epstein seemed to think Wolfe would do better if he wrote about New York , instead of the "Noble Savages," working with what he knows best - status. There were eighteen drawings in *Kandy-Kolored*, some of which Epstein thought to be quite good.

Emile Capouya (*Saturday Review*, 31 July 1965) agreed with Vonnegut that Tom Wolfe knows a lot of stuff about a lot of things, and presents it with a vigor

---

*References to articles reprinted in this text are shown by parenthetical citations, while those not reprinted are cited with endnotes.

reminiscent of Henry Miller. But, he feels we are already "mired to the haunch in facile cultural junk, and may soon sink beneath the ooze. Mr. Capouya called Wolfe's drawings "mean-spirited" and expressed his sorrow at their being published to the world. Turning his back on Wolfe for his wealth of information, Capouya commented that life is too short to contemplate every piece of flotsam brought in by the tide, and Wolfe should tell us something interesting.

The final review of *Kandy-Kolored* in this collection treats Wolfe more kindly than some. William James Smith (*Commonweal* 17 September 1965), after reference to aphoria, ellipsis, neologism, and imitators of the Wolfe Man , credits him with a magical quality that marks his prose as distinctive, a unique voice with something special to say. Smith saluted Wolfe as Emerson did Whitman: "I greet you at the beginning of a great career."

How could one describe Wolfe based on the critical response to his first book? Perhaps looking back, one would say: an overaged teenager who liked to write about the younger generation with such enthusiasm that splashes of ink spilled all over the pages, but who was at his best when making sociological observations about New York and the status-seekers who lived there. What did Wolfe think about his talents at that time? In an interview with Elaine Dundy he responded:

What do you feel you have the greatest talent for?

Drawing.

The least talent for?

Creating stable ties with other people. [4]

Tom Wolfe packed his blue silk blazer and wide ties and headed for San Francisco to interview a phenomenon of the drug-crazed generation - Ken Kesey and his Merry Pranksters. Kesey was a well-known novelist (*One Flew Over the Cuckoo's Nest*) who traded his young career for an International school bus and a place in the woods, and began his movie of how one should go with the flow of life. When Wolfe went west he knew Kesey only as a fugitive from three marijuana arrests. Wolfe's non-judgmental account of this effort was published in three part form in *New York Magazine*, and in 1968, it appeared in book form as *The Electric Kool-Aid Acid Test*, so named after the Pranksters' concoction of kool-aid and LSD, served freely to the attendees of a party intended, ironically enough, to go beyond acid. *The Pump House Gang* was published at the same time in 1968, so the six reviews in this section are arranged chronologically, and some of them discuss both books.

A. Carl Bredahl's "An Explanation of Power: Tom Wolfe's Acid Test," is a wonderfully comprehensive discussion of *The Electric Kool-Aid Acid Test* (*Critique*, Winter 1981-82). Bredahl credits Wolfe with the ability to "look rather than to theorize" and this results in a "functioning narrative voice in an exciting new world." Robert Scholes[5] put Norman Mailer and Wolfe in a stylistic category of writers who reported the hysteria of the '60s, and in doing so became "hystorians." Mailer's *Armies of the Night* is described as engaged, political and ethical, while Wolfe's *Electric Kool-Aid* is detached, social and esthetic. Wolfe reports with a double perspective: simultaneously inside and outside the object of his investigation. Scholes saw this same double perspective present in *The Pump House Gang.*

Margaret Hentoff said the two-year-old articles revitalized in *The Pump House Gang* were "yesterday's cold potatoes." In reference to *The Electric Kool-Aid Acid Test*, she remarked, "There is about Kesey, about the cults and flummery of the Sixties, and about Tom Wolfe, a sense of run-down motion." [6]

Time defined Wolfe's outlook as partly cool, partly hysterical, but most of all, the most talked about and most imitated journalist of the sixties.[7] Yet, Wolfe is charged with distortion and the use of "electric wordmobiles" which make the reader wish for a rest-stop.

Nora Sayre (*New Statesman*, 9 May 1969) thought *The Electric Kool-Aid Acid Test* to be repetitious and sometimes boring, but with less frantic language than *Kandy-Kolored* and certainly the best account of tribal living to be published at that time.

Another review of both books by Peter Meinke (*Christian Century*, 4 December 1968) calls *Electric Kool-Aid* "an important account of an important event in American history; the rise of the psychedelic generation." But Meinke regards *The Pump House Gang* as an "only sporadically interesting collection of essays." Meinke credits Wolfe, as did other critics, with recognizing the seriousness and significance of the hippie movement, and his style of "involved journalism" as an appropriate reporting style.

Paul West (*Commonweal* 20 December 1968) described Wolfe's reporting style as one which makes the reader realize "how it feels to be" a contemporary type, as well as "how it ought to feel." This is done by intrusion into the psyche of his subjects, while using a hyped-up style of writing to report the intrusion.

The overall evaluation of Tom Wolfe as a writer after his first three books was still to regard him as the best "pop" reporter around - easy to recognize by his dandy wardrobe and his super-star reporting; a writer who was breaking down the barriers between fact and fiction.

Leonard Bernstein died in 1991. He will always be remembered as a marvelous conductor and New York socialite. Tom Wolfe captured Bernstein and several other "beautiful people" (Barbara Walters, Otto Preminger, and others) in the latter role, and the phrase "Radical Chic" came into being. On January 4, 1970, Bernstein and his wife held a gathering in their apartment to raise money for the Black Panther Defense Fund. Wolfe attended with notepad in hand, and in June of that year "Radical Chic" appeared in *New York Magazine*. Cries of racism and snottiness went up, just as they did when *The Bonfire of the Vanities* was published in 1987. Later in 1970, *Radical Chic and Mau-Mauing the Flak Catchers* was published, using the *New York* article, and another describing in detail how the ethnic groups dealt with ("mau-mauing") the government civil servants ("flak catchers") of the poverty programs. Five reviews of this book are reprinted here.

The comments about the earlier Tom Wolfe's dandy wardrobe continue to be made, but now one no longer reads about the excess punctuation, ellipses, and aphorisms. Instead, there are such terms as "brilliance," "neutrality," "cleverness," "journalistic virtue," and "best poetry we have around."

Melvin Maddocks (*Christian Science Monitor*, 27 November 1970) captions his review "Dandy in the Ghetto," based on a promotional picture of Wolfe in checked suit and homburg, pointed shoes, and rolled-up umbrella. It is Maddox who credited Wolfe with "obvious brilliance" and a passion to know, and added that "journalism is in no position to do without its super-aware skeptic in the checked suit."

Richard Freedman (*Book World*, 6 December 1970) thought Wolfe combined the talents of Thorstein Veblen, Beau Brummel and Lucrezia Borgia in reporting the Bernsteins' party. Wolfe is praised for his ability to spot the irony and to dissect the underlying history and assumptions of such gatherings as no one else could.

Timothy Foote (*Time*, 21 December 1970) and Phillip French (*New Statesman*, 17 September 1971) made such similar observations that it would seem Wolfe's image was changing from that of a "flop-haired dandy" to one of a serious and extremely capable journalist, or "parajournalist" as the critics preferred to call him.

But Jason Epstein, asserting that Wolfe was an uninvited guest to the Bernstein's apartment that evening, asked the question, "Then why, when he left Mrs. Bernstein's party, didn't Wolfe simply thank his hostess, leave a small check for the bail fund, and depart . . . . Why did Wolfe choose instead to offend his hostess further by writing his own frivolous account of her efforts?" [8]

Alicia Ostriker (*Partisan Review*, Summer 1971) rose to Wolfe's defense against the *New York Times* and *New York Review of Books* articles which criticized Wolfe for being uncaring and insulting. She felt that those reviewers missed the whole point of "Radical Chic" - that in reality the good intentions and high motivations about social and ethnic problems are mostly self-delusion. Wolfe's point is just that the political process is amusing and a joke. Ostriker gave *Radical Chic and Mau-Mauing the Flak Catchers* and *The Electric Kool-Aid Acid Test* very high marks.

It is certainly difficult for a writer to report with a double-perspective, as A. Carl Bredahl credits Wolfe with doing, and still interject no moral judgments. In an interview with Michael Dean (1970), Wolfe addressed involvement and values:

How involved are you with any of the people you write about?

What I really try to do is keep some kind of distance. Some people I'm obviously going to like more than others, some I can identify with more. But then when I'm writing I try to go into a kind of controlled trance. I've often got letters from people asking me if I took drugs while I write - well, I don't, but I can remember actually closing my eyes and trying to imagine myself back into a scene that I witnessed three or four days before. It's not like Wordsworth recollecting in tranquillity: I'm not very tranquil at that time.

You criticise Dwight Macdonald for bringing his values with him as a kind of extra payload.

I really feel that the urge to bring morality into writing at this phase of history has become the greatest cop-out among writers. It's so much easier to come to a subject with your mind made up, or to make a political point on behalf of some cause, than it is actually to going on a voyage of discovery. . . .[9]

The term "new journalism" was seen frequently in reviews of Tom Wolfe, Truman Capote, Gay Talese, and several others since 1962, when Talese published an article on Joe Louis in *Esquire*. But in 1973, Wolfe edited the book *New Journalism*, a collection of articles and essays which included prefaces, written by Wolfe, to each article, as well as three of his own pieces. The reaction of critics to this book ranged from praise to remarks that new journalism was nothing new, so why all the fuss. The death of the novel has been announced many times in many ways. Wolfe was not proclaiming its funeral, and most critics realized this. According to Wolfe, the new journalists were reacting to a type of writing in which the novelist did no research and presented characters with no background and no history - even put them in no particular time period. Wolfe credited the new journalists with creating journalism which reads like a novel - a non-fiction novel - such as Capote's *In Cold Blood*. Wolfe recognized some earlier writers with the same efforts (see "Legend on the License" for John Hersey's comments).

Tom Curran (*America*, 18 August 1973) said that although Wolfe gets carried away with the importance of new journalism, the point he (Wolfe) was trying to make was that this form of writing can no longer be ignored "in an artistic sense." Curran described new journalism as "a breath of fresh air on a summer day," and considered *New Journalism* to be an important step in American literature.

Alan Trachtenberg (*Partisan Review*, July 1974) took issue with many of Wolfe's claims about new journalism. Trachtenberg saw nothing new in writing narratives of firsthand experiences in contemporary society, and cites several early examples. He found the importance of the collection to lie in the relation of the compositions to America in the 1960s and in the absence of social purpose and passion for change. But his final analysis was that Wolfe's revolution "changes nothing, inverts nothing, in fact is after nothing but status."

Wolfe knew the book would not please everyone. Before the reviewers got started, he remarked to Michael Mok:

> In this book [*New Journalism*] I think I have managed to antagonize everybody in the fiction world - plus uncounted members of the nonfiction establishment, who at first I thought would be pleased. But when you pass the fail-safe point in the Alienation Derby, a few more vendettas, derks in the arras, don't really signify.[10]

At about that time, Wolfe viewed the launching of Apollo 17 and he committed to a book on the astronauts. However, *The Right Stuff* did not appear until 1979. In the meantime, the "Alienation Derby" got hotter, because *The Painted Word* was published in 1975. To quote Rosalind Krauss, it "hit the art world like a really bad, MSG-headache-producing, Chinese lunch."[11] Wolfe pointed his ballpoint pen at the "kings of Cultureberg," Clement Greenberg, Harold Rosenberg, and Leo Steinberg, scoring direct hits on all three.

Douglas Davis[12] said the book would not succeed because "Wolfe is no longer out there, mixing it up with his subject. . . . Instead he is sitting back. . .but not so far as to wrinkle his white linen suit. . .Tom Wolfe theorizing about subjects he doesn't understand. . .such as modern art." Douglas continued that *The Painted Word* would not serve anyone but Wolfe, and would not alter the political world of art. Wolfe's thesis was that because of its dependence on critics (Greenberg, et al), art would eventually end up as pure theory, and its stars would be the kings of Cultureberg.

Dennis Leder (*America*, 30 August 1975) wondered why Wolfe should expect to be able to stand in front of "thousands" of modern paintings and expect "crystal clarity," when Matisse himself did not believe this to be possible. Leder thought Wolfe to be eliminating any threat posed from artists by removing them from all privileged status. He regarded *The Painted Word* not as a "cause for celebration" (from the dustjacket), but "a sad wielding of power through cynicism."

It is difficult to imagine a reasonable analogy between Linda Lovelace's *Deep Throat* and Tom Wolfe's *The Painted Word*. Yet, Rosalind Krauss (*Partisan Review*, 42, 1975) found one. Lovelace replied repeatedly to reporters that *Deep Throat* was a "kind of goof." Wolfe, in an interview (unnamed by Krauss) replied in essence that he had no idea what should replace modern art, and did not care if anything did, because if it changed it might not be as funny. For Krauss, that meant the same as Lovelace's "It's kind of a goof." Wolfe's statement that there isn't any "experience" in modern art definitely was a "derk in Krauss' arras."

Albert Bergesen (University of Arizona) rose to Wolfe's defense. Bergesen said, "Obviously Tom Wolfe is on to something. But no one seems to acknowledge what he has seen." (*American Journal of Sociology*, January 1979). Forget all the rest, says Bergesen, Wolfe was really talking about two trends in modern art:

1. The gradual de-objectivation of art, and

2. The corresponding rise in the necessity of some kind of theory.

These two points form the basis for an interesting way of understanding change in artistic style and a way of conceptualizing art as a kind of linguistic code. Essentially, the gradual disappearance of the physical characteristics of art necessitates an increase in art theory, which functions properly in a restricted community (New York), but when that community disintegrates, the physical signs must return.

Bergesen was sufficiently intrigued with this application of the semantic equation to modern art that he wrote another lengthy article based on his review of *The Painted Word*, and proposed a general theory of style-change in art.[13] This paper uses the theory of sociolinguist Basil Bernstein (1975), who identified two kinds of linguistic codes, elaborated and restricted. These codes are applied to the notion that if art exists in a community of shared interests and assumptions, the visual structure of art (language) diminishes, with an understanding that the closed community understands what is being spoken about (theory). If that community becomes, or is in the beginning, loosely associated and widespread, the visual elements (language) must be more obvious and the theory decreases. The former situation is comparable to a restricted code, and the latter to an elaborated code of communication. This is an impressive expansion of Tom Wolfe's approach to modern art.

Tom Ricklefs reviewed *Mauve Gloves and Madmen, Clutter and Vine* (1976) and remarked that "Wolfe has significantly toned down the bizarre writing style that many readers found so annoying."[14] Wolfe is credited with "a really good eye." Ricklefs said, "Wolfe sees things that most people miss - some significant, some quite the opposite." Wolfe's obvious patriotism in several of these articles was also commented upon by this reviewer.

The general reaction of the reviewers to *Mauve Gloves and Madmen, Clutter and Vine* was that Wolfe had moved away from his earlier razzle-dazzle style of writing. The articles in this book were written from 1966 to 1976, and according to Paul Gray of *Time*, Wolfe was still asking the question, "What is going on here," but he was doing a better job of finding unsettling answers.[15] Much of Wolfe's attention was focused on fashion and how it explained the society of the period.

The article "The Truest Sport: Jousting with Sam and Charlie" drew the most praise from critics as a piece of excellent journalism. Wolfe described an aircraft carrier in the Gulf of Tonkin during the Viet Nam war as "a greasy skillet" heaving on the water. The jet airplanes were "bricks" that were not gliding toward the ship, but "falling" onto it with a smash.

In his review of *Mauve Gloves*, Nereo Condini (*The New Leader*, 31 January 1977) said Wolfe had matured, and he compared this book to a Chinese tapestry full of intricate details that one does not at first notice. Condini recognized that Wolfe's sympathy lay with the working class or "woks" as Wolfe calls them, and although he thought Wolfe wrote with the same earlier vitality, Condini said Wolfe made every effort to be "cool, firm and dignified."

Everette Dennis (*Journalism Quarterly*, Summer 1977) found *Mauve Gloves* to be bright and fun to read. He said of Wolfe, "Of course there is no one quite like

Wolfe writing in America today." Almost echoing Kurt Vonnegut, Jr.'s 1965 evaluation of Wolfe, Thomas Powers (*Commonweal*, 3 March 1978) described him as "gifted in almost heroic proportion," a writer with independence of mind and a manner that persuades people to tell him things. Dennis described Wolfe as "not a generous writer," because his choice of subjects was arbitrary and his treatment of them sometimes unkind.

Although America formally gained a foothold in the space race with Alan Shepard's flight on May 5, 1961, Tom Wolfe did not start his novel about the Mercury Project until 1972. *Rolling Stone* sent him to report on the last moon shot, and from that came four magazine articles. Wolfe told Adrianne Blue that he had planned to go through the whole program up to Skylab, but when he reached 450 pages, he realized it was time to quit.[16] *The Right Stuff* was published in 1979. During the writing of the book, Wolfe married Sheila Berger (1978), the art director of *Harper's Magazine*.

The "right stuff" was not defined by Wolfe, but always referred to as something that pilots understood. The early period of the Mercury Program was one of intense patriotism and it was undoubtedly an honor to be selected to the program. But in *The Right Stuff* Wolfe went below the surface (as he usually does) and talked about the astronauts getting drunk, cheating on their wives, and having a good time. None but John Glenn escaped untarnished. Wolfe presented Glenn as a straight-laced Presbyterian who drove an old car, jogged every day, and was constantly deriding the others for their behavior.

The reviews of this book were many, and the comments were generally favorable. Even NASA and the astronauts thought they had been treated fairly. Ted Morgan (*Saturday Review*, 15 September 1979) remarked that Wolfe had finally let go of marginal events and tackled the novel he had talked about for so long. Morgan said of *The Right Stuff*: "a splendid adventure story, an updating of *The Seven Samurai*, but it is more that. It shows our propensity to manufacture heroes, and, just as quickly, to forget them; it shows how a scientific program was exploited for political advantage. . . ."

Chuck Yeager stands out in Wolfe's book as a prime example of the right stuff, and there is clearly an admiration by Wolfe for those who fly test aircraft and for the fighter pilots who entered the space program. *Time* commented that behind Wolfe's inverted-pyramid style of journalism there lurked "the heart of a traditionalist" (*Time*, 24 September 1979).

The *Atlantic* (October 1979) thought *The Right Stuff* to be Tom Wolfe's best and most ambitious book. This staff reviewer commented that his ability to put together the strands of the story without minimizing the courage and virtuosity of its participants is a credit to his skill as a journalist. *The Illustrated London News* (January 1980) said of Mr. Wolfe:

" . . .*The Right Stuff* tells us more about the astronauts than we really want to know, there is no denying its excitement and readability. Mr. Wolfe writes like an American journalist, which he is, and paces his book with the skill of a novelist, which he also is."

Included in the section on *The Right Stuff* is a lengthy article by John Hersey *(Yale Review* Winter 1986). Although not specifically a review of this book, the article has been placed here because considerable attention is given to *The Right Stuff* in his discourse. The article is edited, with the author's permission, at the beginning of his discussion of Norman Mailer's *The Executioner's Song.* Hersey was most disturbed by the blurring of the line between fiction and non-fiction and journalism and fiction. He reminds us that in fiction the reader is aware of the legend on the license, "THIS WAS MADE UP." Journalism, on the other hand must follow the legend on the license that says: "NONE OF THIS WAS MADE UP."

Hersey traces the genesis of the problem to Truman Capote's description of *In Cold Blood* as a "nonfiction novel." He regards the notion that a work can be both fiction and journalism as a serious crime against the public. He also considers Doctorow's statement that there is no such thing as fiction and nonfiction - only narrative as equally troublesome. Hersey calls *The Right Stuff* a "tainted book." According to Hersey, Wolfe is a journalist who cannot resist improving on the material he finds; fabrication. Hersey refers back to Wolfe's two earlier articles on *The New Yorker* and William Shawn (see page one of this introduction) and calls the articles "a collage of shameless inventions." He refers to the coda of the second piece as "a perfect example of a Wolfe fantasy flying out of control."

Hersey said *The Right Stuff* has been accepted by those who know as a fairly accurate portrayal of the events of the space program. He credited Wolfe with becoming more careful and hard-working since the publication of *The New Journalism*, but blames the acceptance of this "tainted" book in part on the indifference of the public to the blurring between fiction and nonfiction. Wolfe is charged with failure to verify details that are verifiable, use of sweeping generalities, and abuse of point of view. In regard to point of view, Hersey remarked, "Each astronaut in turn becomes Tom Wolfe. Without even a little jiggle of lexical sex-change each astronaut's wife becomes Tom Wolfe. Right Stuffers who are alleged to speak nothing but Army Creole are garlanded with elegant tidbits like *esprit, joie de combat, mas alla!* The chimp talks pure Wolfe. God help us, God becomes Tom Wolfe and with His sweet ear chooses the Wolfeish 'ninny.'"

Mr. Hersey concedes that all of this makes for good entertainment and fun reading, but, according to Hersey, it leaves serious doubts about the veracity of such a mode of journalism which really should be addressing the important issues of the space program.

The Painted Word (1975) was highly controversial when published, but in terms of volume and tone of the criticism written about it, the book must rank second to *From Bauhaus to Our House.* I have included eight articles about *Bauhaus*, that being only a small sampling of what was written. A list of some of the titles of articles shown here gives a hint of the attitudes toward the book: "Tom Wolfe vs. Modern Architecture," "White Gods and Cringing Natives: Tom Wolfe's look at architecture gets its half right," "Prose and Prejudice," "Wolfe vs. the Bauhaus Boys." Many of the critics of *The Painted Word* said that Wolfe is writing on a subject about which he knew nothing, and that he was trying to force his own likes and dislikes on his readers. This accusation was very similar to the one made by Wolfe against architects. According to Wolfe, the concrete and glass walls were forced upon the Americans by the Europeans and we surrendered without a fight. The targets were Walter Gropius, Mies van der Rohe, and Le Corbusier.

Hilton Kramer (*Saturday Review*, October 1981) said the purpose of *From Bauhaus to Our House* was "to explain how we came to be hoodwinked into accepting an art that, in Wolfe's opinion, we actually loathe." He noted that although Wolfe asserted the Museum of Modern Art was founded to subvert our native culture, it showed Burchfield and Hopper before it showed Picasso or Matisse. Kramer called Wolfe's writing hyperventilated and hyperbolic and found somewhat repugnant the notion that all of modernist culture must represent "some sort of alien threat to the purity of American life."

Time (19 October 1981) said Wolfe brought nothing new to the argument about modernist architecture except, perhaps, "a kind of supercilious rancor and a free-floating hostility toward the intelligentsia," and that there was nothing to indicate he cared anything about architecture.

Several reviewers of Wolfe's earlier books said he knew everything about everything. Garry Wills was of the opposite opinion when he said, "The list of things Mr. Wolfe does not know is astonishing." Wills thought Wolfe was expressing native prejudices in implying that a ban should have been set up on Bauhaus architects and Wills reminded us that American style was a result of cross-fertilization and not isolation.

The reviews by *Newsweek* and *Book World* were not favorable to Wolfe. *Newsweek* said the book "falls as flat, in the end, as the tower of Pruitt-Igoe. Thud!"[17] Benjamin Forgey (*Book World*, 15 November 1981) said the book contributed nothing to the discussion about architecture.

Crediting Wolfe with a "splendidly witty little book," Peter Grier (*Christian Science Monitor*, 14 December 1981) said Wolfe had found himself a splendid target in modernist architecture, as exemplified by the glass boxes of the World Trade Center and Boston's Prudential Center. However, Grier pointed out not all modernist architecture is deserving of Wolfe's criticism. He cited Hancock Tower as an example. He said Wolfe himself had entered a postmodern phase by changing from his decorative prose of the past to cleaner and more functional sentences.

Blake Morrison (*Times Literary Supplement*, 26 March 1982) wrote that there was nothing new in Wolfe's complaints against architecture. Morrison commented that most of them had been expressed more succinctly by others such as Frank Lloyd Wright and even Dickens. He pointed out some obvious mistakes in the book, such as "Simon Rodia" instead of Simone Rodilla, and concluded that *From Bauhaus to Our House* was "too philistine to carry any real conviction."

From Bauhaus to Our House was described by Stephen Mullin (*New Statesman*, 26 March 1982) as "132 small, wide-margined, double-spaced large typeface pages," for which some historical knowledge would have been useful. He added that some of the observations Wolfe made on elite architecture in the United States could have been developed into a few good essays but, according to Mullin, Wolfe stopped short and tried to pull the book together in other less productive ways. He suggested that Wolfe could profit by a reading of Reyner Banham's two classic books on modernist architecture.

A review of three books which gave very different interpretations of American architecture was made by Richard Guy Wilson (*Virginia Quarterly Review*, Summer 1982). Wilson reviewed Whiffen and Koepper's *American Architecture, 1607-1976*, *The End of the Road:Vanishing Highway Architecture in America* by John Margolies, and Wolfe's *From Bauhaus to our House*. He remarked that Wolfe could be easily dismissed because he is not an architect, a serious critic of architecture, or an historian. Wilson implied that this would be unfair because Wolfe is "an intelligent man with impeccable scholarly credentials, and there is a certain truth, though overstated, in what he says." He concludes that the primary weakness of Wolfe's book is that he offers no solutions to the problems he presents.

According to Albert Bergesen (*American Journal of Sociology*, November 1989) Wolfe consistently raises interesting questions in his works. We may not always like his answers or his questions but they are important. He thought perhaps Wolfe should be called a "social archaeologist" because of the way he always uncovers things we may not want surfaced. Bergesen remarked that for one who is not regarded as a real critic of architecture, Wolfe always stirs up a lot of reaction and perhaps we should pay attention to his presentation of the ironies and contradictions of life.

The Purple Decades: A Reader (1982) was a collection of many of Wolfe's pieces written over the prior twenty years. It included those articles that formed the basis for all of his previously published books. There are four reviews reprinted here by critics not presented earlier in the text.

Commenting on Wolfe's use of punctuation and repetition, Paul Fussell (*New York Times Book Review*, 10 October 1982) thought his method of writing to be appropriate for the material presented. He said Wolfe is able "to notice real merit and quick to respond to real emotional need, even among his urban jerks and hoods." Fussell was less complimentary about the drawings in the book. He thought them to be amateurish and that they should be confined to the company of friends.

According to Jonathan Yardley (*Book World*, 7 November 1982) Wolfe is a master observer of detail and style and his books are interesting and funny, as long as he avoids his "Look at Me" style. He regarded Wolfe as somewhat ineffective when talking about art and architecture because of his use of ridicule and bile. Yet, Yardley called Wolfe "a model of restraint" and a terrific reporter and thought it regrettable that in the introduction Joe David Bellamy had tried to elevate Wolfe into the domain of literature.

A joint review by T. Patrick Hill (*America*, 12 March 1983) of Peter Carroll's *It Seemed Like Nothing Happened: The Tragedy and Promise of America in the*

1970s and *The Purple Decades: A Reader* gave Wolfe high marks for the collection of essays. He thought the drawings from *In Our Time* were "quite brilliant." Hill, unlike Yardley, thought the introduction by Joe David Bellamy was an asset to the book.

Contrary to the opinion of some reviewers, Esmond Wright (*Contemporary Review*, 242, 1983) said Wolfe can write well on architecture, pop art, and space-age-pilots, all with brilliant fashion. He called Wolfe "The Poet Laureaute of Pop" and regarded *The Purple Decades* as "amusing, ironic and splendid reading."

The Bonfire of the Vanities (1987) was originally written in twenty-plus installments for *Rolling Stone*. Wolfe planned the book around Thackeray's *Vanity Fair*. The title was based on a 15th-century religious reformer named Girolamo Savonarola who periodically traveled to Venice and had the people bring their items of vanity and place them in a bonfire. Savanarola himself was eventually thrown into a bonfire.[18] The protagonist of *Bonfire* was a writer in the *Rolling Stone* series. When Wolfe rewrote the articles into his first novel, the writer became Sherman McCoy, vain and adulterous bond trader from Wall Street. There are eight reviews reprinted here, which I consider to be those most representative of the very large amount of criticism published.

To prepare for *The Bonfire of the Vanities*, Wolfe spent considerable time in the Bronx courthouse and in the streets and subways of New York . The old maxim "truth is stranger than fiction" has always rung true for Wolfe, who believes that almost anything extraordinary or bizarre in life can or will be found to occur and outstrip fiction. Although *Bonfire* is fiction, it is also journalistic reporting in the Wolfe/Dickens style. *Bonfire* stayed on the best-seller list for over a year and is still selling well in the bookstores. In 1989, it was released as a movie directed by Brian DePalma and starring Tom Hanks as Sherman McCoy, but did not fare as well as the movie version of *The Right Stuff*.

In the words of Christopher Buckley (*Wall Street Journal*, 29 October 1987), *Bonfire* is a "damned fat slab of a book, herniating to pick up but impossible to put down." He considered the book to be as good as *Radical Chic and Mau-Mauing the Flak Catchers* and *The Right Stuff*, and remarks that Wolfe is getting better and better. Buckley describes the cast as "post-modern Dickensian" and teeming with the vain, greedy, soulless, and self-important. He has difficulty accepting Wolfe's preoccupation with architecture and clothing and finds the ending problematic. Buckley would have preferred to have the characters thrown into a bonfire instead of getting away, as often happens in real life.

A review by David Lehman and Ray Sawhill said *Bonfire* is grounded in solid reporting and close observation, but they expected Wolfe to receive criticism for his handling of racial hostility.[19] His portrayal of the Bronx as a war zone and his depiction of "the Pimp Roll" are certainly inflammatory. Lehman and Sawhill said Wolfe may have written the right book for the wrong reason. Instead of a book about "urban naturalism," Wolfe produced a book that is "a lot more fun than gritty realism," and one that is in keeping with his high-spirited style.

According to James Andrews (*Christian Science Monitor*, 3 November 1987), Wolfe is in splendid control of his first novel. Andrews credits Wolfe with not drawing political conclusions in a novel that may shake the readers trust in the criminal justice system, and one in which the stinging humor "betrays the underlying anger of the idealist . . ."

"Wolfe is a master of social satire; he is in fact, the best of his generation," wrote R.Z. Sheppard.[20] Andrews expected Wolfe to be criticized for creating characters so much like New York's social figures, but concedes that this is part of what has made Wolfe's journalism vital.

Thomas Mallon (*American Spectator*, January 1988) thought that in *The Bonfire of the Vanities* there was some conflict between Wolfe the novelist and Wolfe the essayist in the first part of the book. Mallon said things moved too slowly until after the first third of the book when Wolfe's talents began to cooperate with each other and the descriptive writing disclosed the ability of a novelist who really "knows things." He compared Wolfe to Balzac, calling him a maximalist who uses all his talents to stage his scenes without making moral judgments on any of those characters.

The comments of David Benedictus (*Punch*, 12 February 1988) and George Black (*New Statesman*, 12 February 1988) are strikingly similar, pointing out that Wolfe sets up Sherman McCoy time and again to be knocked down, humiliatingly, by the events of life. Black goes on to say that Wolfe's "linguistic fireworks" become tiresome, making them "one-line jokes." He criticizes as unfair Wolfe's depiction of the underclass in the Bronx and compares *Bonfire* to Charles Bronson's *Death Wish* series.

Peter Quinn's assessment of *Bonfire* resembles Thomas Mallon's (*America*, 2 April 1988). Quinn said Wolfe put together an array of old stereotypes to create this novel and it had difficulty getting off the ground - "The engines backfire with a black exhaust of exclamation points . . ." But then, according to Quinn, the book takes flight and levels its sights on everyone and everything. However, the plot "runs out of propellant" and Wolfe resorts to speech patterns to keep the story moving. Quinn concluded that Wolfe has not created a great novel, but has brought his readers some memorable details and truths of New York.

Luther Carpenter (*Dissent*, Summer 1988) considered *The Bonfire of the Vanities* to be a book about "The Ruling Class," or as Wolfe put it, the "Masters of the Universe." Carpenter's review is a comparison of Lewis Lapham's *Money and Class in America: Notes and Observations on Our Civil Religion* and Wolfe's *The Bonfire of the Vanities*. His conclusion is that neither are really worth reading and calls the claim that Wolfe is "the foremost chronicler" to be pure hype. Carpenter asserts that Wolfe grossly exaggerates the power of certain activist groups and the willingness of the wealthy to give each other up to please those groups.

In 1989, Tom Wolfe published an essay in Esquire, entitled "Stalking the Billion-Footed Beast: A Literary Manifesto for the New Social Novel." Although the essay may appear to be a justification for *The Bonfire of the Vanities*," it is really a summation of Wolfe's attitude toward the novel and the novelist. Wolfe writes about the big issues and wants to make the reader aware of the problems that exist. What he is saying to the novelist is to get out and learn the world - have a social consciousness. Much of what is said here was said in *The New Journalism*, but there is more. Referring often to the realistic novel of the nineteenth-century, he argues that a novel should demonstrate the effects of society on the individual. Taking Lionel Trilling's statement that the nineteenth-century novel produced great characters because they were a portrayal of the "class traits modified by personality," Wolfe then substitutes status for class. This, of course, is the underlying element in all of Wolfe's work.

In *The Bonfire of the Vanities*, Wolfe portrays the city and how the city acts upon the individual. Following the style of Zola, Wolfe went into the city, beyond his personal experience, and reported what he found in the form of fiction. This is how Wolfe has always written. He believes that the reporting of the *petits faits vrais* does more than create verisimilitude; they are the things that build a good novel. The small truths and facts may not please everyone, but they are the essence of Tom Wolfe's work.

Notes

[1] Macdonald, Dwight. "Parajournalism, or Tom Wolfe & His Magic Writing Machine." *New York Review of Books* 5 (26 August 1965), 5.

[2] Ibid.

[3] Epstein, Joseph. "Rococo and Roll." *New Republic* 153 (24 July 1965), 27-29.

[4] "Tom Wolfe . . . But Exactly, Yes!" *Vogue*, 147 (15 April 1966), 152.

[5] Scholes, Robert. "Double Perspective on Hysteria." *Saturday Review* 51 (24 August 1968), 37.

[6] Hentoff, Margaret. "Dr. Pop." *New York Review of Books* 11 (22 August 1968), 30-31.

[7] "Tom Wolfe and His Electric Wordmobiles." *Time* 92 (6 September 1968), 98-99.

[8] Epstein, Jason. "Journal du Voyeur." *New York Review of Books* 15 (17 December 1970), 4.

[9] Dean, Michael. "Pop Writer of the Period - Tom Wolfe Talks to Michael Dean." *Listener* 83 (19 February 1970), 250-51.August 1968), 37.

[10] Mok, Michael. "PW Interviews: Tom Wolfe." *Publishers Weekly* 203 (18 June 1973), 34-35.

[11] Krauss, Rosalind. " Café Criticism." *Partisan Review* 42 (1975), 629-33.

[12] Davis, Douglas. "Crying Wolfe." *Newsweek* 85 (9 June 1975), 88.

[13] Bergesen, Albert. "The Semantic Equation: A Theory of the Social Origins of Art Styles." *Sociological Theory* (1984). Ed. Collins, R.

[14] Ricklefs, Roger. *Wall Street Journal* 188 (22 December 1976), 8.

[15] Davis, Douglas. "Crying Wolfe." *Newsweek* 85 (9 June 1975), 88.

[16] Blue, Adrianne. *Washington Post Book World* (9 September 1979), 9.

[17] Davis, Douglas. "Wolfe Vs. the Bauhaus Boys." *Newsweek* 98 (2 November 1981), 106.

[18] Gilder, Joshua. *Saturday Review* (8 April 1981), 40-44.

[19] Lehman, David and Ray Sawhill. "An Unleashed Wolfe." *Newsweek* 110 (26 October 1987) 84-85.

[20] Sheppard, R.Z. "The Haves and the Have-Mores." *Time* 130 (9 November 1987), 101, 104.

Chronology

1930	Thomas Kennerly, Jr.: born in Richmond, Va. on March 2, 1930; Son of Thomas Kennerly and Helen (Hughes) Wolfe.
1947	Graduated from St. Christopher's School, Richmond, Va.
1951	Graduated from Washington and Lee University, B.A. (cum laude).
1951-57	Attended Yale University, graduating with Ph.D in American Studies. Cofounder of the literary quarterly *Shenandoah*.
1956-59	Worked as a reporter for the *Springfield Union*, Springfield, Mass.
1961	Won Washington Newspaper Guild awards for foreign news reporting and for humor.
1962-66	Worked as city reporter for *New York Herald Tribune* and writer for *New York* Sunday Magazine (now the *New York* magazine), New York , N.Y.
1965	*The Kandy-Kolored Tangerine-Flake Streamline Baby* published in 1965. One-man showing of his drawings at Maynard Walker Gallery, New York in November 1965.
1966-67	Began as a writer for the *New York World Journal Tribune*, New York , N.Y.
1968	Became contributing editor to *New York Magazine*. *The Pump House Gang* and *The Electric Kool-Aid Acid Test* published .
1970	Publication of *Radical Chic & Mau-Mauing the Flak Catchers*. Awarded Society of Magazine Writers award for excellence.
1971	D.F.A., Minneapolis College of Art.
1973	Awarded Frank Luther Mott research award.
1974	One-man showing of his drawings at the Tunnel Gallery, New York , N.Y.
1975	*The Painted Word* published.
1976	*Mauve Gloves & Madmen, Clutter & Vine* published.

1977   Became contributing editor to *Esquire*. Named Virginia Lau-
            reate for literature.

1978   Married Sheila Berger, art director of *Harper's Magazine* on
            May 27, 1978. Became contributing artist to *Harper's Maga-
            zine*.

1979   Publication of *The Right Stuff*.

1980   *In Our Time* published. Daughter, Alexandra Kennerly, born.
            Received American Book Award for *The Right Stuff*; Harold
            D. Vursell Memorial Award for excellence in literature;
            American Institute of Arts and letters. Received Columbia
            Journalism Award. Citation for art history from National
            Sculpture Society.

1981   *From Bauhaus to Our House* published.

1983   L.H.D. from Virginia Commonwealth University.

1984   L.H.D. from Southampton College. Received John Dos Pas-
            sos Award.

1985   Birth of son, Thomas Wolfe.

1986   Received Gary Melchers Medal; Benjamin Pierce Cheney
            Medal from Eastern Washington University; Washington
            Irving Medal for literary excellence from the Nicholas Society.

1987   *The Bonfire of the Vanities* published.

1989   "Stalking the Billion-Footed Beast: A Literary Manifesto for
            the New Social Novel" published.

The Kandy-Kolored Tangerine-Flake Streamline Baby

Infarcted! Tabescent!

Kurt Vonnegut, Jr.

From *The New York Times Book Review*, (27 June 1965), 8, 38. © Kurt Vonnegut, Jr. Reprinted by permission of Kurt Vonnegut, Jr.

Note to the people of Medicine Hat, Alberta, who may not know it: Tom Wolfe is the most exciting - or, at least, the most jangling - journalist to appear in some time. He writes mainly for Esquire and The Herald Tribune. Everybody talks about him. He is no shrinking violet, neither is he a gentleman. He *is* a superb reporter who hates the East and the looks of old people. He is a dandy and a reverse snob.

The temptation when reviewing his works, of course, is to imitate him cunningly. Holy animals! Sebaceous sleepers! Oxymorons and serpentae carminsel! Tabescent! Infarcted! Stretchpants netherworld! Schlock! A parodist might get the words right, but never the bitchy melody. Interestingly: the most tender piece in this collection depends upon a poem by Kipling for depth, and has G. Huntington Hartford 2d, for its hero.

The frightful, public gastrectomies Wolfe performed on Norman Mailer and William Shawn so recently, without anesthetics or rubber gloves, came too late for this book, will no doubt lead off the next. What we have here are 22 of the exercises that built up to such violence: Cassius Clay, Las Vegas, Baby Jane Holzer, automobile collisions as entertainment, automobile racing, nannies, Howard Rushmore, weak, dumb rich divorcees, fag interior decorators, and on and on. Fame has come quickly for Wolfe, and should have, for his is almost certainly the fastest brilliant writer around. Will he blow up? Some people must hope so. Who is a complete stranger to envy and *Schadenfreud?*

Wolfe comes on like a barbarian (as Mark Twain did), like a sixth Beatle (Murray the K being the fifth), but he is entitled to call himself " Wolfe" if he wants to. He has a Ph.D. in American studies from Yale, and he knows everything. He knows all the stuff that Arthur Schlesinger Jr., knows, keeps picking up brand new, ultracontemporary stuff that nobody else knows, and arrives at zonky conclusions couched in scholarly terms. I wish he had headed the Warren Commission. We might then have caught a glimpse of our nation.

He is also loaded with facile junk, as all personal journalists have to be - otherwise, how can they write so amusingly and fast? His language is admired, but a Wolfe chrestomathy would drive one nuts with repetitions, with glissandi and tin drummings that don't help much. The words "tabescent" and "infarcted" appear again and again, and, upon investigation, turn out to be not especially useful or piquant. Young breasts ("Mary Poppins") point upward again and again like antiaircraft batteries, and women's eyes are very often like decals, and transistors are very often plugged into skulls, and feet very often wear winkle-picker shoes.

Then again, America is like that. And maybe the only sort of person who can tell us the truth about it any more is a Ph.D. who barks and struts himself like Murray the K, the most offensive of all disk jockeys, while feeding us information. Advanced persons in religion have been trying this approach for some time. Who can complain if journalists follow?

Wolfe is a Southerner, and he is electric with regional animosity. He feels buoyant in the South and Far West, speaks loathingly of "the big amoeba god of Anglo-European sophistication that gets you in the East." There are some unpleasant pen-and-ink drawings he has made of New York in this book, by the way, caricatured Ashcan School. No girls are pretty, and nobody smiles. (The best drawing by Wolfe that I have seen so far is a Beerbohmish self-portrait that appeared in *Newsweek* a while back. The artist sees himself as an Edwardian fop with a plow-boy's three-by-eight wrists, and loves him.) His particular delight in his New York pieces is to show up the art establishment and its friends as intellectual and moral tinhorns. It's a mild, funny little establishment to bop so hard. For all Wolfe's passion and exclamation points, most of the people he bops are essentially harmless. They make the mistake of having something like an amusing time in New York, or of being no longer young anywhere. There is a built-in joke, I know: Wolfe has proved to himself and to some others that teen-age culture is becoming dominant, so he casts himself as a teen-ager, a razzer of old folks and old establishments, the better to describe that culture. But he sounds hooked to me.

I have been trying to identify the key that winds up his mainspring so tight, and, though he is 33 years of age, I think this might be it: He is, like all teen-agers, terribly embarrassed or annoyed by almost anything an American grown-up not associated with automobiles may wear or say or do.

Verdict: Excellent book by a genius who will do anything to get attention.

The Wolfe-Man

It comes as something of a shock to realize that all of the 22 pieces collected in Tom Wolfe's first book were written in the last fifteen months. In this time he has made, with these articles from *The New York Herald Tribune* and *Esquire*, the biggest impact of any new journalist in years. His recent pieces anatomizing *The New Yorker* polarized the impactees into haters and lovers, and no doubt the brash 34-year-old from Virginia will hear plenty from the former as they come galumphing out of the reviewers' bull pens with horns lowered.

Pow! as Wolfe would say. But the tall, flop-haired, dandified wordpecker will survive the impact. He is full of raw talent, and it is that which has touched so many nerves and created such anger and delight. And he did it with the most primitive of writer's weapons - language. About fifteen months ago, Wolfe, who had been doing what he calls "totem pieces" (talented but square journalism), had a breakthrough. He had written a "totem" story about a custom-car show at the New York Coliseum, but, he writes, "I knew I had another story all the time . . . the real story . . . but I didn't know what to do with it. It was outside the system of ideas I was used to working with . . ."

Well, in one all-night session with his typewriter, his radio blasting rock 'n roll, Wolfe made his breakthrough - who knows how? His cells simply rearranged themselves like Lon Chaney Jr., and he became the Wolfe-man.

Thus metamorphosed, Wolfe found himself outside the "system of ideas," and he began to roam the byways and breezeways of America's pop, bop and slop culture, armed with a new arsenal of language. This book contains most of his trophies from that foray. Almost all are brilliant, baroque mirrors in which Wolfe has caught with his anamorphic prose the grotesque, spastic juggernaut of metropolitan life, or half-life. In a clatter of detail, a char-broil of savory observation, he captures mad memorabilia, from the neon jungle of Las Vegas (where he saw a mental patient making slot-machine motions with her hand) to the ecstatic carnage of auto-demolition derbies, to the St. Vitus's dance of teen-age pop-rock culture, to the world of disk jockeys with its "comic hysteria" and "symbolic logic," to the glossy, silk-slithering sadness of New York's empty young divorcees.

Wolfe instinctively knows that a word is a supercharged mixture of sense and mind stimuli, and he is not afraid to act on that instinct. He hits as many senses as he can with his linguistic bazooka, knowing that the mind will be waiting for the final impact like the scoreboard on a pinball machine. He describes "cable-

knit mohair sweaters, the ones that fluff out like a cat by a project heating duct."
Or an airplane stewardess: "Under a lifebuoy blue skirt, her fireproof legs are
clicking out of her Pinki-Kini-Panty Fantasy."
Great Hairy Ned: He uses comedy as an analytical weapon, as when he relates
how LBJ decided to get his clothes custom-made: "Mr. Johnson was campaign-
ing with John Kennedy in 1960, and he had to look at Kennedy's clothes and then
at his own clothes, and then he must have said to himself, in his winning, pastoral
way, Great Hairy Ned on the mountaintop, my clothes look like Iron Boy overalls. Yus, muh cluths look luk Irun Bouy uvverulls . . ."

Partly, Wolfe belongs to the old noble breed of poet-journalists, like Ben
Hecht, and partly he belongs to a new breed of supereducated hip sensibilities
like Jonathan Miller and Terry Southern, who see the complete human comedy
in everything from a hair-do to a holocaust. Vulgar? A bit. Sentimental? A tic.
But this is the nature of journalism, with its crackling short waves transmitting
the living moment. Wolfe's best pieces have that "fictive music" of the poet or
novelist, as in his piece on Junior Johnson, the ex-moonshiner and stock-car
champion, which has the mythic lilt and velocity of a story by Faulkner, or his
poignantly hilarious little narrative of a Madison Avenue man confronting his
beatnik son and friends in their squalid, shrewd unreachability. This is a book
that will be a sharp pleasure to reread years from now, when it will bring back,
like a falcon in the sky of memory, a whole world that is currently jetting and
jazzing its way somewhere or other. By that time, Wolfe may have buffeted himself through the journalism barrier and produced the work of art that is obviously jouncing around in those kaleidoscopic cells of his.

True Facts and Artifacts

Emile Capouya

From *Saturday Review* 48 (31 July, 1965), 23-24. Reprinted with permission of OMNI INTERNATIONAL, LTD.

Mr. TOM WOLFE has taken as his device the time-honored "Nothing human is alien to me." There is a complete intellectual program implicit in the tag, and at bottom it is generous and democratic. The difficulty is that some human activities are important and others are not, and the ethic of *nihil humanum* does not by itself help us to distinguish which is which.

Now, Mr Wolfe is startlingly well informed. His collection of articles and sketches is a tissue of facts - true facts, as the children say - that I am sure I never suspected. The book also abounds in information that I had managed to misplace. On reflection, it appears to me that Mr. Wolfe's facts are addressed to the country cousins, rural and urban, among us, persons in whom the praiseworthy faculty of wonder is swelled beyond all praise to a promiscuous curiosity about the cultural junk of the modern world. We are already mired to the haunch in the rich gumbo of facts. It is only a matter of time before we sink beneath the ooze and our place knows us no more.

So it is hard to be grateful for Mr. Wolfe's industrious researchs, his eye for the characteristic triviality, and his very lively style. That style, incidentally, sometimes reaches a pitch of colloquial vigor that suggest the influence of no less a master than Henry Miller. But mostly it is exclamatory and goes on too long. To my mind, the best piece in the book is the article on stock-car racing, Southern style, that treats the drivers as the heroes of a new *Iliad;* but the epic is about twice as long as the subject can support.

For the rest, those things that Dante advises us to look upon and pass by, Mr. Wolfe elects to linger over and celebrate - in a curious tone that wavers between sarcastic paean and sentimental complaint. Things the Jonathan should be ashamed to know the names of, Thoreau said of the type of artifact that take up so much of Mr. Wolfe's attention: customized - wonderful word - cars, hyperthyroid disc jockeys, corporate airplanes, publisher of petty slander, stretch pants, girls-of-the-year, winklepicker boots, Wall Street Beau Brummels, Las Vegas architecture. The reasons, in short, that led Mr. Auden to picture the Sphinx as "turning a vast behind on shrill America," and the reasons for which we Americans ought to present our smaller bottoms to the same scene.

An album of drawings is included in the book. If the reader misses the point made so voluminously by Mr. Wolfe's prose - and I confess I missed it for a time - the drawings will repair that misfortune. They are astonishingly mean-spirited. As a gloss on the text, they lend another surprising face to Mr. Wolfe's linguistic exuberance. What I took at first to be energy and ebullience now look more like bilious compulsiveness and a neural itch. I am sorry that Mr. Wolfe made the drawings, and having made them, published them to the world.

Mr. Wolfe's mission is to inform and when he mentions Hotchkiss he adds a parenthetical identification: a private school for boys. Now the great unwashed can breathe easy; they are less likely to eat their soup with a fork when the talk turns on prepschools. As it happens, I'm a city boy myself, familiar with the name of Hotchkiss and that of many another school I never attended. But, with the best will in the world, it is hard to be proud of that kind of information. It seems not to have occurred to Mr. Wolfe that this is a very short life, and our time is valuable. The kind of knowledge that makes us knowing is not of much use in our losing fight to get through life with some smack of honor. The notion that every fact, activity, mannerism, detail of costume is significant, is a vulgar error. It is not so much that you cannot be a saint if you give your soul to contemplating whatever flotsam the tide brings in. Thus preoccupied, you cannot be a sensible man, paying reasonable attention to the shape of your life. And why should a talented writer compose dithy-rambs on the manners and morals of the underbred, undereducated, and underevolved? One wants to say to Mr. Wolfe: you're so clever, you can talk so well, tell us something interesting.

The Kandy-Kolored Tangerine-Flake Streamline Baby

Reviewed by William James Smith

From *Commonweal* 82 (17 September, 1965), 670-72. Reprinted with the permission of *Commonweal Magazine*. © *Commonweal*.

Tom Wolfe is undoubtedly the most parodied writer alive. Two years ago he was unknown and today those who are not mocking him are doing their level best to emulate him. Magazine editors are currently flooded with Zonk! articles written, putatively, in the manner of Wolfe and, by common account, uniformly impossible

Oddly enough, none of his parodists - and even fewer of his emulators - has successfully captured much of the flavor of Wolfe. On the surface he seems a natural for the imitator - exclamation, aporia, ellipsis, neologism, the esoteric vocabulary, the wild comparison - but somehow the imitations never quite come off. They go too far or they do not go far enough. Most of them, in the fashion of parodies, go too far, but even the best fall short in a peculiar way - they miss the spark of personality that is more arresting than the funny punctuation. Wolfe has it, that magical quality that marks prose as distinctively one's own. It is not just a matter of tricks.

Few writers, even among the best, find a unique voice, and among journalists the tendency is to blend into the common, shirt-sleeve, hat-on-the-head anonymity. Wolfe, at the age of thirty-two, realized that he had something special to say and his praised and excoriated style, I suspect, was merely an outgrowth of the realization. His comic, horrified, and yet affectionate, observations on the American scene have been appearing prolifically in *Esquire* and in the New York *Herald Tribune's* Sunday magazine. This first book of Wolfe's is a collection of those articles and, unlike most journalistic collections, it is lively ready from start to finish.

Wolfe has a Ph.D. in "American Studies" from Yale, and whatever American Studies may be the phrase sums up his journalistic interest - Las Vegas, demolition auto racing, Murray the K, the Peppermint Lounge, Kustom Kars, Baby Jane Holzer, Cassius Clay, wayout beatniks, the art gallery gang, all the bizarre outposts of our culture and its strange spokesmen. Wolfe has a vision, not an original one perhaps but chillingly and wonderfully documented, of all these weird forces taking over, closing in, not with any particular vicious impulse but moving with a relentless, half-conscious, force - "arising, slippy, shiny, electric - Super Scuba - man! - out of the vinyl deeps."

Wolfe is appalled and at the same time fascinated by the sight of Super Scuba-man advancing on us. What he has done is simply to describe the brave new world of the "unconscious avant-garde" who are shaping our future, but he has described this world with a vividness and accuracy that makes it something more than real. There is something of Super Scuba-man about Wolfe himself. His voice is one that has never been heard before and the intonations are the kind that raise the hair on the back of your neck.

All new voices in writing are apt to be reprobated. The reasons for this are implicit in human nature. Tom Wolfe's *New Yorker* articles are an interesting case in point. These two articles (they do not, unfortunately, appear in the present collection) came out in the *Herald Tribune's* Sunday magazine and attacked the denizens of the *New Yorker* magazine offices as "tiny giants" and "living mummies." The *New Yorker* itself shuddered visibly, Eustace Tilley dropped his monocle, and all tiny giants from J. D. Salinger on down wrote white-lipped letters of scorn to the *Herald Tribune*. The furor was an interesting one. An upstart crow had shaken the plumage of the great bald eagle with apparently little effort or compunction - or even bad temper. The reaction was not so much to what Wolfe said as to the way he said it. Wolfe could be "heard," he had a voice that made you listen, he had a style. And it was a style that was no more a mere collection of gimmicks than, say Whitman's was a hundred years ago when he raised a similarly raucous and self-confident voice.

It is a little early to predict whether Wolfe will develop into a major literary figure. It is hard, in fact, to decide whether what he is saying is significant in itself because of his assertiveness and his talent. Usually, however, when we say of a first book that it is promising we mean that it displays a little something that may mature, develop, establish a personality. Wolfe is promising in quite a different way. He's got, the something that puts you in the running, makes you a contender. It's not a question of his finding his feet, he's on them, or of finding his voice or his attitudes, he's found them. It is, in fact, merely a question of production, and whether he can slip effectively over into the fictional works that he has promised. But no one who has read "The Last American Hero is Junior Johnson. Yes!" or any of the other pieces, indeed, in this collection can say that the possibility is not a hopeful one. It is too bad there is not on the current scene an Emerson to say, as he did to Whitman: "I greet you at the beginning of a great career."

I'll say it. Why not? I greet you at the beginning of a great career. Yes!

The Electric Kool-Aid
Acid Test
The Pump House Gang

Go With the Flow

Nora Sayre

From *The New Statesman* 77 (9 May, 1969), 660. Reprinted with the permission of New Statesman and Society and the author.

Read amongst the brisk spring sounds of clubs on skulls, the shouts of pain, the explosions of small bombs in schools and libraries, and the hoarse faculty voices in debate, while the sun glints off policemen's plastic visors and riot helmets, this book seems almost as remote as a Bloomsbury memoir; and the Beats seem merely Victorian. In 1959, Herbert Gold wrote:

> The hipster doesn't want to feel; he keeps cool. He has checked up on experience and found it wanting; he . . . doesn't dig overmuch. He carries books without reading them, drives cars without going anyplace, goes places without arriving anywhere . . . He . . . is the delinquent with no zest, the gang follower with no love of the gang . . . the youngster with undescended passions . . .

Who has lately seen such a creature? True, one meets a few querulous relics in New York, but their fatigue is no longer distinguished: being tired and numb is no longer a style in sensitivity. Those I've encountered have complained about the noise, the heat, the cold, the food, the young, and the air-conditioning; they said that everyone talks too quickly, and implied that anger and enthusiasm have 'gone too far'. Carping as creakily as suburban parents, few seemed to have kept pace with Allen Ginsberg - a decade-vaulter who will probably bury us all.

As for the hippies, 1967 seems very long ago. Lots of love beads got broken and rolled out of reach; horoscopes went awry; the moon betrayed Virgo; murders and diseases and threatening drug merchants drove them from their neighbourhoods. The Diggers, who ran a Free Store in NY, were raided by toughs and beaten up several times, even though they kept no cash and boasted that nothing could be stolen because everything was free. Finally, they painted out 'Love' on their window, painted in 'Hate', and departed. Many others have left the cities for rural communes.

There are still urban hippies, of course. But they are mainly the instant variety who arrived yesterday from Westchester, or the more militant brand, who further Revolution by undressing during political speeches, or prevent speakers from finishing a sentence. Recently, Norman Mailer was stopped from describing his platform as a mayoral candidate by a few of The Crazies. In passing, he remarked that he wouldn't call cops pigs, 'because they've got balls.' 'No, they haven't, Norman.' 'Yes they have.' 'Stop bullshitting!' 'I'm not bullshitting!' 'Yes you are.' 'He is!' 'I'm not!' 'You are!' We were never allowed to hear his fantasies of uniting the Left and the Right.

At any rate, one misses the hippies of two summers past. The Beats were never funny - was that their tragedy? - but many hippies were nimble comedians. Endearingly uncool, beguiled and beguiling, they were ready to be zonked by the gritty world; acid detonated all those feelings that the hipsters shunned. Many hippies were delightful company, amazingly gentle and generous. Hence some of *The Acid Test* makes one rather nostalgic - as for those brief, flowery fables about levitating the Pentagon.

In 1964, Ken Kesey, a gifted novelist who had dropped into acid, assembled his Merry Pranksters for a 'group adventure'. They toured the US in their psychedelic bus, inviting others to 'Go with the flow!' In their California commune, even the woods were wired for sound, and the trees were striped with orange and green Day-Glo paint. Wolfe credits the Pranksters with the beginning of the whole Haight-Ashbury scene, the invention of mixed media, and even the style of psychedelic posters. Meanwhile, moments of horror tunnelled through the gaiety. Amidst all the footloose clowning and the snuggling atmosphere of group therapy (such excitement but little apparent sex), there was the toppling paranoia that often accompanies LSD, plus scenarios of madness. Naturally, Wolfe makes no moral comments; he simply unleashes the Prankster 'allegory of life' in all its defiance, naivete, and freaking charm. Parts of the book are as repetitious and exhausting as some LSD trips must be; there are even blurts of boredom. But it does take you 'into the pudding', as they say, by bestowing the experience of 'the Group Mind', where even reading or smoking are selfish acts, since they gratify only one person and give nothing to the group. The concept of life as a movie, where you pull others into your script, or play into theirs, is skillfully filmed in prose. Those who can't read Wolfe's other books may well enjoy this one. Minus much of the frantic filigree of his earlier language, this is the best account of tribal living that's yet appeared.

Throughout this celebration of technology, one irony is hard to miss: the Pranksters and their heirs have been so dependent on *equipment*. Projectors, tapes, slides, cameras, loudspeakers, microphones and amplifiers were essential to their spiritual or sensory liberation. Yet, last month, when the Living Theatre troupe disrupted a symposium at NY's Theatre for Ideas, the uproar included screams of fury against technology. Last fall, as a TV network tried to record an anti-war speech, the equipment broke down each time the speaker patiently repeated that 'technology is looting the universe.' Perhaps machinery is tolerable only when you play with it; for some, it may be a desperately necessary toy.

Thus, *The Acid Test* freezes and preserves the immediate past. And if history is hurtling, it's pleasing to remember that Emerson anticipated one key maxim; in an 1841 essay, he wrote, 'But do your thing and I shall know you.'

The Pump House Gang

Reviewed by Louis M. Savary

From *America* 119 (31 August, 1968), 136-37. Reprinted with permission of America Press, Inc., 106 W. 56th Street, New York, NY 10019. © 1968, 1973, 1975, 1977, 1983 and 1988. All rights reserved.

In his first collection of essays on American pop culture, *The Kandy-Kolored Tangerine-Flake Streamline Baby* (1965), Tom Wolfe started a new way of writing about the contemporary scene that was violent, free-wheeling, unexpected and delightfully exhausting to read. *The Pump House Gang* is another collection of Wolfe's essays, written in the same explosively unbelievable kind of language as *Kandy-Kolored*.

The theme of *Kandy-Kolored* is social style. The theme of *The Pump House Gang* is social status. For the past three years Wolfe did much cultural field work among the noble savages in America and England - from Carol Doda, the girl who "blew up her breasts with emulsified silicone, the main ingredient in Silly Putty," to Hugh Hefner, the patriarch of the playboys, "now a recluse." In his research Wolfe uncovered a strange phenomenon in contemporary life: a conscious turning away from conventional social standards among young people. This phenomenon Wolfe calls "starting your own league." Except for the die-hards living according to the book of etiquette in the sclerotic social worlds of New York and London (read the chapters "Bob and Spike" and "The Mid-Atlantic Man"), the youth culture is filled with people ready to start their own leagues.

They write their own rules, too. Surfers, motorcyclists, hippies, the boys with long hair, are all creating for themselves new styles of life. If society won't invite them into the party, the new-leaguers thumb their collective nose at society. They take with them their money, machines and muscle, they split from society and put together their own hermetically sealed little worlds. If the new-leaguers lacked status in the old neighborhood, they see to it that they are kings in the new spheres they create. Whoever invents the rules creates the "statusphere," as Wolfe calls it. Southern California, for example, is a hothouse of nestling statuspheres.

It's not that no one has ever created his own league before. "Robin Hood did it," says Wolfe. "Spades, homosexuals, artists and street gangs have done it. All sorts of outlaws, by necessity or choice." Today, however, the surprise is that many young Americans who are not outlaws or outcasts are doing the same thing.

For example, the Pump House Gang (also title of chapter one) is a group of boys and girls who banded together to "start their own league" based on the expertise of surfing. Surfing was their statusphere. Living in garages, they looked much like a street gang. In reality, they came from homes in a high-class beach community in California. "They had very little sense of resentment toward their parents or 'society' and weren't rebels." They just felt they were "being prodded into adulthood on somebody else's terms." So they split off from society. They live as though youth were a permanent state, or at least they try to preserve the mental atmosphere of the surfer as they move into adulthood. Wolfe gives one example of how they exist outside society. "They attended the Watts riot," he said, "as if it were the Rose Bowl game in Pasadena." They came to watch.

The crucial point of *The Pump House Gang* lies below the surface of Wolfe's scintillating stories: there is a significant minority of young people in America and England who are not status-seekers but status-creators. As the influence of this trend grows - like Carol Doda's breasts - all eyes turn and each one wonders: where is the reality? Are the people who are starting their own leagues destroying society or giving it a healthy shot of vitamin B-12? Wolfe makes no moral judgment on the case. He merely reports the facts as a good journalist should.

Interestingly enough, however, Wolfe's own writing style is so different from anyone else's that one wonders if he is also starting his own league.

Involved Journalism

Peter Meinke

From *The Christian Century* 135 (4 December, 1968), 1545. Copyright © Peter Meinke. Reprinted by permission of author.

+SPLAT--the Serious Reviewer smashes the Wolfe book with its Day-Glo Acidy cover on the library steps of Columbia University, jumps on it scruush black--shoelaces snapping like crazy. . . .But that's a mistake. Because Tom Wolfe's *The Electric Kool-Aid Acid Test* is an important account of an important event in American history; the rise of the psychedelic generation.

On the other hand, *The Pump House Gang*, published simultaneously, is an only sporadically interesting collection of essays dealing with surfers, Marshall McLuhan, Hugh Hefner, silicone-inflated topless go-go girl Carol Doda and other "now" manifestations. Its jazzy style simply gets in the way.

In *The Electric. . .*Wolfe recognizes the essential seriousness of the LSD-hippie movement. Arising like a new religion from the midst of a middle class that "has screened out the richest and most wondrous part of its experience" (McLuhan), this movement soon split into a passive-contemplative Zen-oriented wing (Leary and the east) and an active-bacchanalian electronic-rock wing (novelist Ken Kesey and the west coast). The book traces Kesey's "discovery" of LSD, the gathering of his disciples (the Merry Pranksters), the wild proselytizing bus trip across the U.S., the acid tests, the bust, Kesey's escape to Mexico, his return and capture, and his announcement of the "new step" beyond LSD.

Kesey emerges from these pages as a sort of pop Christ or Captain Moses, though he tries to avoid any such identification: "We're not on the Christ Trip. That's been done, and it doesn't work. You prove your point, and then you have 2,000 years of wars. We know where that trip goes." But through sheer force of personality he performs "miracles" such as taming and controlling groups as disparate as a Unitarian conference and the infamous Hell's Angels. Kesey and the Pranksters are in many ways the other side of the Puritan coin. While not anti-Puritan, they are opposite to the Puritans in some ways (being permissive, gay, sexually amoral) but strikingly similar in others; a feeling of being chosen, a shared experience (here, LSD), a sense of mission, a belief that everything in everybody's life is significant (what the Puritans called "special providences," the Pranksters call "synchronizations").

In some ways, too, Kesey represents the apotheosis of the Romantic revolution; the emphasis on feeling and spontaneity (intensified by drugs), the cult of the individual pushed to anarchy, the attempt to render repressions harmless by getting them "out front," the insistence that everything is holy and love is the answer.

Wolfe's style of "involved journalism" (though, like Mailer's in *The Steps of the Pentagon*, sometimes irritating) is the proper medium for this hippie epic. The LSD experience, as Kesey recognizes, is already somewhat passé, and this is probably good; but America will never be the same again. Future generations will read *The Electric*. . .to find out what kind of trip it was.

The Pump House Gang
The Electric Kool-Aid Acid Test

Reviewed by Paul West

From *Commonweal* 134 (20 December, 1968), 413-16. Reprinted with permission of author. © Paul West, c/o Elaine Markson Agency.

For the last half-dozen years this nearly visionary journalist has been remedying an omission perpetuated by Ernest Hemingway, who chose not to write about American popular culture and so deprived himself of abundant materials as well as denying intelligent American readers something they very much needed, and needed, it is now clear, not in the form of fiction. The something is How It Feels To Be this or that contemporary type; not just observation of but penetration into the type's distinctive performances and even into his head. Eyeball invasiveness; the metamorphoses of an inquisitively adaptable personality; the wire-tapping of a thousand individual psyches - call Wolfe's own freewheeling performance what we will - it tells Americans what is going on in such a way that, even at two removes, they feel part of the scene.

Not only that: Wolfe's own dizzymaking pyrotechnical prose style - curt and lissom, hepped-up and contemplative - somehow tells them, even as they are reading him, *how it ought to feel* while they are reading him. Here comes the prose, ogling and cavorting and aflash with gorgeous virtuosity, and with it a built-in response-kit; Wolfe *possesses* not only his surfers, fine art tycoons, London dollies, Carol Doda the tit-dancer and Hugh Hefner and Marshall McLuhan and Ken Kesey and the lumpen-dandies and the Mid-Atlantic Man; he takes possession of the reader too, so that you either go along with him in everything, letting him dictate the timbre and duration of even every buzz or whoop emitted (such is the acoustical insistence of his style), or you close the book at once, feeling like Mike Hammer after he inch-lifted the lid of that heavy box containing a nuclear reactor (or whatever it was). Slam shut or (what Wolfe wants) open up wide: woo death with Hemingway or go beyond acid with Ken Kesey. In motive at least, I keep thinking, Wolfe and Hemingway are pretty close.

They both seek to draw us out of ourselves (fitting us out with selves if we haven't any), Hemingway into delicious pastorals and exotic townscapes, Wolfe into the off-beat, the far-out, the extreme, the super, the It: faultless surfing, the biggest known bust, the Hardest Head in the West. They both - as well as specializing in deeds done and poses struck according to a code that is also a life-style - deal in ecstasy in the strict sense of the word, which is 'displacement,' always from where you are to where the weather is somehow more relishable, say the track at Auteil, or to where there is the most putrid-smelling red tide ever, off Manzanillo, say. Except that, really, the weather at Auteil and the red tide off Manzanillo aren't half as potent where they are as in prose reports which, in effect, mobilize us to appreciate any weather and any red tide and quicken us into a best awareness way short of millennary ecstatics but coming under ecstatics all the same, one end manifest in "this *ecstatic* in Columbus, Tom Reiser - the stud who rides a motorcycle with an automobile engine in it - Liberation!" (Wolfe) or (Hemingway) "Linart, the great Belgian champion that they called 'the Sioux' for his profile, dropping his head to suck up cherry brandy. . . when he needed it toward the end as he increased his savage speed."

That's the secular end. At the other (less finite) there is what happens when Ken Kesey and his Merry Pranksters serve up a punch laced with LSD or when a man and a woman together under a blanket feel the earth move. Secular or mystagogical, this is the ecstatics of getting out of oneself, of maximizing each moment, of burning with a gem - or laser-like flame, of not being confined to (although starting from and maybe regaining) prosaic social rigmaroles, of realizing we have one life only, and without guarantees, and had therefore better do all we want while there is time. Neither Hemingway's tight-lipped sensuousness nor Wolfe's nearspastic intensity amounts to anything new; but what is a welcome change is Wolfe's scope over Hemingway's. The one is choosy, omitting most of the trash of living, whereas the other - well, he wolfs it and so achieves an ecumenical lyricism that never reads like a falsification of the world we live in. An open mind denies entry to nothing and can thus arrive at - what *The Kandy-Kolored Tangerine-Flake Streamline Baby* (national), *The Pump House Gang* (international) and *The Electric Kool-Aid Acid Test* (supranational) add up to - the "Scene individable, or Poem unlimited" of which Polonius incongruously speaks to Hamlet.

Free to observe or ignore the rules (syntactical, punctuational, typographical), Wolfe might easily have gone wrong, manufacturing trendy-looking but tame portraits of orthodox and unorthodox status-seekers. But, as well as logging all the pertinent trivia and working hard his ear for goofy chatter and his lepidopterist's eye for any kandy-kolored tangerine-flake on the move, he also indulges in the gutsy, volcanic joy of writing to please himself. The fun he's had doing it comes through almost always. "What struck me throughout America and England," he writes in one of his less hectic moments, "was that so many people have found such novel ways of . . . *enjoying,* extending their egos way out on the best terms available, namely, their own." Tom Wolfe too, of course; and it's his own epicurean ego that gives all those other egos that extra patina. For what he does is meta-reporting, something creative and inventive which releases a lot of his own static into their ecstatics and demonstrates time and again that imagination (which he has in abundance) wasn't given us to make copies with but to help us masticate actuality (as if the universe were lazily at play with itself).

Of course, what it *is*: Tom Wolfe himself plainly reports that white Norway rats behave consistently under consistent experimental conditions, and there is no place for imagination in describing that behavior. But for what lies "beyond acid" - what Wolfe approaches via "the mental atmosphere or subjective reality" as distinct from the Pranksters' apparatus and paraphernalia, patois and garb - there is only imagination to use and only imagination to judge by (and judging here is guessing, for imagination do not police other imaginations). So you just have to take or leave drug-induced encounters with "the Management" and Kesey's won discovery that "It's kind of hard, playing cello on a hypodermic needle and using a petrified bat as a bow." The individable scene that includes the convention of counting 1-2-3 also includes imagination the unknown 'x,' not to mention quasars and DNA, curved space and Leptis Magna, voodoo and LSD, dollars and dinars and drachmas, belly-dancers and computers, $6.95 semi-spread Pima-cotton shirts and No-Kloresto egg substitute and Telstar and *Queen Magazine . . . . Endless.* I don't know what 'making sense of' it all could possibly mean, but I think there are many ways of marveling at it, among which Tom Wolfe's is one of the most exciting because, primarily, he knows how much of it there is, as well as knowing how little of it many of our most esteemed writers - novelists as well as essayists and playwrights and documentary men - confront. In addition to having that Huck Finn thing, the sense of adventure, he also has - never mind what the girl called Doris Delay said was missing from his appearance - the colors of the world in his coloratura poem unlimited.

The Electric Kool-Aid Acid Test

Reviewed by Rollene W. Saal

From *Saturday Review* 22 (27 December, 1969), 32. Reprinted with permission of OMNI INTERNATIONAL, LTD.

Mention all the names you want - Andy Warhol, Viva, the Rolling Stones, Roman Polanski, Claes Oldenbourg, anybody - Tom Wolfe is still the Pop of the Superpop-journalist, hyped-up super-star reporter, refiner and inventor of words when need be.

He's easy to recognize. Here it is winter and he's wearing a white suit, white vest, white shoes, a blue and green plaid shirt, a flowered pocket handkerchief. His blond hair is straight and Beatle-length. He's a superb dandy in the Wildean tradition-and it's all camp and a Wolfe put-on. "Actually, I discovered clothes are a harmless form of aggression," he says. "I once had a white suit made for summer, but it was too hot so I wore it one winter day. It annoyed people and they stopped me to tell me about it. After all, it was only a suit. 'Gee,' I thought, 'this is nice.' " For Wolfe it opened a whole world, a way of being at once aggressive and harmless.

"My tailor is a Hungarian and a painter. He can sew any fantasy I happen to think up."

But Wolfe is not merely a sartorial gadfly. He likes it when his books and articles produce abrasions. In *The Electric Kool-Aid Acid Test*, a piece of brilliantly explosive reportage on novelist Ken Kesey and the whole mad psychedelic world of California's Merry Pranksters, Wolfe's own feelings about the drug-happy hippie scene never intrude for a moment. The articles in *The Pump House Gang* soar like butterflies and sting like bees, whether he's writing on Hugh Hefner, Marshall McLuhan, or Carol (the Silicone Girl) Doda. "I hate easy emotional appeal. I like it if I can inspire equal and passionate reactions." His Hefner piece aroused a variety of responses. Says Wolfe: "I heard Hefner himself liked it, while others told me, 'Boy, you really got him.' " As in most of Wolfe's pieces, the subject is treated as a representative of a certain life style; here it's the quintessential dropout. "I'm always happy if people can't figure out my attitude," Wolfe declares. "I'm much more interested in making the reader understand what Caligula is doing than to make him hate him."

Those Wolfe tries to make us understand range from surfers, motorcyclists, and hippies to advertising men and political activists. "So many people today lead extraordinary lives. They have more money and more free time so that they can carve out their own life styles. The New Left, for instance. I think it's at least

70 per cent life style with its own semi-military dress, hair styles, vocabulary - and only 30 per cent political passion."

Until he was out of his teens Wolfe, who grew up in Richmond, Virginia, wanted passionately to be a baseball pitcher. He was even scouted by the N.Y. Giants. "I showed him sliders, screwballs, curves. The scout said, 'All you really need is the high hard one.' " So Wolfe went to Washington and Lee University, and then took a Ph.D. in American Studies at Yale.

What Wolfe does is to break down barriers between fact and fiction. "If you do enough reporting, you can get the accents, the scenes, the dialogue, like fiction. Part of my technique I call the 'controlled trance.' I close my eyes and try to put myself into the situation that I'm writing about. If I'm really into it things start happening, phrases and thoughts begin to spin off."

"Lots of people have asked if I use drugs when I write. Of course I don't. That would alter your ability for self-criticism. Sometimes, like after I wrote *Kool-Aid*, I end up in a strange mental state, really drained."

Maybe even Pop-eyed.

An Exploration of Power: Tom Wolfe's Acid Test

A. Carl Bredahl

From *Critique* 23 (Winter 1981-82), 67-84. Reprinted with permission of the author.

Tom Wolfe's writing is the most vivid instance of the role of the journalist in American literature, a role that has played a major part in the development of twentieth-century prose fiction. Unfortunately, even Wolfe himself, in his introduction to *The New Journalism* (1973), seems content to distinguish his world from that of novelists and to look for influences in "examples of non-fiction by reporters." He does not but should recognize that the novel is a dynamic form, that in the hands of such journalists as Stephen Crane and Ernest Hemingway the novel has developed in this century just as it did in the eighteenth and nineteenth centuries. In the novel the imagination has always been concerned with particulars of a real world, a concern that has only been intensified in the twentieth century. The journalist, once depicted in literature as a mere observer and thus only a second-rate artist, has begun to emerge as an individual especially well trained to work with particulars. Certainly, all journalists are not suddenly novelists, but in several significant ways New Journalism is actually in the mainstream of the developing American novel. In *Green Hills of Africa* Hemingway speaks of pushing the art of writing prose fiction much further than it has ever gone before, and Wolfe, like Hemingway, is a writer who, instead of reporting facts for the consumption of a mass intelligence, is consuming the physical world as a part of his own nutriment. Like Hemingway eating the kudu's liver, this new journalist is thriving on the materials available to him: Ken Kesey and the Pranksters.

The Electric Kool-Aid Acid Test (1968) is a story of individuals keenly sensitive to the fact that they live in a new world and delighted by the prospect of exploring it. Tom Wolfe's story describes individuals anxious to say "Shazam", and draw new energies into themselves. Ultimately, however, they fail to become Captain Marvel:

"We blew it!"
". . . just when you're beginning to think, 'I'm going
to score'. . ."
"We blew it!"

Henry Adams dreamed of the child of power, but the twentieth century child has discovered that power is not enough: the excitement of Eugene Gant must be combined with the cool skills of Hemingway. *The Electric Kool-Aid Acid Test* reflects Gant's exuberance in its free use of the medium, the language and syntax; but it is at the same time a carefully structured work. Neither an uncontrolled celebration of drugs nor an ordered documentary on Ken Kesey and the Pranksters, *The Electric Kool-Aid Acid Test* is an expression of a narrative imagination that sees the possibilities of the twentieth century embodied in the Pranksters. That imagination has discovered the need and ability to integrate both the exuberance and the structure if it is to function in a world characterized by electric energies.

Wolfe's values are evident in the book's opening sequence:

> That's good thinking there, Cool Breeze. Cool Breeze is a kid with three or four days' beard sitting next to me on the stamped metal bottom of the open back of a pickup truck. Bouncing along. Dipping and rising and rolling on these rotten springs like a boat. Out of the back of the truck the city of San Francisco is bouncing down the hill, all those endless staggers of bay windows, slums with a view, bouncing and streaming down the hill. One after another, electric signs with neon martini glasses lit up on them, the San Francisco symbol of "bar." - thousands of neon-magenta martini glasses bouncing and streaming down the hill, and beneath them hundreds, of people wheeling around to look at this freaking crazed truck we're in, their white faces erupting from their lapels like marshmallows. . . .Kneeling in the truck, facing us, also in plain view, is a half-Ottawa Indian girl named Lois Jennings, with her head thrown back and a radiant look on her face. Also a blazing silver disk in the middle of her forehead alternately exploding with light when the sun hits it or sending off rainbows from the defraction lines on it. (1-2)

As one of several reporters covering Kesey's story, Wolfe comes to San Francisco with a pre-arranged idea of what his story will be - "Real-life Fugitive" - and interviews Kesey with all the usual questions. In spite of these limitations, Wolfe is moving, fascinated with the Pranksters, and able to focus on the details of the physical world. That world is one of objects that explode with an energy all their own. Nothing is static in the opening scene - faces erupt, lights explode, and the city bounces out of the back of the heaving, billowing truck. The description is, of course, that of the narrator Wolfe in contrast to the reporter Wolfe; but even as a reporter, Tom Wolfe is himself moving West, attracted to Kesey and the Pranksters.

"Stolid," and two years out of date as a result of being from the East, Wolfe enters a world that stimulates his senses rather than his mind. He has only a limited amount of information about Kesey, and his rational questions of what, when, and why are distinctly out of place in the world of day-glo paint and marshmallow faces - but he sees a great deal: Kesey

> has thick wrists and big forearms, and the way he has them folded makes them look gigantic. He looks taller than he really is, maybe because of his neck. He has a big neck with a pair of sternocleidomastoid muscles that

rise up out of the prison work shirt like a couple of dock ropes. His jaw and chin are massive. (6)

His first encounter with Kesey takes place in a jail, a sterile, rigid, and confined environment that contrasts sharply with the physically healthy individual who responds immediately to Wolfe's interest. That same contrast is also evident in the "conversation" between Wolfe and Kesey. Tom Wolfe, like the television reporter who interviews Kesey but does not get the answers he is looking for, does not hear what Kesey is saying: "The ten minutes were up and I was out of there. I had gotten nothing, except my first brush with a phenomenon, that strange up-country charisma, the Kesey presence." (8) The early relationship between Wolfe and Kesey is imaged in the telephone they use to speak to each other:

> Then I quickly picked up my telephone and he picks up his - and this is truly Modern Times. We are all of twenty-four inches apart, but there is a piece of plate glass as thick as a telephone directory between us. We might as well be in different continents, talking over Videophone. The telephones are very crackly and lo-fi, especially considering that they have a world of two feet to span. (7)

Physically they are close, but imaginatively they are miles apart. Wolfe is a note taker and instigator of talk, and Kesey's responses about moving and creativity lose Wolfe: "I didn't know what in the hell it was all about" (7). Little is *answered*, but Tom Wolfe has been "brushed" by Kesey's energy.

After leaving Kesey, Wolfe continues his journalistic efforts and investigates the environment of the Merry Pranksters: "Somehow my strongest memories of San Francisco are of me in a terrific rented sedan *roaring* up hills or down hills, *sliding* on and off the cable tracks. *Slipping* and *sliding* down to North Beach." (8, italics added). Moving enthusiastically but not with much control, Wolfe discovers that an old world is vanishing: "But it was not just North Beach was dying. The whole old-style hip life - jazz, coffee houses, civil rights, invite a spade for dinner, Vietnam - it was all suddenly dying" (9). Wolfe's "blue silk blazer and . . . big tie with clowns on it" reflect that hip world, a world that Wolfe understands and enjoys. Now he stands on the edge of a new world and is "starting to get the trend of all this heaving and convulsing" (9); he is, however, one of the few. The straight world of the cops and the courts thinks in terms of keeping Kesey trapped and forcing him to preach their cause or be denounced by his friends - and the "heads" are unable to understand Kesey's talk about "beyond acid."

While these two groups want to "Stop Kesey," their efforts in essence directed at stopping movement, we get an insight into values in the actions of his lawyers who are able to pull off the   miracle of his release. They make things happen, in contrast to the efforts of those who try to stop activity. In the best Ben Franklin sense of the word, Kesey "uses" people. The cops and heads are using Kesey as a tool to keep a structured environment rigid, but Kesey - like Ben -

sees a world of continuous possibility in which individuals [and drugs and machines) can be of use to each other in realizing that possibility. The opening situation of the book, Kesey coming out of jail, thus embodies two major impulses in the narrative: the explosive activity of Kesey to make things happen and the efforts of those who fear change   and wish to lock him up.

Tom Wolfe is responsive to his new world: "Well, for a start, I begin to see that people like Lois and Stewart and Black Maria are the restrained, reflective wing of the Merry Pranksters" (11). Wolfe is beginning to see actions and a world that glows; he also hears- "From out of the black hole of the garage comes the sound of a recording by Bob Dylan and his raunchy harmonica and Ernest Tubb" (11) - and knows what he is hearing. Wolfe has possibilities of doing more than just recording data since he is both responsive and knowledgeable, but he is still unsure as to what is happening: "that was what Kesey had been talking to me about, I guess" (9).

"For two or three days it went like that for me in the garage with the Merry Pranksters waiting for Kesey" (15). Kesey is the unifying and stimulating ingredient; without him the Pranksters do not function. As Wolfe gets further into their life. he sees them as a gathering of individuals who, without Kesey, live amid a piled up "heap of electronic equipment" (21) and talk, however eloquently, about abstractions. Above all else, they wait.

> Through the sheet of sunlight at the doorway and down the incline into the crazy gloom comes a panel truck and in the front seat is Kesey. . . . Instead of saying anything. however. he cocks his head to one side and walks across the garage to the mass of wires, speakers. and, microphones over there and makes some minute adjustment. . . . As if now everything is under control and the fine tuning begins. (22)

Kesey enters the gloom of the garage through a doorway of light and with his fine tuning. Wolfe himself feels the electricity: "despite the skepticism I brought here. *I* am suddenly experiencing *their* feeling" (25).

> "Don't say stop plunging into the forest," Kesey says. "Don't stop being a pioneer and come back here and help these people through the door. If Leary wants to do that, that's good, it's a good thing and somebody should do it. But somebody has to be the pioneer and leave the marks for the others to follow." (27)

Kesey's drive is to keep moving, to explore new energies. He has no question about *whether* possibility exists or *whether* it is demonic; the energy is there, and Kesey wants to use it, go with its characteristics rather than impose his requirements on it. These qualities also characterize Wolfe's art, a skillful exploration of the possibilities of prose fiction. Together, the book and Kesey tremble with energy that can either transform Billy Batson into Captain Marvel or blow a fuse.

With Chapter Four Wolfe begins a flashback which carries through much of the book. We should remain aware, however, that though the focus is on Kesey, we are really seeing Wolfe "evaluate," take the strength from, Kesey and the Pranksters. The flashback is, then, a continuation of the narrative fascination with Kesey, a fascination that leads to Wolfe's own growth. Both Kesey and *The Electric Kool-Aid Acid Test* focus on physical objects that sparkle with life:

> That was the big high-school drive-in, with the huge streamlined sculpted pastel display sign with streaming streamlined superslick A-22 italic script, floodlights, clamp-on trays, car-hop girls in floppy blue slacks, hamburgers in some kind of tissuey wax paper steaming with onions pressed down and fried on the grill and mustard and catsup to squirt all over it from out plastic squirt cylinders. (34)

No corresponding attention is paid to the talk *about* life. The Perry Lane sophisticates turn "back to first principles" (31) of Greece, but Kesey is into the modern western hero who is capable of transformation into a being of superhuman energies: "A very Neon Renaissance - And the myths that actually touched you at that time - not Hercules, Orpheus, Ulysses, and Aeneas - but Superman, Plastic Man, The Flash" (35). The power of the verbal "Shazam," like the new drug LSD, sparks an electrical power surge which makes an individual begin "traveling and thinking at the speed of light" (35). Attuned to this new power, Kesey is able to see detail and movement:

> The ceiling is moving - not in a crazed swirl but along its own planes of light and shadow and surface not nearly so nice and smooth as plasterer Super Plaster Man intended with infallible carpenter level bubble sliding in dim honey Karo syrup tube not so foolproof as you thought, but, little lumps and ridges up there, bub, and lines, lines like spines on crests of waves of white desert movie sand each one with MGM shadow longshot of the ominous A-rab coming over the next crest for only the sinister Saracen can see the road and you didn't know how many subplots you left up there, Plaster man, trying to smooth it *all* out, *all* of it, with your bubble in a honey tube carpenter's level, to make us all down here look up and see nothing but ceiling, because we all know ceiling, because it has a *name*, ceiling, therefore it is nothing but a ceiling - no room for A-rabs up there in Level Land, eh, Plaster man. (36-37)

He can also see the muscles in the doctor's face or his pulse as an accurate measure of his life or Chief Broom as the key to his new novel. As his perception is altered, Kesey becomes aware of a potentially frightening world where few people want to go but which is also a place where a moving line can suddenly become a nose, "the very miracle of creation itself" (40).

Kesey's early activities after taking LSD are burstings forth of "vital energy" (41). The move to La Honda, the appearance of the intrepid traveller, and the bus trip are all forms of this eruption. The bus trip "Further," like the flashback technique Wolfe uses in his narrative, is a movement back in preparation for new directions. The bus heads *East* toward the old intellectual world of the Lea- ryites and Europe. The trip carries the Merry Pranksters down through the pressure-cooker heat of the South, something like the first stages of a sauna bath where the body is flushed of internal poisons. The trip back culminates in "the Crypt Trip" where the pressure is of a different kind. The Pranksters expect to be received joyously, but all along the road they encounter a variety of threaten- ing responses. When they visit the Learyites, they discover that the "Pranksters' Ancestral Mansion" (94) is not a home; rather its "sepulchral" atmosphere and "Tibetan Book of the Dead" (95) emphasizes that the Pranksters have broken off from the intellectual Eastern world:

. . .the trouble with Leary and his group is that they have turned *back*. But of course! They have turned back into that old ancient New York intellectual thing, ducked back into the Romantic past, copped out of the American trip. New York intellectuals have always looked for. . .another country, a fatherland of the mind, where it is better and more philosophic and purer, gadget-free, and simpler and pedigreed. (100)

The Pranksters are a new group, living in a new world. They have no roots and must seek their life in constant discovery. When they emerge from their crypt, they turn westward, but the bus now takes the cooler, Northern route. The trip ultimately integrates and unifies the Pranksters; they become a special group rather than a collection of idiosyncratic individuals.

Kesey's interest in energy and art have also been developed while on this "risk-all balls-out plunge into the unknown" (78). Simply becoming aware, sen- sitive to power is not enough:

Kesey said he wanted them all to do their thing and be Pranksters, but he wanted them to be deadly competent, too. . . . They should always be alert, always alive to the moment, always deep in the whole group thing, and be deadly competent. (88)

Being alive to the moment is integrally related to Kesey's understanding of art. For him art is a way of getting totally into the now, a world where one experi- ences an event at exactly the same time it is occurring: "The whole other world that LSD opened your mind to existed only in the moment itself - *Now* - and any attempt to plan, compose, orchestrate, write a script, only locked you out of the moment, back in the world of conditioning and training where the brain was a reducing valve" (52). While Kesey wants to be the artist, who can organize such an experience, he also wants an art form that does not determine the experi- ence. Being trapped in the rules of syntax and the referential properties of lan- guage, while it allowed him to break through the "all-American crap," earlier, would destroy his present commitment to the now. In pointing to the bus and in creating the miracle in seven days and the acid tests, Kesey imagines an artist

who can artificially create conditions but not the experience of the work, Each
individual must do that - get on the bus - for himself.

"It could be scary out there in Freedom land. The Pranksters were friendly,
but they glowed in the dark" (107). The tightening power of the new electricity is
epitomized in the Hell's Angels:

> The Angels brought a lot of things into sync. Outlaws, by definition, were
> people who had moved off of dead center and were out in some kind of
> Edge City. The beauty of it was, the Angels had done it like the
> Pranksters, by choice. They had become outlaws first - to *explore*, muvva -
> and then got busted for it. The Angels' trip was the motorcycle and the
> Pranksters' was LSD, but both were in an incredible entry into orgasmic
> moment, *now*. (152)

As the Angels' motorcycles roar into La Honda, the energy that has been discovered and explored thus far surges forth. It is not just a test of the Pranksters; it is
an event which embodies just how far the Pranksters have gone in their exploration of power. No group in America could seem more demonic than the Angels,
but their tremendous energies are now being taken into the Pranksters and used
by a group of highly skilled individuals. What could have been a "time bomb"
(159) becomes instead a vibrating two-day party.

With all the energies of the Angels in their movie, the Pranksters are now
able to achieve a "miracle in seven days." This chapter is at the center of the
book and culminates the effects of Kesey to get in tune with his environment,
discover the Power that is available, and use that Power through his own art to
bring others to see what it [is] like out on Edge city. What the conference allows
Kesey to do is demonstrate that he is able to make his current fantasy work.
When it is all over, "it's like all the Pranksters' theories and professed beliefs
have been put to a test in the outside world, away from La Honda, and they're
working now, and they have . . . Control" (170).

So that creative impulse to burst forth from the all-American crap, an impulse that is the driving force during the first part of the book, culminates in an
artistic production that is non-verbal and unprogrammed. The actors and audience become one movie - but something is wrong:

> Kesey also had his court appearances to contend with and more lying,
> finking, framing, politicking by the constables than a body could believe -
> he looked like he had aged ten years in three months. He was now some
> indeterminate age between thirty and forty. He was taking a lot of speed
> and smoking a lot of grass. He looked haggard, and when he looked
> haggard, his face seemed lopsided. (172-73)

The final word of the chapter is "Control," and the last few pages stress "Power," but the lives of the Merry Pranksters are soon to become like a nuclear
reactor that has gone beyond critical mass. The image of energy bursting forth,

impulsing outward, which dominates the first half of the book, is the same image which dominates the second, but that energy is rapidly getting out of control.

Kesey's efforts have been to discover and release energy; he beginning to find, however, that energy may not be easily handled. Two chapters demonstrate what is happening: the one which closes the first part of the book, "The Hell's Angels," and the one which opens the second, "Cloud." In the Hell's Angels chapter the Pranksters welcome tremendous outlaw energies into their movie - "The Merry Pranksters Welcome the Hell's Angels." The situation is the same in "Cloud" - "The Merry Pranksters Welcome the Beatles" - but what had worked in the earlier chapter becomes ugly and dangerous in the second. The Beatles fantasy is an effort to continue moving, but now the vibrations are bad because the value that Kesey has been striving for - Control - is absent:

> It is like the whole thing has snapped, and the whole front section of the arena becomes a writhing, seething mass of little girls waving their arms in the air . . . and they have utter control over them - but they don't know what in the hell to do with it. (182)

Instead of energy working, the Pranksters find themselves in a pen in which "mindless amok energy" (185) threatens to become a cancer, uncontrolled and self-consuming.

The implications of that cancer are developed in the chapters after "Cloud," but one would be mistaken to suggest that the first part of the book does one thing and the second part something different. Rather, the factors that result in the blown fuse are present during the early successful activities of the Pranksters; they have just gone unrecognized by Kesey (but not by Wolfe - since they are part of his narrative). They are integral aspects of some of Kesey's major assumptions. The problem is evident in the opening of "Cloud," the chapter in which the energy becomes cancerous.

> They lie there on the mattresses, with Kesey rapping on and on and Mountain Girl trying to absorb it. Ever since Asilomar, Kesey has been deep in to the religion thing. . .on and on he talks to Mountain Girl out in the backhouse and very deep and far-out stuff it is, too. Mountain Girl tries to concentrate, but the words swim like great waves of. . . . Her mind keeps rolling and spinning over another set of data, always the same, Life - the eternal desperate calculation. In short, Mountain Girl is pregnant. (177)

Kesey has gotten so completely into his current fantasy that he has lost touch with the physical environment he is seeking to touch. Mountain Girl is pregnant, but Kesey is unaware. She is about to bring forth life, but Kesey is sensitive only to ideas.

Evidence of the difficulty appeared in Chapter Eleven when the Merry Pranksters returned from their trip East having discovered a new unity: "What they all saw in . . . a flash was the solution to the basic predicament of being *human*, the personal *I*, *Me*, trapped, mortal and helpless, in a vast impersonal *It*, the world around me" (114). Kesey began with the urge to create from within himself and to involve himself in his world, drives which suggest a need to experience fully what it means to be human. But in Chapter Eleven the implication is that being human has become a "predicament" that needs to be altered. At the same time, however, the movie is demanding some very human skills if it is not to become its own uncontrolled cancer:

> But the Movie was a monster . . . the sheer labor and tedium in editing forty-five hours of film was unbelievable. And besides. . . much of the film was out of focus. . . .But who needs that old Hollywood thing of long shot, medium shot, closeup, and the careful, cuts and wipes and pans and dolly in and dolly out, the old bullshit. Still, plunging in on those miles of bouncing, ricocheting, blazing film with a splicer was like entering a jungle where the greeny vines grew faster than you could chop them down in front of you. (122)

The cutting needed in the jungle or in the editing of the movie *requires* a human response that is not just a submersion of the individual into the physical, a submersion that is implied in the statement, "Suddenly! - All-in-one! - flowing together, *I* into *It*, and *It* into *Me*, and in that flow I perceive a power, so near and so clear, that the whole world is blind to" (114). These words have Emersonian overtones, where the individual is in danger of losing his individuality - or where he can lose his ability to see the particular because he has become intellectual. Chapter Eleven explores the human "predicament" as Kesey understands it, talking of Cassady:

> A person has all sorts of lags built into him. Kesey is saying. One, the most basic, is the sensory lag, the lag between the time your senses receive something and you are able to react. . . . He is a living example of how close you can come, but it can't be done. You can't go any faster than that, You can't through sheer speed overcome the lag. We are all of us doomed to spend our lives watching a movie of our lives. . . .That lag has to be overcome some other way, through some kind of total breakthrough . . . nobody can be creative overcoming all those lags first. (129)

Kesey's statement that no one can be creative - that the creative impulse cannot burst forth and fully express itself - without overcoming this lag, this humanity, invites a potentially destructive conflict between his beliefs and the physical properties of his environment. Once the lag is ended, the individual will be completely in tune with the pattern "one could see the larger pattern and move with it - Go with the flow! - and accept it and rise above one's immediate environment and even alter it by accepting the larger pattern and grooving with it" (129). However, they are left with "the great morass of a movie, with miles and miles of spiraling spliced-over film and hot splices billowing around them like so many intertwined, synched, but still chaotic and struggling human lives" (131).

Such a life is Mountain Girl's and in all the theory and talk, Kesey has missed that individual. The loneliness and pregnancy of Mountain Girl, an individual who is so thoroughly a Prankster, calls attention to the dependency upon Kesey that most, if not all. the Pranksters have developed. "Kesey was essential to Mountain Girl's whole life with the Pranksters" (149) just as he was essential to the success of the party with the Hell's Angels. Kesey's initial urge had been personal, and he sought to extend his own perception while also stimulating others to begin perceiving for themselves. The Pranksters - as well as those drawn into their movie - should be developing that individuality, but their dependency on Kesey's energy has apparently limited their ability to concentrate and explore their own. What was to have stimulated the individual to discover himself has become a social enterprise where the group is dependent on the leader. If such a problem is developing, the removal of that leader ought to bring movement to a halt and perhaps to cause that tightly welded unit to disintegrate. These problems develop in the second part of the book, the section that begins with power out of control at the Beatles concert and with the power surge in New York that blows all the city's fuses and transformers (190).

Events in the book, then, have begun to anticipate the breakup of the Merry Pranksters. In "Departures" Kesey prepares to head for Mexico, for the first time responding to the actions of others -the police - rather than initiating action himself, and Mountain Girl goes to New York to try to get herself back together. Sandy also leaves for New York, again the victim of what for him will apparently always be "the demon Speed." As if to emphasize the social thrust of their recent activities, the two chapters preceding Kesey's trip focus on the skills of the Pranksters "to extend the message to all people." with Kesey prominently at the controls. No longer is each individual Prankster striving to become deadly competent, a functioning individual alive to the moment. Rather each is concentrating entirely on the collective enterprise of conveying their "message" - with all the verbal and social connotations of that word - to a group. Instead of the effort of the individual to go "further," the Pranksters create an authorized, organized Now.

The Mexican chapters parallel in many ways the earlier bus trip. but where the pressure cooker had then been restricted to the heat the sun, now Kesey and those with him are subjected to disease, filth, and death. What had been an intellectual crypt trip now becomes almost too real. Wolfe's handling of the opening scene in Mexico is both a vivid description of the paranoid state into which Kesey has fallen and a major indicator of the developing difference between Kesey and Wolfe. Earlier, Wolfe had been stimulated by Kesey's skill, but now Wolfe himself is demonstrating that skill. Kesey's helpless mental state is presented with an incredibly sharp eye for detail:

> Kesey sits in this little rickety upper room with his elbow on a table and his forearm standing up perpendicular and in the palm of his hand a little mirror, so that his forearm and the mirror are like a big rear-view mirror stanchion on the side of a truck and thus he can look out the window and

see them but they can't see him. . . . Kesey has Cornel Wilde running
Jacket ready hanging on the wall, a jungle-jim corduroy jacket stashed
with fishing line, a knife, money, DDT, tablet, ball-points, flashlight, and
Grass. (200)

Kesey is seeing very little - his mind is alive largely to the details of his latest
fantasy - but Wolfe is able both to focus on the reality of Kesey's world and to
convey the quality of Kesey's paranoid experience, each second of which lasts no
more than a minute and is agonizingly detailed and examined in the best Prankster day-Glo color. Wolfe is in control, and in his hands the verbal medium
comes alive.

Kesey's energies are also alive but trapped within himself - the artificial rules
of syntax. His tremendous energies are still there and they continue to pull
people back to him: Black Maria and Mountain Girl , now back with the Pranksters and eight months pregnant - as well as some Pranksters left at La Honda -
begin to regroup in Mexico. What they find there is the ugly world in which
Kesey has been living: "All the vibrations outside were bad. Corpses, chiefly.
Scrub cactus, brown dung dust and bloated corpses, dogs, coyotes, armadillos, a
cow, all gas-bellied and dead, swollen and dead. . . . This was the flow, and it was
a sickening horrible flow" (275).

The intensity of the Mexican experience is epitomized in "The Red Tide," "a
poison as powerful as aconitine" which is produced by the plankton in the ocean
waters and which is death to the fish. That death mirrors the death on the land
where the Pranksters are "stranded like flies in this 110-degree mucus of Manzanillo" (280-81). The red tide and the Mexican disaster are less efforts at journalistic accuracy than metaphors for the Prankster experience at a time when death
and stagnation are as much a part of their lives as they are in the filthy pressure-
cooker world of the environment. The drugs which were opening doors earlier
are now only a means to escape the heat.

Under these same conditions, however, Mountain Girl has her baby, her dyed
hair gradually returns to its natural state, and Kesey begins to see what is happening to them: "they have made the trip now, closed the circle, all of them, and
they either emerge as Superheros, closing the door behind them and soaring
through the hole in the sapling sky, or just lollygag in the loop-the-loop of the
lag. . . either make this thing permanent inside of you, or forever just climb
draggled up into the conning tower every time for one short glimpse of the horizon" (290) . The "current fantasy" has become just that, a fantasy: they have lost
contact with reality. "Mommy, this movie is no fun any more, it's too real,
Mommy" (299). That reality - in the form of the Mexican police - reaches out to
capture Kesey but succeeds only in spurring him into activity: "It was time to get
the Movie going on all projectors. And the bus." (301)

Kesey's return to California is a curious mixture of continuing live-in fantasy
and yet wanting to get back in touch with the environment, separate values
that mirror Kesey's own state of mind - "Kesey veering wildly from paranoia

and hyper-security to extraordinary disregard for his own safety, one state giving way to the other in no fixed order" (312). His commitment is once again to movement, this time beyond acid and beyond the stagnant condition of tests which have quickly become the thing, the sport of college students and New York intellectuals. Kesey is once again probing the "western-most edge of experience" (323), and that scares those who are content to remain where they are. It is the Hell's Angels side of the Kesey adventure that panics the hip world because the Angels are "too freaking real. Outlaws . . . the heads of Haight - Asbury could never stretch their fantasy as far out as the Hells Angels" (326).

Kesey is also having to work his imagination: at the moment he is theorizing and playing a game of cops-and-robbers with the California authorities:

> It will be a masked ball, this Test. Nobody will know which freak is who. At the midnight hour, Kesey, masked and disguised in a   Super-hero costume, on the order of Captain America of the Marvel Comics pantheon, will come up on stage and deliver his vision of the future, of the way "beyond acid." *Who is this apocalyptic* - Then he will rip off his mask - Why - it's Ken Kee-zee! - and as the law rushes for him, he will leap up on a rope hanging down from the roof at center stage and climb, hand over hand, without even using his legs, with his cape flying, straight up, up, up, up through a trap door in the roof, to where Babbs will be waiting with a helicopter, Captain Midnight of the U. S. Marines, and they will ascend into the California ozone. (328)

This seems less movement than fantasizing, less Captain Marvel than a child who is exercising his power to defy authority. Once again Kesey finds that "the current fantasy . . . this movie is too real, Mommy" (329). Appropriately, Kesey's capture is put in terms of a little boy with torn pants.

The last chapter of *The Electric Kool-Aid Acid Test* details the anticlimax of Kesey's efforts to go beyond acid; they blow it. In the final scene, the Pranksters who are striving to move are sitting on the floor of the Warehouse surrounded by too much noise and too many TV cameras. Whatever Kesey has been driving for is imaged as a much publicized stagnation: "It's like a wake" (366). Wolfe has said that during the abstract expressionist movement of the 1950's

> The artists themselves didn't seem to have the faintest notion of how primary Theory was becoming. I wonder if the theorists themselves did. All of them, artist and theorists, were talking as if their conscious aim was to create a totally immediate art, lucid. stripped of all the dreadful baggage of history, an art fully revealed, honest, as honest as the flat-out integral picture plane. [1]

To a Prankster as well as an abstract expressionist this passage might pear an irritatingly inaccurate evaluation of their activities, but it indicates much about Wolfe's own artistic values and does indeed point to the crucial weakness in the

---

[1] Tom Wolfe, *The Painted Word* (New York: Farrar, Straus and Giroux, 1975), p. 63.

Prankster way of life. The emphasis in the passage is on the Word in its most sterile form: and it is this that would annoy the Pranksters because their whole effort is dedicated to going beyond an abstract verbalization which is the epitome of the distance between the event and the experiencing of it.

The desire to open oneself up to the world, not unique with Pranksters, allows us to see them in the mainstream of American thought and literature reaching back through Hemingway, Whitehead, Melville, Thoreau, and Emerson to Franklin and the Puritans. Whitehead's emphasis on creativity and novelty illustrates, potential vitality of the Pranksters:

> "Creativity," is the Principle of novelty. An actual occasion is a novel entity diverse from any entity in the "many" which it unifies. Thus "creativity" introduces novelty into the content of the many, which are the universe disjunctively. The "creative advance" is the application of this ultimate principle of creativity to each novel situation which originates. [2]

The world is continually being "renewed"; there is no stasis, biblical Garden of Eden. Kesey's concern with "beyond acid" is absolutely right, for it indicates continuing novelty; however, when he says that we are "doomed" to watch our lives and that without overcoming lag "nobody can be creative" (219), his stress is not on movement but on goal, one that is disturbingly Edenic. At such a theoretical point, the world might be moving but the individual would be carried along with it. Kesey points to Cassady as someone "going as fast as a human can go, but even he can't overcome it. He is a living example of how you can come, but it can't be done. You can't go any faster than that" (129). Cassady, however, is an individual who burns himself out and Kesey's praise of Cassady should warn us of dangers implicit in Kesey's drives. When Kesey starts to talk about overcoming rather than opening, his drives become self-destructive rather than liberating. In addition, the existence of Wolfe's art indicates that far from limiting creativity, lag is what makes creativity possible. Kesey urges the Pranksters to "go with the flow," but the danger, as any defensive tackle will verify, is always that such movement can result in being swept along. Kesey's interest is in the ability to perceive and evaluate flow so as to develop not dissolve individuality. Such perception necessitates lag. The discovery and assertion of personal skills - "The most powerful drive in the ascent of man," says Jacob Bronowski, "is the pleasure in his own skill" - is not a goal but a process that demands vision and objectivity. Kesey has all the right impulses, but when he begins to talk about overcoming lag, he is danger either of becoming self-destructive or of being swept along by the flow.

While Kesey sees goals and ideas, Wolf sees objects:

[2] Alfred North Whitehead, *Process and Reality* (New York: The Free Press, 1969), p. 26.

> But my mind is wandering. I am having a hard time listening because I
> am fascinated by a little plastic case with a toothbrush and toothpaste in it
> that Hassler has tucked under one thumb. . . Here Hassler outlines a
> pyramid in the air with his hands and I watch, fascinated, as the plastic
> toothbrush case shiny shiny slides up one incline of the pyramid. (18)

Ultimately, the difference between Wolf and the Pranksters is evidenced in
Wolf's ability to keep his narrative eye focused on the physical world of the
Pranksters and to unify *The Electric Kool-Aid Acid Test* in contrast to the talk
and endless feet of film and electrical wires that the Pranksters can never man-
age to bring together. Kesey worries that his experience cannot be verbalized:
"But these *words*, man! *And you couldn't put it into words*. The white Smocks
tried to put it into words, like *hallucination* and *dissociative phenomena*" (40).
Wolf, however, goes for the vitality rather than intellectual abstraction, a quality
that distinguishes him from writers who come to cover the story of redeveloping
Perry Lane.

> The papers turned up to write about the last night on Perry Lane, noble
> old Perry Lane, and had the old cliche at the ready, End of an Era,
> expecting to find some deep-thinking latter-day Thorstein Veblen
> intellectuals on hand with sonorous bitter statements about this machine
> civilization devouring its own Past. Instead, there were some kind of nuts
> out there. They were up in a tree lying on a mattress, all high as
> coons . . . . but they managed to go back with the story they came with,
> End of an Era, the cliche intact. (48)

These men see with their clean, structured minds; thus the cliches. But Tom
Wolf is able to open his eyes and see the vitality of Prankster world. His willingness to look rather than to theorize allows him to perceive "shape and pattern"
in his verbal exploration of the Pranksters. The result is a functioning narrative
voice in an exciting new world: "That's good thinking there, Cool Breeze. Cool
Breeze is a kid with three or four days' beard sitting next to me on the stamped
metal bottom of the open back part of a pickup truck. Bouncing along. Dipping
and rising and rolling on these rotten springs like a boat" (1). Good thinking
and movement and concrete objects - these are Tom Wolfe's values.

Kesey and Wolfe share many of the same values, but Wolfe is able to look at
physical laws as something to be used to one's advantage - evaluated - rather
than as frustrations to be overcome. *The Electric Kool-Aid Acid Test* is thus a
book about art, about the individual's effort to get it all together. Telling one's
story and getting one's skills finely tuned are finally the same thing. Kesey has
the skills to tune a piece of machinery, but he is also interested in fine tuning
himself. Ultimately, he and the Pranksters fail to look at themselves or at each
other as individuals (the Who Cares girl) just as they prefer to look at the physical world as metaphor rather that object. Games, roles, metaphors, and abstractions become Prankster values in spite of their talk about opening doors and
going further. Tom Wolfe's uniqueness is his recognition that perception and

skill must be developed together, that one can only discover his strengths by evaluating his environment.

Radical Chic & Mau-Mauing the Flak Catchers

Dandy in the Ghetto

Melvin Maddocks

In the portrait that promotes his new book, Tom Wolfe is wearing a checked suit with vest. In his left hand he holds what looks like a black homburg. His right hand is clasped over a tightly rolled umbrella on which he leans with elaborate casualness so that his right leg can cross over his left and balance on one pointy-toed shoe. An old vaudevillian taking his curtain call. Behind Mr. Wolfe lies the rubble of a gutted building.

Caption the picture, "Dandy in the Ghetto," or words to that effect. The photograph accurately, insolently suits the book it goes with: *Radical Chic & Mau-Mauing the Flak Catchers*.

Mr. Wolfe is the dude who is not going to let the messy old 20th century ruffle one hair on his parted-just-so head. Vietnam and smog. Hell's Angels, Ken Kesey's Merry Pranksters, the Black Panthers. Nothing and nobody is about to blow Tom Wolfe's cool.

Mr. Wolfe is an anthropologist from another planet, putting all the panic into perspective. Show him a mob scene. Stage an assassination for his private benefit. His response would be the same: It's "an American custom, like talk shows, Face the Nation, marriage counseling, marathon encounters, or zoning hearings."

Mr. Wolfe has seen Everything. His game is to believe nobody and, above all, never to be shocked. Be patient. He will find the con behind the con, for he never doubts it is there.

"Radical Chic," of course, is the title of his celebrated essay on the party Leonard Bernstein threw in his rather posh apartment to raise funds for the Black Panthers. "Mau-Mauing the Flak Catchers" is a parajournalistic account of how the "certified angry militants" of minority groups competed, scowl by scowl, for poverty program money in the San Francisco-Oakland area.

Poverty. Racism. Eldridge Cleaver. Is nothing sacred to Mr. Wolfe? Of course not. His instinct is for comedy, and he reduces everything to the ridiculous - white liberals nibbling caviar while signing checks for the revolution with their free hand; civil service employees trembling in their $4.99 Hush Puppies as they judge the charisma of a Black Spokesman according to how fast he makes their hearts beat below the shirt pockets full of ball-point pens.

Mr. Wolfe's brilliance is obvious - and so is the case against it. "He doesn't *care*," the Wolfe critics cry. His flip cultural-historian neutrality is monstrous, they complain. Why, he fails to blame evil actions or credit good intentions. He is more interested in his cool pose than in that rubble behind him.

All partly true, no doubt. But to leave Mr. Wolfe there - pat and a touch cruel - is to ignore his passion. Behind his mere knowingness he has a deeper urge to *know*. There is nothing too cool about his refusal to do business with cultural cliches. Along with the visible cleverness, he has a fierce determination not to be taken in - that curiously old-fashioned journalistic virtue. In the age of the put-on - the managed event and the just-invented trend - journalism is in no position to do without its super-aware skeptic in the checked suit.

That Night at Lenny's

Richard Freedman

From *Book World* 4 (6 December, 1970), 5-6. ©1970, 1982, 1987, The Washington Post. Reprinted with permission

On the night of January 4, 1970, Maestro and Mrs. Leonard Bernstein threw a bash in their thirteen-room Park Avenue pad to raise money for the Black Panthers Defense Fund. New York society will probably never play Lady Bountiful in quite the same way again, because among the Beautiful People present was Tom Wolfe, pop-sociologist and parajournalist supreme.

Combining the talents of Thorstein Veblen, Beau Brummell and Lucrezia Borgia, Wolfe here regales us with every detail of the evening's débâcle in his richest baroque style. If ellipses, italics and exclamation points are ever banished from English prose, Wolfe might find himself out of a job, but with their help his remorseless ear catches every verbal fatuity of limousine liberal and rabid revolutionary alike.

His equally penetrating eye sees that only white servants will do for such gatherings, that the Bernstein pianos are laden with framed family pictures, achieving what decorators call "the million-dollar *chatchka* look," that the latest snob-status thing is to donate to non-tax-deductible causes. He spots the nut-studded Roquefort canapés nestled in the silver salvers, and they haunt the memory long afterward in much the same way as Princess Mary's infinitesimal moustache haunts the reader of *War and Peace*.

"Radical Chic" is high social comedy - possibly Wolfe's finest performance to date - largely because Bernstein's motives were undoubtedly as pure and guileless as those of Candide, the appropriate hero of his ill-starred opera of a few years ago.

Wolfe nevertheless dissects the underlying history and assumptions of such gatherings (he alludes in passing to several others of the same stripe) with a fine scalpel. He sees them as arising from society's "*nostalgie de la boue*" - nostalgia for the gutter - although I daresay a certain romantic nostalgia for the Noble Savage is involved as well.

Bernstein's particular misfortune was that at the time he gave his wingding, black anti-Semitism had recently been inflamed by the New York public school teacher's strike. The party - Bernstein insisted it was a "meeting," canapés and all - ended with Otto Preminger questioning, in his richly Teutonic accents, a bit of Panther palaver to the effect that "this country is the most oppressive. . .maybe in the history of the world," and getting down to the nitty-gritty of Panther attitudes to Israel.

This hidden issue had some bizarre aftereffects. *The New York Times* saw fit to run a knuckle-rapping editorial on the party, and "In Miami, Jewish pickets

forced a moviehouse to withdraw a film of Lenny conducting the Israel Philhar-
monic. . .in celebration of Israel's victory in the Six-Day War."

When "Radical Chic" appeared last June in *New York*, that worthy magazine
was deluged with letters accusing Wolfe of the twin sins of racism and snottiness
(the latter, one gathered, being more the heinous), but a careful reading reveals
that in fact his attitude is that the Panthers are demeaned by such occasions. The
attitude to Bernstein is simply that being a great musician is no guarantee that
one has the social sense of a campfire girl.

Doubtless, both Bernstein and the Panthers will survive, but it may be some
time before Wolfe is invited back to sample those luxurious canapés *chez* Lenny.

The companion piece eking out this slim volume lacks the formal perfection
of "Radical Chic," but is almost as much fun. "Mau-Mauing the Flak Catchers"
shows in gruesome detail how the government's poverty programs have neutral-
ized the ghetto gangs of San Francisco by the simple expedient of cutting their
leaders in on the swag. Wolfe thinks this was the original intention, but doubt
that Washington is capable of such cynicism.

"Mau-Mauing" is the witty ethnic term for confrontation politics, the arm-
twisting which in earlier days brought such Americans as John D. Rockefeller
and Al Capone all the cookies they wanted. The Flak Catchers are the Civil
Service "lifers" who are left in their local offices to cope as best they can with the
manifold abuses to their masculinity handed out by the poverty parishioners,
while their bosses are in Washington, gobbling up the gobbledegook. A horrifying situation, rendered the more so by Wolfe's consistently objective, empathetic,
urbane wit.

Wolfe is above all the poet of the quotidian. His purple passages list the variety of pens and pencils bristling from the pockets of a civil servant's "August
end-of-summer sale" white sleeveless shirt, and they read like the catalogue of
spears in the *Iliad*. His highest pitch of eloquence comes in this catalogue of
every Jewish liberal's composite nightmare: "Mitchell and Agnew and Nixon and
all of their Captain Beefheart Maggie & Jiggs New York Athletic Club troglo-
dyte crypto-Horst Wessel Irish Oyster Bar Construction Worker followers."

It may not be Wordsworth, or even Whitman, but it's about the best poetry
we have around.

Fish in the Brandy Snifter

Timothy Foote

From *Time* (21 December 1970), 72,74. Copyright 1970 Time Warner, Inc. Reprinted by permission.

What Tom Wolfe has done - with a touch of malice and more than a pinch of cheek - is create an appallingly funny, cool, small, deflative two-scene social drama about America's biggest, hottest and most perplexing problem, the confrontation between Black Rage and White Guilt.

Scene 1 (large portions of it originally printed in a June issue of *New York* magazine) centers on that now famous money-raising party for the Black Panthers given in Conductor Leonard Bernstein's Manhattan apartment last January. For the Occasion (*Time,* Jan. 26), Wolfe coined the phrase "radical chic." He thus described the tendency among bright blooded, moneyed or otherwise distinguished New Yorkers - lately grown weary of plodding, *via media* middle-class institutions like the Heart Ball, the U.J.A. and the N.A.A.C.P. - to take up extreme, exotic, earthy and more titillating causes. To hear Wolfe tell it, radical chic lays some deliciously agonizing stresses upon the Beautiful People. How do you dress, for instance - funky or fashionable? And what does a hostess giving a Panther party do about Claude and Maude, her normally indispensable Negro couple?

Ragging the rich is an old, though declining sport. If Wolfe merely ran on like that, he might be dismissed as a frivolous type who has done little more than shoot fish in a brandy snifter. Happily, the gathering - and with it Tom Wolfe's look-homeward-recording-angel prose - soon begins to reflect depths of confusion and true social comedy. There is a remarkable moment when Panther Defense Minister Don Cox talks of police harassment, evoking the Reichstag fire (blacks now, Jews next is the thought), then reads the Declaration of Independence to justify talk about Revolution Now. Eventually Bernstein and Guests Otto Preminger and TV Reporter Barbara Walters, somewhat apologetically and with few results, try to pin down the Panthers about what they really have in mind for the future beyond ghetto breakfasts and the high cost of bail.

Few scenes could better reveal the painfully comic convulsions that beset old-fashioned, dead-serious liberalism in the age of the rip-off, the put-on, and the total acceptance of verbal overkill. Wolfe's Leonard Bernstein is neither a freak nor a fool. Following the sound old American principle of defending civil liberties, wherever threatened, he winds up with the Panthers in his drawing room. Where bail was concerned, their legal rights certainly were threatened. But how is a good Jewish liberal to take a group that cheerfully talks about destroying his society and is, at the very least, linked to gang shakedowns of Jewish merchants in the ghetto and black nationalist propaganda against Israel?

Wolfe's second target is far from Park Avenue - in the ghettos of San Francisco, about which, Wolfe asserts, bureaucrats in the Office of Economic Opportunity "didn't know any more than they did about Zanzibar." As a result, when they wanted to find black leaders to receive OEO grants in 1968, "they sat back and waited for you to come rolling in with your certified angry militants, your guaranteed frustrated ghetto youth, looking like a bunch of wild men." If the bureaucrats got so shook up that "their eyes froze into iceballs. . .they knew you were the right studs to give the poverty grants and community organizing jobs to."

That was "mau-mauing." Chameleon-voiced as usual, and still given to Homeric catalogues and hang-ten metaphors, Wolfe inhabits an imaginary mau-mau character as he gleefully recalls some of the finer techniques. First, aspect: "You go down there with your hair *stickin' out!*" Second, mien: "Don't say nothing. You just glare." Then, tactics - which include bringing along some ringer Samoans who all look ten feet tall. One of Wolfe's master mau-mauers, like some Pied Piper of litterbugs, threatens to devastate city hall at the head of a horde of kids all armed with packages of sticky candy and plenty of wrappers. Another mau-mau Ph.D. didn't even need a gang. He would just turn up at the OEO office with a crocus sack full of "ice picks, switchblades, straight razors, hand grenades and Molotov cocktails and dump it on a desk, claiming he's just taken the stuff off 'my boy last night.' " Concludes Wolfe: "They'd lay money on this man's ghetto youth like it was now or never."

For Wolfe, as for any satirist, manner is matter. To reduce his scenes to message is to miss both his point and his quality. Still, given the high-voltage polarity of the age, Wolfe is already being unfairly abstracted for message and misread something like this: the black movement is a put-on; the poverty program is a feckless giveaway; white liberals are pure patsies. As a result, he will endure not merely the embarrassing approval of the Neanderthals ("You see! you see!") but the threat of stoning at the hands of enraged reformers and black extremists alike. When a *Time* reporter recently asked a minister of the Panther Party's shadow government about the truthfulness of Wolfe's Radical Chic account, the reply was ominous: "You mean that dirty, blatant, lying, racist dog who wrote that fascist disgusting thing in New York magazine?"

Wolfe's peculiar blend of artistic omniscience and journalistic detail has often troubled readers who cannot decide where reality leaves off and Wolfe begins. These two pieces are not entirely proof against such doubts. *Radical Chic* frequently goes too far in Wolfe's "Everybody there felt. . ." generalizations. Still, it is generally so accurate that even some of the irate guests at the Bernsteins later wondered how Wolfe - who in fact used shorthand - managed to smuggle a tape recorder onto the premises. Satire is no way to win friends. If the Panthers ever do take over and Wolfe winds up behind bars, who will want to give a bail party for him?

Dandy Monocle

Philip French

From *New Statesman* 82 (17 September 1971), 404-05. Reprinted with permission of the author.

Tom Wolfe's latest exercise in the frenetic 'New Journalism' is a victory of the mean-minded over the well-intentioned. In the second of the book's two essays he observes the way in which unemployed Negroes in San Francisco extract money from welfare agencies by the process of 'mau-mauing,' i.e., playing on the fears and superstitions of white bureaucrats by theatrically aggressive (yet basically harmless) dress, speech, and gesture, which represents its practitioners as belligerent community leaders and spokesmen. Such confrontational tactics, he argues, are not only a predictable means of exploiting poverty programmes, but a positive result of the sociological thinking behind them.

In the first, longer and more calculated provocative of the essays, he reports on the now well-known 1969 cocktail party in Leonard Bernstein's elegant Upper East Side Manhattan apartment to raise bail and defence money for the 21 Black Panthers then detained on charges of conspiring to destroy various public buildings in New York. Nothing escapes Wolfe's vulpine eyes, from the 'perfect Mary Astor voice' of the hostess to the host's insistence on the correct *Jewish* pronunciation of his name. He describes with deadly accuracy the way this smart set - a sort of NW1 writ large in moon-lighting along the East River - falls over itself to comfort and agonize with its revolutionary "pet primitives," so different, so much more *real*, more stylish than the middle-class, baggy-trousered 'Civil Rights Negroes' who had been fighting the good fight hitherto. No one present gets away without a personalized poison-dart in his back - no one, that is except the unseen Wolfe who's cranking the candid, *cinema-vérité* camera at 24 truthful frames a second. Characteristically he puts a price-tag and a manufacturer's label on everything like a compulsive off-duty window-dresser or comparison-shopper; equally characteristically he has a phrase to encapsulate the whole scene - 'radical chic,' which ought to get him into the next edition of Bartlett.

'Radical Chic' is a sprightly American filly by the dependable continental stud *Nostalgie de la boue* out of the ageing mare *Epater le bourgeois*, and food for a few brisk furlongs in the next couple of seasons, but to be kept away from the sticks. Trained by Seymour Martin Lipset under the guidance of Thorstein Veblen, this horse suffers from erratic, too frequently changed jockeys and usually sports the traditional colours of new gold and varying shades of red.

Leonard Bernstein has already paid dearly for his cocktail party - or 'meeting' as he's insisted upon it being called after the first report of the occasion by the *New York Times's* fashion-page correspondent brought the wrath of the *Times's* heavy-handed editorial writers and international derision down upon his silvery head. Unfortunately neither he nor his critics (including Wolfe) were ready to go directly to the principle involved and stand upon it. Which is at once a proof of the accuracy of Wolfe's observation and a condemnation of the superficiality of his technique. However one regards the Panthers - as pathetic or tragic, as symptoms or examples of the failure of black leadership - they needed and deserved money. America *is* in a critical situation, though perhaps not a revolutionary one. One way or another America is going to undergo radical social change in the next decade: to think otherwise is to be the victim of far more dangerous illusions than those embraced by the representatives of Radical Chic. Moreover, the political claims of the Puerto Ricans, the Chicanos and the American Indians are not, as the author glibly asserts, to be placed on the same footing as those of the Panthers. Viewing America through Tom Wolfe's dandy monocle is a lot of fun and rather comforting, but of limited utility. His detached lorgnette-vignettes are largely refractions in a jaded eye, proffering the illusion of three-dimensional reality.

Cry Wolfe

Alicia Ostriker

Reprinted with permission of the author. From *Partisan Review* 38 (3 November 1971), 335-58.

Wolfe of course is a "parajournalist." Besides writing the hippest fop's English since Oscar Wilde, he is the finest amateur sociologist in the business. From car customizers, to surfing teenies, to the New York art world, the subculture he can't mimic doesn't exist. Like Wilde, he does it by relentlessly probing the surfaces. And in moral America, this makes some people uneasy.

The book consists of two complementary essays, "Radical Chic," a shorter version of which first appeared in *New York Magazine*, takes off from the party given by Felicia (Mrs. Leonard) Bernstein in the Bernstein Park Avenue duplex, to raise bail money for New York Black Panthers. It invites us to amuse ourselves over some interesting ironies in the soul kissing of Beautiful People and Raw Primitives:

> For example, does that huge Black Panther there in the hallway. . .the one with the black leather coat and the dark glasses and the absolutely unbelievable Afro, Fuzzy-Wuzzy scale, in fact - is he, a Black Panther, going on to pick up a Roquefort cheese morsel rolled in crushed nuts from off the tray, from a maid in uniform, and just pop it down the gullet without so much as missing a beat of Felicia's perfect Mary Astor voice . . .[?]

The essay traces, all too briefly, the history of this flirtation and of analogous fashionable impulses, under the generic nineteenth-century label of *nostalgie de la boue*, nostalgia for the mud. In case we didn't know, the proneness of the idle rich to associate themselves with the life styles of the vital poor is not exactly a new thing under the sun. As for the particular issues involved in *l'affaire* Bernstein, the narrator has no doubts whatever about the sincerity of all concerned: "One's heart does cry out - quite spontaneously! - upon hearing how the police have dealt with the Panthers, dragging an epileptic like Lee Berry out of his hospital bed and throwing him into the Tombs." We then hear Lenny Bernstein, Otto Preminger and Barbara Walters of the "Today" show pursuing the Panthers with some heavy queries about their program. They sound like a seminar full of the goodest bright students all listening to the seriousness of their own voices as they ask really hard questions. But in fact, just as things are getting rather warm,

> "Power to the people!" says Leon Quat. . .and all rise to their feet. . .and Charlotte Curtis puts the finishing touches in her notebook. . .and the

white servants wait patiently in the wings to wipe the drink rings off the Amboina tables.

So much for dialogue. As a piece of writing, "Radical Chic" isn't Wolfe's best. In fact it reads a little like stretched bubble gum (though to my palate Wolfe bubble gum is tastier than most writers' steak and potatoes - in fact, a hack job, like, stretch it out for that deadline and the dodos will never know the difference. I attribute this, actually, to authorial boredom. The Beautiful People are not going to teach *Wolfe* anything about style. And alas, the rhetoric-laden Panthers, though they do succeed in hooking a corner of his admiration, are not going to teach him anything about revolution. More on this below.

The companion essay, "Mau-Mauing the Flak Catchers," describes a less exalted form of mutual hustle. When the Office of Economic Opportunity wanted to give money to ghetto leaders in 1968, how could they find the true leaders? Well, says a San Francisco character named Chaser, getting his boys set for a bureaucratic meeting,

> Y'all wear your *ghetto rags*. . . .You wear your *combat* fatigues and your leather *pieces* and your shades. . . .You go down with your hair *stickin' out*. . .and *sittin' up!* Lookin' wild! I want to see you down there looking like a bunch of *wild niggers!*. . .He'll try to get you to agree with him. He'll say "Ain't that right?" and he wants you to say yes or nod your head. . . see. . . It's part of his psychological jiveass. But you don't say nothing. You just glare. . .Then some of the other brothers will get up on that stage behind him, like there's no more room or like they just gathering around. Then you brothers up there behind him, you start letting him have it. . . . He starts thinking, "Oh, good God! Those bad cats are in front of me, they all *around* me, they *behind* me. I'm *surrounded*." That shakes 'em up.

Mau-mauing was a ghetto term for what the press called "confrontation"; flak catchers, the Hush Puppy civil service functionaries begging for symbolic castration so they could know who the real *bad* boys were and could ladle the funds out to them. Wolfe estimates hundreds of militant confrontations in San Francisco, thousands in the nation. He runs through a few of these, and incidentally performs a stunning analysis of the poverty-money scene in these innocent States.

If the publishers ever reissue this bright-tincted ephemerid, they should do so with an appendix of quotations from the reviews, which surely confirm the author's point beyond his fondest dreams. In response to these fleeting joys, one reviewer after another finds Wolfe insufficiently committed to justice and humanity. Why, asks the *Times* anxiously, doesn't he suggest what to do about racism? *New Republic* sort of approves, but still feels he needs more "sense of ethical alternative." And *New York Review of Books,* slamming "Radical Chic," gets into a terrific sweat over the noble motives of the Bernsteins and their guests, the dignity of the Panthers, and the nastiness of Tom Wolfe, who is a voyeur, and makes fun of people's Jewish accents, and is no better than Spiro

Agnew, and should have signed a check like a decent human being instead of insulting his hostess by writing such a mean story!

I hope Wolfe enjoyed that review. It should have felt like digging a hole and having real heffalumps fall in. But even benign reviewers mostly make sure to display their own Serious Concern about the issues of poverty and racism. In brief, everybody still wants to bark up the tree of Good and Evil - and so the message is missed.

What message? William Blake needled humanitarianism in eighteenth-century England, "Pity would be no more/If we did not make somebody poor,/And Mercy no more could be,/If all were as happy as we." In the August 1971 issue of *Social Policy*, M.I.T. sociologist Herbert Gans outlines a theory of the social functions of poverty. Poor people, he observes, do useful things for others. They create automatic status and self-respect for the non-poor. They offer votes to liberal politicians and a handy scapegoat for conservatives. More interestingly, they provide work for armies of penologists, criminologists, social workers, public health officials, OEO paraprofessionals and so on - all those people who are supposed to be "helping" the poor and who would lose their reason for existence if the poor were ever actually helped - and of course they provide an object for the benevolence of the wealthy, a sacred cause for radical intellectuals and a lifejuice culture exploitable by the arts. What would we do without them?

This dovetails nicely into *Radical Chic and Mau-Mauing the Flak Catchers*, which suggests, similarly, that good intentions, high motivations and serious concern about social evils and "ethical alternatives" - whether we are chic like the Bernstein gang or nonchic like the lowly flak catchers - are a charming form of self-delusion. We are pleased to suppose that the political process of the nation is an important matter. Wolfe thinks it's a joke. The present book should probably be read alongside his earlier work, the LSD epic of Ken Kesey and the Merry Pranksters called *The Electric Kool-Aid Acid Test* (which is not only the best thing available on the counterculture, but maybe the most exciting treatment of the American Dream since *The Great Gatsby*). Stylistically, *The Acid Test* is every kind of amazing indescribable. But here the author is not merely bored or amused. He is captivated by that *other* revolution: it's amoral, apolitical, carried on in a wilder high style than anything on Park Avenue, and cuts the heart out of our comfortable categories of right and wrong more than any existing political radicalism, black or otherwise.

If you are a hard man to impress, here was "*quelque chose de nouveau*," as Baudelaire says. After the *Acid Test*, one can see why the games played by socialites and Panthers, Mau-mauers and civil servants, might seem merely entertaining.

The New Journalism

When Fiction Is No Stranger To Fact

Arnold Beichman

From *The Christian Science Monitor* 65 (20 June 1973), 11. Reprinted by permission from *The Christian Science Monitor* © 1973. The Christian Science Publishing Society. All rights reserved.

Tom Wolfe, my favorite arbiter elegantiae, believes that thanks to the arrival of the New Journalism, "the most important literature being written in America today is non-fiction." This school of writing, he says, has developed because of "the retrograde state of contemporary fiction" and represents "the first new direction in American literature in half a century."

So far as I'm concerned, there is only one New Journalist in America, Tom Wolfe, and I am his prophet. As for some of those upon whom he bestows that title, they lack in large measure the utterly essential ingredient for serious journalism, the quality of that social-political, intelligence which informs Tom Wolfe.

Anyone who has read the author's "Radical Chic" (or his recent series in Rolling Stone on the Apollo-17 moon-shot) will appreciate the distinction between a Balzacian observer of humanity and a writer who piles detail upon infinite detail without discernible end.

The purpose of new journalism, he says, is "to give the full objective description, plus something that readers had always to go to novels and short stories for: namely, the subjective or emotional life of the characters." The 1966 publication of Truman Capote's "non-fiction novel," "In Cold Blood," gave new journalism "an overwhelming momentum."

The standard for the "non-fiction novel," however, is not Capote but according to Mr. Wolfe, Dostoevsky's "The Possessed," Balzac's "Human Comedy," Lionel Trilling's "Middle of the Journey," and books by Stendhal, Flaubert, Dreiser, Bierce, Tolstoy, Gogol, Joyce, Dickens.

What these writers possessed was a point of view about man, a theory of human nature, a sense of tragedy and irony, an understanding of culture. They were philosophers, psychologists, political theorists, novelists, yes, even New Journalists.

The anthology which forms the second half of the book, contains some of the finest feature-writing to be found in a single volume. Few of the articles, however, can be called New Journalism. Rex Reed's interview with Ava Gardner is delightful reporting but it falls short of the kind of creative and sustained intelligence which can make the leap from New to Great - to what I would call journalism of transcendent imagination.

Yet is such journalism possible? In "Honor Thy Father," Gay Talese tells us everything about some Mafiosi except, as Mr. Wolfe wryly puts it, "their criminal activities themselves." The limitations Mr. Talese was working under are understandable and are precisely the reason that few NJ's can function properly: the intractability of nonfictional material. Balzac created Vautrin, the greatest criminal character in fiction, and made him far more real that Vidocq, the actual 19th-century French criminal whose memoirs Balzac used as a basis for his unforgettable character.

Until another Balzac comes along, we will happily make do with the enormously talented "non-fiction" writers represented in this anthology. The greatest assignment for novelist and new journalist is still ahead. When the time comes, who will write - and in what form - the great "non-fiction novel" of the 1970's: the Watergate story?

Tom Wolfe - A Prophet Looks Back on the Good Old Days of the New Journalism

Melvin Maddocks

From *The Christian Science Monitor* 65 (8 August 1973), 9. Reprinted by permission from *The Christian Science Monitor* © 1973 The Christian Science Publishing Society. All rights reserved.

"Real buttonholes. That's it! A man can take his thumb and forefinger and unbutton his sleeve at the wrist because this kind of suit has real buttonholes there. Tom, boy, it's terrible. Once you know about it, you start seeing it. All the time! . . ."

This is how Tom Wolfe might begin a profile of himself - literally feeling for the cut of the man in the cut of the clothes he wears (In fact, this description inimitably belongs to him: an act of self-description).

Or he might start with the handwriting - flourishing, baroque, curlicueing out of the 18th century, making the reader wonder if "The Kandy-Kolored Tangerine-Flake Streamline Baby" had been composed with a quill.

Starting with gestures

Style is what our man seems to look for as if every portrait-sitter were the sum total of his successful gestures, minutely recorded. All right then, start with the real-buttonhole suit, start with the Your-Obedient-Servant signature, and, like a novelist, predicate a character, a rather marvelous paradox of a character. A Southern dandy (with the image of crumbled white pillars at the back of one blue eye) attending to the '60's like an extraordinary carnival barker.

A writer is the sum of what he perceives? Start then with Tom Wolfe's subject matter. California surfers. Stock-car racers. Disc jockeys. Ken Kesey and his Merry Pranksters. Why doesn't everybody else see these things? - this Youth Culture, this Great Awakening, this sophisticated new world created by children, this civilization gone pop, like bubble gum under everybody's nose.

Chronology is out

Start there, with the phenomena and the eyewitness recorder of the phenomena. Don't say: Tom Wolfe went to St. Christopher's in Richmond, Va., where he took five years of Latin. Then he went to Washington and Lee, where he took one course in journalism. Then to Yale, where (as in a dream) he whiled away five years of graduate study in American Civilization.

Bad, very bad - chronology is out with the New Journalism.

Say maybe (as Wolfe did): Graduate school is like "being locked inside a Seabord Railroad roomette, sixteen miles from Gainesville, Florida, heading north on the Miami-to-New York run, with no water and the radiator turning red in an amok psychotic overboil, and George McGovern sitting beside you telling you his philosophy of government."

How to go bohemian?

Or still better, start with New Journalism itself, or at least journalism. Say that Tom Wolfe, after five years in graduate school, was starved for the Real World. He determined to go bohemian, but after all those semesters at Yale, he really didn't know how. (The year was 1957: write the date in italic scroll but make nothing of it.) So he ended up loading trucks in New Haven, hungering for "insights from the lower order." Famine!

What to do? Once an academic, always an unregenerate academic. He read a book. It was called "How to Land the Job You Want." The argument reduced itself to a single axiom: "You only need one job." To young Wolfe, at that moment, it seemed "one of the golden apercus of Western thought."

The system worked

What sort of job with no special qualifications could an overqualified super-graduate qualify for? Journalism, of course. Following the instructions of the manual, Wolfe sought his one job with 200 letters of application. He got three answers: Two noes and one yes, from the *Springfield* (Mass.) *Union*. What do you know? The system worked, just barely. For $55 a week, plus $9 for night differential, Wolfe was a (gulp) real reporter in the Real World. Church suppers. Lost dogs. Bent fenders at Elm and Main. "Front Page" - the whole bit.

The first volunteer

Wolfe's memories are gilded: "I thought it was 1923, and I was in Chicago. I worked nights. I worked weekends. I accepted up to six assignments a day. I even volunteered for the police beat - the first volunteer in the history of the paper. I thought it was the thing to do."

After the *Springfield Union*, Wolfe moved onward and upward to the *Washington Post*, then, in 1962 arrived at the late and properly lamented *New York Herald Tribune*. Let the journalist, on his way to becoming a New Journalist, put it in his own words: "This must be the place!. . .I looked out across the city room of the *Herald Tribune*, 100 moldering yards south of Times Square, with a feeling of amazed bohemian bliss. . . . Either this is the real world, Tom, or there is no real world. . . . The place looked like the receiving bin at the Good Will. . .a promiscuous heap of junk. . . Wreckage and exhaustion everywhere. . . ."

These were giants

In a word, Nirvana. There were giants in those days: Jimmy Breslin, Dick Schaap, Charles Portis, later to write "True Grit," and, of course, Tom Wolfe - all competing for "a tiny crown the rest of the world wasn't even aware of: Best Feature Writer in Town." And don't forget Gay Talese, then competing in the uniform of the *New York Times*.

What a derby! In nine months during 1963-64 Wolfe, working as *Tribune* city-desk reporter for two days and as contributor to *New York* magazine (then part of the *Sunday Tribune*) the rest of the week, turned out 20 magazine-length pieces for the pages of *New York*, plus three long articles for *Esquire* in his spare time.

Those were the golden days for Wolfe. A demolition car-bash on Long Island one day. Off to Las Vegas for a tale-of-Babylon the next. The whole goofy panorama of '60's Americas spread out before him, wilder than a novelist's imagination.

And here is where all the tailored threads, all the elegant signature swoops, all the exuberantly agonized races against deadline lead to. Here is the vision. From a 10-years-after perspective the early '60's not only look golden to Wolfe but patterned, as if a curious, common impulse had been at work in himself and the other high-flyers. A veritable *zeitgeist*.

Obsessed with actuality (that "real world"), equally obsessed with making actuality entertaining, Wolfe and his fellow feature-stars were writing, as he now sees it, short stories out of fact. Constructing scenes. Depicting character. Recording interior monologue. *Beginning in the middle.*

Monument established

Every self-respecting Southern town once had its monuments to the past - the soldier with three names on the pedestal; the cannon; the little plot of grass. Wolfe, a charming romantic - curiously gentle, certainly less flamboyant in person than in prose - has now erected his monument to his past: *The New Journalism*, an anthology edited with E. W. Johnson. All the aces of today's journalism seem to fit under the "New" umbrella: Norman Mailer and Joan Didion; Truman Capote and George Plimpton; "Adam Smith" and Terry Southern; Hunter Thompson and Rex Reed.

Like most monuments, Wolfe's has a credo to go with it. He is a fundamentalist (in literary terms), believing in that oldest and most rejected of orthodoxies, realism. He has an abiding faith in what he calls "status details": the "specifics of dress, fashion, language, gesture." Writers, he complains, are always substituting their emotions for their data: "Moral outrage is a basic strategy for endowing the idiot with dignity." The true moral duty of a writer is to collect details the way philatelists collect stamps - with a passion. A writer should want to *get it all down*, like Dickens, like Trollope - like the novelists that used to be.

Best of both worlds

Ah, the novelists today, gentlemen. They are fabulists who have fed on Kafka, Beckett, Borges. They have lost their appetite for fact. "Great literature gets to essences, cheap literature deals with surfaces." So goes the operative criterion, and they have fallen for it, - even Philip Roth in "The Great American Novel." A race of pale allegorists - that is what "experimental fiction" has led to, leaving the scene to the New Journalist, the man who writes like a novelist and records like a reporter and has the best of both worlds.

Wolfe has made a career out of recording society's minirevolutions. He is participating in at least one himself: to shake up the literary hierarchy that place fiction writers at the top ("creative") and journalists at the bottom (the hacks!). If it doesn't take - well, Southerners are specialists at surviving lost causes in winner's style.

Targets missing

Is the New Journalism itself a phenomenon of the '60's? The targets - the absolutely right topics - seem to be missing for the moment. Where are the '70's equivalents of the Rolling Stones, the Black Panthers, Baby Jane Holzer? The men aren't biting the dogs the way they used to.

With the atmosphere hazy, the aces are grounded. Schaap, the traitor, has turned to television and to sports. Breslin, the traitor has turned novelist. Talese is researching the Sexual Revolution - a 60's topic, after all - on a $1-million-plus advance, so the gossip goes. And Tom Wolfe is writing about the New Journalism instead of writing it.

Goal: spontaneity

But only for the moment. A book on the astronauts is in the making. There are the raw notes in one binder, all paged. Then there is an outline of the raw notes in another notebook. In a third notebook an index to the outline organizes the refined notes by "concepts" and "categories." And so on. The trick is to produce that most artificial of effects, spontaneity. The trick is to melt all those notebooks away, to make the end result appear a case of serendipity.

Are the astronauts another '60's topic? No matter. Wolfe has his eye on other outer-spaces, like the various religious revivals - real, pseudo, and Satanic. Will he be the man to chronicle Shri Guru Mahafaj Ji and the Divine Light Mission?

Momentum, that's the final trick. Beside reading Savonarola ("Bonfire of the Vanities"), Wolfe is into Balzac, that prodigy of productivity who drank his coffee, ate his plums, and *wrote*. Ten pages a day out of the typewriter is Wolfe's dream. Not nine. Not eleven. When you hit the last line of that tenth page, end it, even if you're in the middle of a . . . And if you're diligent and if you're blessed, one day the new New Journalism will streak into sight like the return of "The Kandy-Kolored Tangerine-Flake Streamline Baby." Varoom! Varoom!

The New Journalism

Reviewed by Tom Curran

From *America* 129 (18 August, 1973), 98. Reprinted with permission of America Press, Inc., 106 W. 56th Street, New York, NY 10019. © 1968, 1973, 1975, 1977, 1983 and 1988. All rights reserved.

To hear Tom Wolfe tell it, it all began with frustrated novelists who worked as feature writers for New York newspapers and magazines. In the fall of 1962, Gay Talese published an article on Joe Louis in *Esquire* and the new journalism was born. Now more than 10 years later, Wolfe presents us with an anthology of some of the best non-fiction writing of the decade.

The New Journalism was an easy book to put together, but because the task was easy, the value of the result is not diminished. Wolfe took three essays he had published before, reworked them and selected pieces from Rex Reed, Truman Capote, Hunter Thompson, Norman Mailer, Joe McGuinness, George Plimpton, Joan Didion and other "new journalists" and came up with a textbook that makes fascinating reading.

At times, Wolfe gets carried away with the importance of new journalism. He says this new form is "causing a panic, dethroning the novel as the number one literary genre, starting the first new direction in American literature in half a century." This may be hyperbole, for later on Wolfe admits that what he really meant to say was "New Journalism can no longer be ignored in an artistic sense." The main point in new journalism is to write journalism, reportage if you prefer, that reads like a novel. But it is still journalism and the heart of any good journalism, new or old, is hard work. The journalist must be willing to "go through the doors marked Keep Out," camp on people's doorsteps, get the facts and write the story.

In writing the story, if the author employs the novelist's techniques, like dialogue instead of quotations, insight into the motivations behind actions instead of simple descriptions of them, the "techniques of realism" as Wolfe calls them, then he is writing new journalism.

If this anthology, compiled with E. W. Johnson, author and editor, is any indication, new journalism is good writing. The articles selected range from personality sketches of Ava Gardner, Joshua Logan and Viva, the Warhol superstar, to Michael Herr's terrifying account of the war in Vietnam and Wolfe's own devastating portrait of the party at Leonard Bernstein's for the Black Panthers.

Wolfe prefaces each story with an editor's note, explaining how each piece fits into the jig-saw puzzle of new journalism. He admits the name "new journalism" might be disconcerting: "Any movement, group, party, program, philosophy or theory that goes under a name with 'new' is just asking for trouble." But if trouble comes, it is undeserved because *The New Journalism* is a breath of fresh air on a summer's day. This is an important book about an important step in American literature.

What's New?

Alan Trachtenberg

From *The Partisan Review* 31 (July 1974), 296-302. Reprinted by permission of the author.

The New Journalism heralds an epos. Fiction is dead. The novel is out as "literature's main event." Long live New Journalism. Twenty-three "examples of the genre" make up Part Two; two of them are by Tom Wolfe, who also takes up all the space in Part One. It is really Wolfe's book throughout: his blurbs present each selection, calling roll like an announcer at the fights. "Hunter Thompson's career as a 'Gonzo Journalist' began after he wrote his first book, *The Hell's Angels, a Strange and Terrible Saga*. Infuriated because *Playboy* wouldn't run a story they had commissioned. . ." The blurbs tell the story of the story. And they point out the thing to notice. "The up-shot was a manic, high adrenal first-personal style in which Thompson's own emotions continually dominate the story." Or they thrust bits of know-how at the reader, making sure he doesn't miss such fine points of the new genre as "any time a nonfiction writer uses an autobiographical approach, he is turning himself into a character in the story." This shrewd observation gets us into Mailer's contribution, *Armies of the Night* - "quite a charming book," considering that the author is normally a "very shy reporter, reluctant to abandon the safety of the Literary Gentlemen of the Grandstand."

Your true New Journalist has long since abandoned the safe grandstand. Only a decade or so back you joined a newspaper to see the world, thinking all the while that the job was "a motel" you checked into overnight on the road to the final triumph. The idea was to get a job on a newspaper, keep body and soul together, pay the rent, get to know 'the world,' accumulate 'experience,' perhaps work some of the fat off your style - then at some point, quit cold, say goodbye to journalism, move into a shack somewhere, work night and day for six months, and light up the sky with the final triumph. The final triumph was known as "The Novel." Then sometime in the sixties the tables turned. Mysteriously the novel drifted from its path, turned its back on "experience," on how people really live, and became "New-Fabulism" - "a puzzling sort of fiction. . .in which characters have no background, no personal history." Meanwhile, feature writers for mass-circulation newspapers and their Sunday supplements were making an extraordinary discovery: "It just might be possible to write journalism that would. . .read like a novel." For Wolfe himself the moment came in 1963, unexpectedly, serendipitously. "A great many pieces of punctuation and typography [were] lying around dormant when I came along. . . .[my ellipses] I found that things like exclamation points, italics, abrupt shifts (dashes) and syncopations (dots) helped give the illusion not only of a person talking but of a person thinking." But the main discovery came when he "started playing around with the device of point-of-view." This led him on, and soon he realized that all "this extraordinary power" of social realism comes from "just four devices." No. 1 is "scene-by-scene construction"; No. 2 is dialogue - the best thing going for involving the reader; No. 3 is "third-person point of view," getting inside your character, showing each scene through someone's eyes. The whole game could come a cropper on this device, for how can a journalist claim to be inside characters he didn't invent but only just met? "The answer proved to be marvelously simple: interview about his thoughts and emotions, along with everything else." And No. 4, the device gleaned from Balzac of recording minute detail of gesture, habit, furniture, clothing, food, decor, all the symbols of "status life": "the entire pattern of behavior and possessions through which people express their position in the world or what they think it is or what they hope it to be."

As for the rest, "from character to moral consciousness (whatever that may be)," that depends on what you have in the way of "genius." The argument is only that "the genius of any writer - again, in fiction or nonfiction - will be severely handicapped if he cannot master, or if he abandons the techniques of realism." All the power of "Dickens, Dostoyevsky, Joyce, Mann, Faulkner, is made possible by the fact that they first wired their work into the main circuit, which is realism."

So much for technical explanations. There is a social explanation as well, an explanation from history. Wolfe is describing a revolution in aesthetics, in culture: a take-over by the sansculottes of the world of letters. New Journalists are the *lumpenproles*, the Low Rent crowd, "ignoring class lines," and they have had "the whole crazed obscene uproarious Mammon-faced drug-soaked mau-mau lust-oozing Sixties in America all to themselves." *The New York Times Book Review* and the *New York Review of Books* disapprove. They are trying to protect the old class structure which has the novelist at the top and the Grub Streeters below.

Waxing prophetic Wolfe foresees "a tremendous future for a sort of novel that will be called the journalistic novel or perhaps documentary novel." And it will not be an isolated event. In Wolfe's world revolution from below has been the main event in American society since World War II, and New Journalism is part of the uproarious scene. Wolfe wants to align the new kind of writing with all the mad energies bursting the old social styles at the seams.

Behind all this is a coherent vision. It came to Wolfe while he was trying to write up a California "Teen Fair." He found in California an "incredible combination of form plus money" taking place among teen-agers and altering history. "Practically every style recorded in art history is the result of the same thing - a lot of attention for form, plus the money to make monuments to it." But always "it has been something the aristocracy has been responsible for." Think of Inigo Jones's designs, Versailles, Palladian classicism: "These were the kinds of forms, styles, symbols. . .that influence a whole society." Now, it comes from below, where least expected. "Suddenly classes of people whose styles of life had been practically invisible (even to themselves?) had the money to build monuments to their own styles. Among teen-agers, this took the form of custom cars, the twist, the jerk, the monkey, the shake, rock music generally, stretch pants, decal eyes - and all these things, these teen-age styles of life, like Inigo Jones' classicism, have started having an influence on the life of the whole country." Not only teen-agers; it is happening all over. For example, racing has replaced baseball, and "this shift from a fixed land sport, modeled on cricket, to this wild car sport (a water, air, or fire sport?). . .[my ellipses] this symbolizes a radical change in the people as a whole."

Radical changes in "the people as a whole" is what Wolfe is after, where his subject lies. Because nobody else seems to notice. A "built-in class bias" gets in the way. "Nobody will even take a look at our incredible new pastimes, things like stock car racing, drag racing, demolition derbies, sports that attract five to ten million more spectators than football, baseball and basketball each year." Presumably all those people themselves noticed, but "nobody" means "the educated classes in the country," those who "control the visual and printed communication media," and who are still "plugged into what is, when one gets down to it, an ancient, aristocratic aesthetic." But the truth is that Las Vegas is our Versailles, the neon skyline "the new landmarks of America, the new guideposts, the new way Americans get their bearings." The sixties were a time, Wolfe teaches us in another book fleshing out his sociohistorical vision, of "a . . . Happiness Explosion." Our "serious thinkers," our "intellectuals and politicians" resist this "scary" notion, that the proles are swimming in affluence, are learning "sheer ego extension," against all the ancient rules - the workers are learning to be happy.

Without New Journalism we might not know all this. Without New Journalism we might go on thinking that the sixties were another decade of war and political assassination, of activism and reaction, instead of "the decade when manners and morals, styles of living, attitude toward the world changed the country more crucially than political events." The recent "revivals" of the thirties and forties should set us straight: movies, pop songs, makeup, hair styles - these were the true changes, not unions, fascism, world war. It is style that matters, not politics; pleasure, not power; status, not class; the illusion of thinking, not thought. New Journalism is the noticing of the new way.

What about the twenty-three examples of "the first new direction in American literature in the last fifty years?" Let it be said on behalf of most of the contributors, the claim is Wolfe's, not theirs. It is a mixed group, some of it journalism only in the loosest construction. Capote's *In Cold Blood* appeared several years after the events, had no relation to what we normally call news, and belongs to an older practice of picking up stories in the press and *imagining* them into novel form. It is the kind of novel of which *An American Tragedy* is the most distinguished example; Henry James's notebooks show him fascinated with similar sources. Capote and Mailer are smuggled into the book. *Armies of the Night* is a sustained reflection on events and their meanings, and reflection is one kind of thinking, or the illusion of such, notably scarce elsewhere in the book. Some of the pieces grow out of news-making events, such as Vietnam; others are examples of what we can still call political reporting, interviews with celebrities, "in-depth" stories of specific social types (the detective, the Hollywood producer), "human interest" accounts of murderers and their backgrounds. Some are fine jobs of reporting, written with insight, sympathy, conviction, and a desire to communicate a point of view. The Vietnam stories (especially Michael Herr's), Gary Wills's "Martin Luther King is Still on the Case," James Mills's "The Detective," and Joan Didion's "Some Dreamers of the Golden Dream" are the best. Judged as writing, journalism new or old, fiction or nonfiction, these are good, worthwhile pieces of work.

In fact there is nothing new in writing narratives of firsthand experiences in contemporary society with dialogue, scene, dramatization. Edmund Wilson did it better than anyone in the book in his trial coverages in the twenties and in "American Jitters." Wolfe has a section in his pseudoscholarly appendix called "Is the New Journalism Really New," and lists earlier "Not Half-Bad Candidates." He mentions some obvious names: Mark Twain in *Innocents Abroad,* Stephen Crane, John Reed, Orwell. (Agee is dismissed earlier as "a great disappointment." True, "he showed enterprise enough, going to the mountain and moving in briefly with a mountain family." But "reading between the lines I would say that his problem was extreme personal diffidence. His account abounds in 'poetic' descriptions and is very short on dialogue.") But Wolfe misses the point of the examples. They exist because the phenomenon is as old as the newspaper. Moreover, since the late nineteenth century it has been associated with a zest for enlarging the social experience of readers, often with reform as a plain motive. See Jacob Riis, *How the Other Half Lives.* Or Jack London, *People of the Abyss.* Or the muckrakers. Or the reportage of the 1930s (Wolfe might start with William Stott's recent book, *Documentary Expression and Thirties America*, where he will learn just where Agee went and lived). Many of the selections in *The New Journalism* fit a familiar, well-tried mold.

If not a "new thing," there is still something special, something that needs pointing out, in the composition of the collection. It lies in the relation of the ensemble to its presumptive subject, America in the 1960s. Although there are exceptions, the dominant social voice in *The New Journalism* is degrees cooler than was true in past reportage, less outrage, more understatement, juxtaposition, irony. There is less undisguised social purpose, less passion for exposure, for change. And less concern simply for "the facts." Wolfe writes: "When one moves from newspaper reporting to this new form of journalism, as I and many others did, one discovers that the basic reporting unit is no longer the datum, the piece of information, but the scene, *since most of the sophisticated strategies of prose depends upon scenes"* [my italics]. The motive revealed here might clear up a puzzling point that appeared earlier. Why should Wolfe worry about whether literary intellectuals and other class-biased souls take notice of the wave of new styles that occupy so many millions of people? Because the cutting edge of his kind of writing is the claim that he is seeing what others, the rulers of taste, the intellectual elite, refuse to see. The assumption behind this kind of writing is that until somebody notices an event, it is not real. But the somebody has to be somebody other than the people in the event, somebody who by noticing thereby gives the event what it needs to become real: status, prestige. The same thing is true about the writing itself; it asks to be noticed, to have conferred upon it the status of "style," and now of "art."

In Wolfe's works, including his present claims to a new kind of writing, the mechanisms of a middlebrow mass culture are transparent. In *Electric Kool-Aid Acid Test,* his book about Ken Kesey, the Merry Pranksters, and the California LSD scene, Wolfe writes: "I have tried not only to tell what the Pranksters did but to recreate the mental atmosphere or subjective reality of it. I don't think their adventure can be understood without that." Unquestionably a clever mimic, a shrewd observer, and sometimes pretty funny, Wolfe performs neat jobs of ventriloquism with his "downstage" voices. The gimmick is that all the words are authentic, taken from observation, correspondence, interviews, publications. They are ingeniously reassembled and appear as if they are the spontaneous generation of the narrated action itself. This way Wolfe seems to merge with his subjects, to be speaking their thoughts, feelings, words. Wolfe is at pains to authenticate his sources, but the claim matters little except as a device to keep the reader from noticing that the true facts of the genesis of the work - the interview, research, listening to tapes, even being on the scene - are kept hidden. Unlike Terry Southern and Hunter Thompson, Wolfe does not dramatize his own participation. He is almost not there. This means that along with the actual apparatus of journalism, anything like a substantive perspective is impossible to locate. The corrugated verbal surface, the hyped-up prose, its tachycardiac speed, its fevered illusion of thinking and feeling, all disguise the *reporter*. That is why the direct quotations from a letter by a woman recounting her first experience with LSD comes with such relief: at last, a real voice. The rest is illusion of a group subjectivity, only and sheerly verbal, never complete, never completing itself in the reader's imagination, except as display, as spectacle.

What Wolfe gains by his pyrotechnics is an easy experience for the reader: just lean back and let it happen to you. But it is deceit: by disguising itself and its procedures, by mystifying the presence of the author as a merely neutral recorder when he is in fact the only active producer of the product, Wolfe's work is a revealing instance of mass culture. The appearance of spontaneity is the product of the most arch manipulation and manufacture. By pretending to render the world always as someone's experience, from the inside, Wolfe may seem to be revitalizing the craft of journalism and preventing the loss of experience that comes with hardened journalistic formulae. But just the opposite results. He converts experience into spectacle, fixes it, reifies it as a reader's vicarious experience. He cheats us with illusions of deeper penetrations into segregated realities but the illusion is a calculated product that disguises what it is we are actually reading.

Wolfe's genre is a cool Flaneur's version of the comic journalism practiced by Mark Twain and his brethren. He dons the guise of the Low Rent rebel, speaking on behalf of those who have been deprived of their status by the literary, intellectual, and political elite. His devices include a bogus erudition and intellectuality, an OED vocabulary of technical terms, outrageous but "learned" neologisms, and catalogue after catalogue of the names and things that fill the days and hours of American popular life, all presented without punctuation, as a kind of synchronistic pop mandala. He panders to both a hatred and an envy of intellectuals. His *lumpenprole* revolution is no more than a botched theft of what he thinks is the prize jewel of the intellectuals, the label of "art." Far from revolutionary it is a conformist writing, whose message at a low frequency is that you have never had it so good. Wolfe cannot see beyond the "chic" in middle-class radicalism, nor beyond the gamesmanship in confrontation (made into slick theater in "Mau-Mauing the Flak-Catchers"). Hardly a vision to disturb the sleep of the proprietors and managers. In many ways it is also their vision. Wolfe's revolution changes nothing, inverts nothing, in fact is *after* nothing but status. It is full of half-baked versions of ideas in currency. The best that might be said for it is that it is a put-on. But I doubt it. I think he is dead serious.

The Painted Word

Crying Wolfe

Douglas Davis

From *Newsweek* (9 June 1975), 88. Copyright © [1975], Newsweek, Inc. All rights reserved. Reprinted by permission.

In one of his many defenses of "the new journalism" - and his own slam-bang, verbal-socko style - Tom Wolfe once wrote: "We developed the habit of staying with the people we were writing about for days at a time. It seemed all important to *be there*. . .to get the dialogue, the gestures, the facial expressions, the details of the environment. . .the emotional life of the characters." Exactly! This is why Wolfe's writing used to succeed. That it does not - particularly in his latest book, "The Painted Word" - is precisely because Wolfe is no longer out there, mixing it up with his subject, reporting directly off the streets. Instead, he is sitting back. . .Tom Wolfe sitting back, but not so far as to wrinkle his white linen suit. . .Tom Wolfe *theorizing* about subjects he doesn't understand. . .such as modern art. Imagine! The *enfant terrible* of the '60s suddenly becomes. . .old doggie!

But that doesn't mean *THE PAINTED WORD* isn't going to be a big seller, and stir up readers everywhere. For one thing, Wolfe by now is more of a celebrity than the celebrities he describes. And the book blasts away at a fat and luscious set of targets: avant-garde art (always easy to attack, since by definition it is difficult to understand); posh museums; Andy Warhol, the hero-villain of pop art; Willem de Kooning and Jackson (the dripper) Pollock. But Wolfe's major target is a whole set of disagreeable difficult highbrow art critics like Clement Greenberg, Harold Rosenberg and Leo Steinberg (the kings of "Cultureburg," as he puts it) who - according to Wolfe - are dominating art with their theories.

Add a set of photographs of strange-looking works of art of a few deft Tom Wolfe drawings and you've got a little tract that everybody will love, from middlebrows to antiabstract-act highbrows who have been feuding with American art since 1945. Attaboy, Tom!. . .go get'em, in the name of social realism!

Shaky: Unfortunately, "The Painted Word" will not serve anybody - except Wolfe - well. Its base in its subject is so shaky and its psychology so wrong that it will never alter either the *realpolitik* of the art world or the enormous personal power wielded by the three kings of Cultureburg - though I agree that such changes are needed. Nor will "The Painted Word" enlighten its readers as to why new art looks the way it does and why it elicits so much enthusiastic support throughout the world. Wolfe's case is fatally flawed by three major fallacies:

1. He believes not only that theory is antithetical to art but also that it is somehow corrupting. "The Painted Word" begins with a lengthy quote from *New York Times* critic Hilton Kramer, in which Kramer faults the new realism because it lacks a verbal rationale ("to lack a persuasive theory is to lack something crucial"). Wolfe leaps upon this text with eurekas, claiming to have found the Rosetta stone for the corrupting success of modern art. "Modern art," he explains breathlessly, "has become completely literary: the paintings. . . exist only to illustrate the text." In brief, the critics have put modern art over on us. But theory has been part of the success of any art as far back as we can go - Victorian, neoclassical, Renaissance, medieval and even Greco-Roman art were surrounded by written analyses and statements, some of them still surviving. Michelangelo, Leonardo and Delacroix were prodigious talkers and writers. So was Picasso. So is Jasper Johns. And every one of them was promoted and defended by critics.

2. Wolfe is convinced that modern art is not "popular" as are film, literature or theater. But his only proof is descriptions of "chaotic" paintings by de Kooning and Pollock, a quote from Greenberg ("all profoundly original work looks ugly at first"), and reference to the high cost of original works of art. But the facts run the other way: museum attendance, print buying and cheap reproduction sales have soared during the very period when "Cultureburg" came to life. The truth is either that the public enjoys the provocation inherent in new art or that it no longer considers this art "ugly."

3. Wolfe is horrified by the thought that art can be made, shown, supported and defended by a handful of people. The "elite" art world, he contends, numbers no more than 10,000, living in seven or eight major cities. This is a conviction proper to the man who first told us in the 1960s that tail fins and surfing were art forms, but it is totally wrong. All forms of art begin with the few, then proceed to the many. Populists and Stalinists to the contrary, art starts alone - and convinces society later.

Tang: Why did Wolfe go wrong? The singular lack of wit and dialogue in "The Painted Word" gives the game away. Wolfe did not get away from the typewriter and out into the thick of his subject. Imagine Wolfe dining with Greenberg, drinking with Rosenberg, going to an opening with Steinberg - and reporting it all. Then we would have the tang of reality, the feel of what is it like to be *inside* Cultureburg, instead of outside peering in, through the lens of theory.

"The Painted Word" ends with a prophecy that can be turned around and aimed at its author. Led further and further toward dependence on critics, modern art will end up as pure as word, says Wolfe. He foresees in the year 2000 a Metropolitan Museum survey of American Art 1945-1975 that will be devoted not to pictures but to critical texts ("huge copy blocks, eight and a half by eleven feet each"), with tiny reproductions of the paintings they discuss. "The three artists. . .featured will be not Pollock, de Kooning, and Johns," predicts the author, "but Greenberg, Rosenberg, and Steinberg." But who must therefore take credit as the discoverer, promoter and theoretician of these "artists"? None other than Tom Wolfe himself, who by the year 2000 will be the curator of this exhibition, the critic of the critics, the Last Word on the Painted Word. Zounds!

The Painted Word

Reviewed by Dennis Leder

From *America* 133 (30 August, 1975), 98-99. Reprinted with permission of America Press, Inc., 106 W. 56th Street, New York, NY 10019. © 1968, 1973, 1975, 1977, 1983 and 1988. All rights reserved.

Material success has often been interpreted as God's favor for man's resourcefulness. A subtle ploy for obtaining such favor was evidenced early in our history in the form of a work ethic. But power has usurped God's favor as the contemporary motivation to work: control over one's fellow humans and over the universe.

Whatever its motivation, the work ethic has damaged an important aspect of the interior life. Fantasy, thought by early Americans to be time ill-spent in a life of work devoted to God, is now equally misunderstood, being considered a harmless diversion amid the important matters of life. At what cost is our contemporary society "succeeding" when the process seems to demand a sacrifice of the precious gift of wonder? Freud tells us that every soul longs for dreams, but ". . .inexorable repressions prevent the enjoyment of all but the meager daydreams which can become conscious." It is the true artist, he says, who has a unique consciousness of fantasy. When modified and expanded, this gift ". . . opens out to others the way back to the comfort and consolation of their own unconscious sources of pleasure."

The French painter Henri Matisse said: "Each century seeks to nourish itself in works of art, and each century needs a particular kind of nourishment." But the 20th century is notable for ambivalence and even hostility towards its own artists and their work. Is this, in fact, the fault of the work, or the result of man's quest for control in which mystery in the deepest sense is unacceptable and contemplation ("sitting with") is intolerable?

I raise these questions because they are crucial to the life of the spirit, which Freud believes the artist unlocks for us, and also because they are notably lacking in Tom Wolfe's treatment of the evolution of modern painting in *The Painted Word*. He is quick to reject most 20th-century painting, but at the same time exhibits little concern for why painters work in a particular manner, and no awareness of the disposition necessary for viewing modern painting, among which are an interest in the very process of putting paint to canvas and a willingness to live with mystery. (Matisse: "When a painting is finished, it's like a newborn child, and the artist himself must have time for understanding. How, then, do you expect an amateur to understand that which the artist does not yet comprehend?")

Wolfe, however, demands crystal clarity as he stands before "thousands" of modern paintings ". . .waiting, waiting, forever waiting for. . .it. . .for it to come into focus, namely, the visual reward. . ." And upon finding no reward he concludes there is none. Critics supply all the meaning. "Modern art has become completely literary; the paintings and other work exist only to illustrate the text." With this view as his basis, Wolfe goes on to describe the artist's process as similar to our power ethic society. Power comes from living a bohemian life style in reaction to bourgeois values ("The Bohemian Dance"), while at the same time keeping alert for recognition by that very bourgeois society, and submitting gracefully to it when it does arrive ("The Consummation"). Freud mentions power, fame and wealth as part of the creative person's interior desires. Usually finding them unattainable, the artist sublimates them and finds gratification in the process of creation. But anyone failing to fit Wolfe's pattern of the "Bohemian Dance" and "The Consummation," and choosing instead a process of sublimation (authenticity or spirituality), is assumed to be unbalanced or fraudulent.

Cynicism is indeed prevalent among us because it so well conceals what we do not or will not understand about ourselves and our world. The true artist, then, who sees deeply, is bound to be as much a threat to some as a blessing to others. Wolfe counters this threat by removing the artist from any privileged status, and assumes that art is now a business like any other, with its manufacturers (the artists), its publicity men (critics) and its consumers (the wealthy elite). Though introducing issues that could warrant further discussion (Is there a universal preference for realistic painting? Does the critic amplify a visual statement or actually give it meaning? Is participation in creativity reserved only for a privileged few or open to all? What constitutes the true artist?), Wolfe takes from these only what suits his purpose, which is to expose the myth of modern painting. Far from being a "a cause for celebration" as the dust jacket announces, *The Painted Word* is a sad wielding of power through cynicism by one who has apparently misplaced his sense of wonder.

Café Criticism

Rosalind Krauss

"Café Criticism" by Rosalind Krauss first appeared in *Partisan Review*, Vol. 42, no. 4, 1975, 629-33.

"It's kind of a goof." That is what Linda Lovelace said to every question a journalist put to her about starring in the first-run pornography of *Deep Throat*. And that, in essence, is how Tom Wolfe responded in a recent interview about his latest book, *The Painted Word.* The interviewer had supposed that the book's flamboyant attack on modern art - its makers, its critics, its patrons - issued from some sort of position on the part of its author. If Mr. Wolfe thought modern art empty, what kind of art did he support in its stead? If he thought the criticism misdirected, what kind of writing would serve its subject better? If he thought those institutions, corrupt, what should replace them? "I don't *care*, frankly," was Wolfe's consistent reply. "I don't care if the situation never changes. Because if it changes, it might not be as funny. I've had a good time writing about it." In short, it's kind of a goof.

The Painted Word hit the art world like a really bad, MSG-headache-producing, Chinese lunch. It hit it at a time when - after a decade of activity during which work of consistently focused ambition and high quality was produced - a sense of diffuseness and transition pervades the art world. But transition is not the same as decline. So those readers of Wolfe's book who have any serious interest in the state of modern painting and sculpture did not think it such a goof; they tended, instead, to think it something of an affront.

The thesis of *The Painted Word* is that modern art, long ago emptied of any intrinsic content, functions solely as a medium of social exchange. Through its purely honorific value, the work is able to add a specialized luster to the cultural lives of the rich, in exchange for which they are willing to lionize its makers. In order for this exchange to take place, Wolfe's argument continues, someone has to create a value for these meaningless objects of trade. This is where the critics come in. Part middlemen, part shamans, they are the ones who validate these fetishes by endowing them with a meaning they would never otherwise obtain. In order to concoct this meaning, the critics invent special brews of aesthetic theory that are as elaborate as they are obscure.

The Painted Word sets itself the task of "exposing" this arcanum of theory, and for this endeavor its author considers the best technique to be ridicule. So, for example, Wolfe decides to make sport of the notion of "flatness," a concept he identifies as the theoretical property of Clement Greenberg. He begins by quoting from an essay on the work of Jackson Pollock in which Greenberg, pos-

tulating that the general concern of modernist art is to reveal, rather than con-
ceal, its material means, states that one of the ways painting can do this is by
declaring its own flatness, and describes Pollock's work in those terms. To these
statements by Greenberg, Wolfe then adds his own set of interlineal riffs: *"That
thick, fuliginous flatness got me in its spell,"* he starts to jeer. *"That constructed,
re-created flatness that you weave so well. . .; Those famous paintflings on that
picture plane,"* Wolfe finishes, counting on the comic exposé to mock both art
and theory out of existence.

But when the laughter subsides, there is left, for some people, an image. It is
an image of one of Pollock's great canvases from the late 1940s, the Metropolitan Museum's *Autumn Rhythm* perhaps; and those people are remembering a
particular experience they had in relation to that work. That experience would
have been one of enormous sensuous immediacy in which there was also an
appeal to thought. For they would have seen a certain kind of transformation of
the physical substances (pigment, canvas) that form a painting, which occurred
without ever having denied those substances. They would have seen a materially
self-evident web of paint generate a very special sense of luminous depth. It was
special in that it did not belong to any particular known space, like a landscape;
and it had no chartable dimensions. Instead it was space seen abstractly as the
property of paintings (the way colors or textures are the properties of objects),
rather than as their illustrated content. Since space or depth is the opposite of
flatness, it is paradoxical that depth should be seen as a property of the flat surface of Pollock's paintings. But the energy of Pollock's work was generated by
that paradox. The luminous flatness of *Autumn Rhythm* was space turned into an
abstract idea which could shape the material givens of a work and its contents
into a single, continuous, object of perception. What those people are remembering, then, is a particular moment of intuition which is sometimes called an
aesthetic experience, and which Wolfe renders in his text, with a sputter of italics
and fancy punctuation, as ". . .it. . . ."

For those people, the ones who have had that kind of immediate experience
in relation to works of modernist art, who have felt grateful for and convinced by
its affirmation of the seriousness of a certain kind of human enterprise, who have
been affected by the forms it has found to embody the moods and modes of
consciousness, Wolfe's thesis remains consistently beside the point because
Wolfe is charging in *The Painted Word* that they have not had that experience -
that *"it."* According to him, there really isn't any experience to be had. But there
are many people who have responded to modern works of art, and for them that
fact is completely beyond argument.

The point that it is beyond argument needs to be emphasized. Because whatever knowledge one might want to see as being established by that primary experience - and different writers about art have obviously had different conceptions
of the directions a critical response might take - critical response begins and
ends in the authenticity of that experience.

By implying that with respect to modern art, specifically modern abstract art, there isn't any experience, Wolfe creates the inference that those who make it and those who respond to it are simply shamming; and in order to cover up this deceit they have either constructed or become dependent upon a barrage of words known as critical theory. In relation to the elaborate con they are pulling, this critical theory functions as an emotionally feeble but politically powerful substitute for the experience that isn't there. Further, their motives for engaging in this game range from self-aggrandizement and self-flattery, through the basest kind of venality and economic self-promotion to a witless credulity and self-deception. Through the flash and filigree of Wolfe's orchestration of this theme, one hears the throb of that *basso ostinato* by which he repeats: there isn't any experience; there isn't any experience.

Now, if one is looking at the kind of social and economic fallout that surrounds the making of high art in our culture (and some of it is very noxious indeed) but one is looking at it from the vantage of having experienced the seriousness of that art, the situation becomes a little more complicated than Wolfe wants to allow. It becomes, one might want to say, morally complex. But if what informs one's perspective is the absence of any experience of that work, then the moral issues begin to shift ground.

From the position from which Wolfe writes, a position informed by his own professed lack of aesthetic experience of this work, there is no central intuitive response for which one has to take any particular responsibility and, therefore, no brake on what one might say. Wolfe feels free to describe the art in just about any way he chooses. Pop art, we are told, was a realistic style all along and held out the pre-cubist pleasures of narrative painting, a point one finds quite baffling in a text illustrated with Jasper Johns' deadpan *American Flag* and Roy Lichtenstein's *Yellow and Blue Brushstrokes,* neither of which function narratively. Larry Poons's painting can be likened to the optical illusions from "Ripley's 'Believe It or Not' "; Frank Stella's work can be described as frames hung on the wall with nothing in the middle; and minimalist sculpture can be characterized as room dividers.

That is how art gets treated; the vulgar cannibalizing Wolfe performs on the body of art criticism is done with even greater insouciance. Given his contention that there is no experience, it is possible for him to describe the men and women who write about modernist art as a monolithic cult, performing the ritual of self-promoting obscurantism out of uniformly contemptible motives. It is possible for Wolfe to ignore, in the case of the three critics he parodies at greatest length, the fact that Harold Rosenberg, Clement Greenberg, and Leo Steinberg are men whose response to works of art have led them to conceive of the project of writing about those responses in ways that are entirely diverse. Rosenberg, who works in an area between art criticism and social history, uses the possibility of an authentic experience of art as a model for authenticity in general, and has been consistently attentive to the dangers of alienation from experience. Greenberg, with an entirely different focus, has engaged in a long and patient labor to build a normative criticism based on a language of description in which what one says about a work is completely verifiable within the manifest features of the object itself. And Steinberg has wished to codify what might be called a psychology of response: a written enactment of the process of careful and sustained attention to works of art. But if these three critical tasks are different, their motivating energies are not. In all three cases there is a primary sense of responsibility to the truth of intuitive experience.

If I keep returning to the question of truth or authenticity, it is because that is both the real subject and object of *The Painted Word*. Tom Wolfe has looked around the art world without having been able to detect a single flicker of it; and if we are to trust his account, that is because his book purports to be the very model of what is missing in the world he observes. Wolfe's language, with its insinuating tone, its confessional hysteria, its performance of immediacy, the fake spontaneity of its asides, is held up to us as the genuine article: feelings at a pitch of intensity, the ego continually triumphing over the threat of alienation.

But as is the case with most of the new journalism, what we are confronted with in *The Painted Word* is the totally theatricalized self. In attempting to present us with a subjective account of the event, the writer has simply substituted himself for the event, which is in this case the work of art.

Yet it is natural to works of art that they exclude the interventionist ego. For like most of the things we take seriously, they are independent entities with meaning of their own to which we must attend. And if Wolfe asks, *"Why* must one attend to them? On pain of *what*?"* then the only answer one can give is this: on pain of not getting *"it."*

The function of criticism is simply to aid the process of that response, suggesting ways of looking and things to look for. It cannot invent something that is not there. But it can describe the vision of experience for which the choices displayed by a particular work are both enactments and emblems.

If there is any real charge that can be leveled at the art criticism of the past few years, it is not that it has conjured up something from nothing, but that it has not responded fully enough to the richness of its subject. Contrary to Wolfe's argument, we are faced at this moment with a poverty rather that a surfeit of criticism with any fresh theoretical energy. The sensibility and the sets of ideas out of which the sculpture of the 1960s was made has never adequately been described. Because this sculpture has generated much of what is being done at the present time, the absence of a coherent body of theory by which to clarify its choices has made the art of the 1970s seem much more fractured and inchoate than it actually is. We are therefore in a situation where current art has moved, temporarily, beyond the reach of a critical language relevant to its terms. It is into that situation that Wolfe has inserted *The Painted Word*, a book that has troubled certain critics, not because (as it contends) they have done too much but because, of late, they have done too little.

The Painted Word

Reviewed by Albert Bergesen

Reprinted from *The American Journal of Sociology* 88 (January, 1979), 1021-24.
Reprinted with permission of the author.

Obviously Tom Wolfe is on to something. But no one seems to acknowledge
what he has seen. The critical reviews of *The Painted Word* all seem to go on
about his superficiality and lack of knowledge about modern art. Considering the
fun he makes of two very sacred institutions, modern art and New York intellectuals, I suppose it is no wonder that the critics should reply in kind. But the
significance of *The Painted Word*, at least for sociologists, lies not so much in
Wolfe's moral evaluation of recent trends in art or in his descriptions of the
various social types which make up the art world as in his insightful observation
of two trends in modern art: the gradual de-objectivization of art - its becoming
more and more abstract, and the corresponding rise in the necessity of some
kind of art theory. These two points are worth pursuing for they suggest ways of
understanding change in artistic style, and more generally, a way of conceptualizing art as a kind of linguistic code.

In discussing the history of modern art from early modernism through abstract expressionism, pop, op, minimal, earth art, and conceptual art, Wolfe
observed the more or less general trend of removing more and more content
from the art object itself. "In the beginning we got rid of nineteenth-century
storybook realism. Then we got rid of representational objects. Then we got rid
of the third dimension altogether and got really flat (Abstract Expressionism).
Then we got rid of airiness, brushstrokes, most of the paint, and the last viruses
of drawing and complicated designs (Hard Edge, Color Field, Washington
School)" (pp. 97-98). He points out how we next got rid of the picture frame
altogether (Frank Stella's shaped canvases). Then we got rid of the picture altogether and painted on the walls of the gallery (Robert Hunter and Sol Lewitt).
Then we got rid of the walls themselves, creating sculptures which filled the
museum (Carl Andre, Robert Morris, Ronald Bladen and Michael Steiner).
Then we got rid of the gallery and museum with earth art, such as Robert Smith-
son's *Spiral Jetty* in the Great Salt Lake. And finally, with conceptual art, we got
rid of the idea of a permanent work of art itself, so that, ". . .there, at last, it was!
No more realism, no more representational objects, no more lines, colors, forms,
and contours, no more pigments, no more brushstrokes. . . .Art made its final
flight, climbed higher and higher in an ever-decreasing tighter-turning spiral
until. . .it disappeared up its own fundamental aperture. . .and came out the
other side as Art Theory!. . . Art Theory pure and simple, words on a page, literature undefiled by vision. . .late twentieth-century Modern Art was about to

fulfill its destiny, which was: to become nothing less than Literature pure and simple" (pp. 107-109). While I do not feel entirely comfortable with this sort of broad sweeping account of the changes in modern art, I do feel that there is enough truth to his point about increasing abstraction to provide some crude evidence for a conception of art as language and for extending our understanding of changes in sign systems in general.

What Wolfe has captured here is the complex relationship between the vocabulary and syntax of an art object, as expressed in questions of color, form, line, brushstrokes, and so on, and the larger cultural context, art theory, in which the art object is embedded. Wolfe has described what Basil Bernstein refers to as elaborated and restricted linguistic codes. Bernstein argues that the meaning of a linguistic act (or in this case an artistic act) comes in part from the actual internal substance and structure of the speech act (vocabulary and syntax) and partly from the more general set of understandings the group holds as to the meaning of these linguistic signs. What Bernstein calls restricted codes develop in situations in which there is a smaller lexical pool and a narrower range of syntactical alternatives from which to construct a speech act. These codes arise in groups where there is a high degree of solidarity, where people know each other on a face-to-face basis, and where there are many commonly held assumptions so that there is little need to spell things out. Hence the restricted code. Elaborated codes, on the other hand, arise in social situations where there is less solidarity, less face-to-face contact, and accordingly fewer commonly held assumptions. Here meaning derives from the internal structure and substance of the language as found in the complexity and variety of vocabulary and syntactical arrangement. Since people do not know what you are about, you have to spell out your intentions. Hence the code is more elaborate. There is an implicit equation here, what I will call the semantic equation. On the one side is the linguistic act, or art object itself, and on the other side are the assumptions the group takes for granted. The dynamic part of this equation centers on the fact that changes on one side of the equation are reflected in changes on the other. If the pool of vocabulary and syntactical alternatives decreases, then the broad cultural understandings must increase so that the semantic equation can remain in some sort of equilibrium, that is, the sentence or art object can still be a meaningful act to some audience.

How does all this apply to Wolfe and modern art? Modern art - in becoming increasingly abstract--throwing out line, color, brushstrokes, and picture frames - is reducing its artistic vocabulary and syntax and, as a means of communication, is becoming an increasingly restricted code. Since the origin of meaning for an art piece is found decreasingly within the actualities of the painting itself, there has to be an increase in art theory to give the art object meaning. The semantic equation remains balanced. As content declines, theory increases. In effect, if a person says less through a speech act or a painting, you have to know more about what he is talking or painting about to make sense out of it. This reliance on the broader cultural context, here art theory, to make sense out of a restricted code is nicely captured in a observation of Hilton Kramer's: "Frankly, these days without a theory to go with it, I can't see a painting."

How restricted can a code become before a crisis in the semantic equation is reached? In the case of modern art the continual removal of elements from the art object can seemingly reach a point where all the meaning in the semantic equation resides on the side of the cultural context, giving us object free art, as in conceptual art where we have art without any sort of visual experience. "Art. . . disappeared up its own fundamental aperture. . .and came out the other side as Art Theory!. . . Art Theory pure and simple, words on a page, literature undefiled by vision" (p.109). Now the emergence of a new realism in the 70s, such as what Wolfe terms "photo-realism" in his epilog, suggests that there may be a cyclical character to these changes in the semantic equation. As a code becomes more and more restricted, as visual free art is reached, so to speak, the semantic equation is no longer balanced because the cultural context now carries virtually all of the meaning. This kind of system is unbalanced, collapses, and then begins again. The new realism, therefore, may be the product of the completion of a cycle of ever restricting codes, which become so restricted that they disappear, with the whole semantic machinery resetting itself in some sort of new equilibrium.

There is still the question of why the semantic equation should move in one direction or another. The world of New York art, with the close contact and familiarity of artists, critics, intellectuals, gallery owners, patrons, and museum directors represents the same sort of intimate and closed society that Bernstein found in his working-class neighborhoods. To the extent that the New York art world was this sort of close intimate community, it seems reasonable that it developed a restricted code in its artistic expression - for example, the various sorts of abstract, minimal, and conceptual art. The decline of New York's role as an intellectual and cultural center represents a weakening of that community's sense of centrality and, as such, a movement away from artistic communication through restricted codes like abstract and minimal art to more elaborated codes, such as the photo-realism mentioned by Wolfe.

All of this, of course, is highly speculative. But we do know that at the height of New York's fame as the center of modern art in the 40s and 50s, we had the emergence of abstract expressionism as a highly restricted code and the increasing necessity of art theory (Clement Greenberg and Harold Rosenberg) through which abstract art was interpreted, and more fundamentally, made into something that could meaningfully be understood as "art." The decline of New York's importance is also associated with the collapse of the secret language, the rise of the new realism - photo-realism - and the increased attention being given to photography. As the community withers, its commonly held assumptions similarly dissipate and the burden for meaning falls on the other side of the semantic equation, that is, on the system of signs rather than on the larger cultural context of art theory. What is to be artistically spoken can no longer be hinted at, or activated by an abstract clue or gesture. It must be said in full by the coherent ordering of the vocabulary and syntax of the art object itself. In some sense, I suppose, the appearance of Wolfe's essay is also part of this process, for with the larger cultural context which gave meaning to abstract forms dissolving, the abstract forms now stand somewhat naked, without a larger purpose and meaning, and, as such, open to ridicule.

Mauve Gloves &
Madmen, Clutter
& Vine

Imprisoned in the Sixties

Garry Wills

From *New York Review of Books* 23 (20 January,1977), 22. Garry Wills.

The Vietnam war returns in these books, not to haunt us but to amuse. Everyone who touches that war gets tarbabyized by it. Gloria Emerson manages to trivialize by her very concern. She feels it her duty to be outraged that a perfume is now called Charlie - once the Americans' nickname for the Viet Cong. Wolfe celebrates America's flyers over Vietnam in a long piece on "Jousting with Sam and Charlie." The "Sam" of that title, a snaky missile seeking out the airplanes' animal heat, makes dramatic appearances in Wolfe's prose. But "Charlie" never does show up. These books are unconsciously aimed at each other; and both miss the target. They remind me of a "Doonesbury" strip from the war days. Phred the Terrorist is screaming up at the bomber pilots, calling them vicious monsters. Meanwhile, in the clouds, Americans rehash the latest Knicks game.

Emerson's book crawls along with Phred, from splutter to splutter, attributing every kind of malice to the colonizers, unable to understand that the war machine worked automatically, without malice, with a dutiful attention to technique. Wolfe's prose soars with appropriate skill and moral obtuseness. You would never know from this chronicle of battle with the SAMS that his flyers risked death in order to deal it.

Wolfe made his mark by celebrating the wacky styles of the Sixties. Some who admired that aspect of his work were dismayed when they found, late in the game, that this stylistic radical was also a right-winger. They felt much as admirers of early Waugh or Eliot did, when they learned that *Vile Bodies* and *The Waste Land* were meant to speak not for this century but against it. Yet Wolfe is no Waugh or Eliot. They were recognizably "conservative" by almost any thoughtful definition. Wolfe is that American kind of "conservative" who is in love with change and all the explosive powers of capitalism. He does not resemble the Waugh who pictured modern life as a speeding race car out of control, but the William Buckley who established God's existence, in a recent essay, from the intricate gadgetry on his yacht. Wolfe's love of style is like Goldwater's love of gadgets as the ornaments and trophies of capitalism.

Wolfe celebrated the Sixties as "a happiness explosion" caused by an economy that "has pumped money into every class level of the population on a scale without parallel in any country in history." The poor are as invisible to Wolfe as Charlie was to the pilots. When Michael Harrington reminds us that there still are poor people, Wolfe uses his customary tactic of dismissal, the invention of a spurious new category - in this case the Adjectival Catch Up: "We have relative poverty (Michael Harrington's great Adjectival Catch Up of 1963)." Wolfe is always discovering some new social phenomenon for which he must invent, on the spot, a new social law. He likes to predict what "historians will say" about us. Flying so high and at such great speed, he spots only the outsize and exotic. He tells us blacks split from whites on the left because the blacks wanted Superfly clothes and the whites insisted on dungarees. He misdates as well as misplaces the split, which was precipitated by the resolutely dungareed SNCC kids.

Wolfe's most famous "new" category was Radical Chic, which was as old as the Abolitionists of the nineteenth century. Radicalism has always had an elitist set of sponsors (if not originators) in America. He makes the Big Insight operate almost like the Big Lie. Call it something new and no one will notice that what is true is old, while only the new is false. Another technique for his sleight-of-hand is the flourishing of odd bits of learning, like distracting hankies of perfumed lace. He likes to explain behavior in linguistic metaphors, drawing heavily on rhetorical devices. But he defines epanadiplosis incorrectly as the equivalent of chiasmus. He supplies us with the etymology for charismatic ("Literally: God-imbued"), unaware that he has confused charismatic with enthusiastic. His love of catchy slogans make him invent one category ("serial immortality") which could not possibly mean what he wants it to.

His history is slapdash - usually irrelevant, and often wrong: St. Paul's rebuke to the Corinthians does not establish (as he thinks) that "the early Christians used wine for ecstatic purposes." In arguing that the Jesus Freaks have inaugurated America's third Great Awakening, he ignores evidence that the religious "revival" of recent years has been a recognition that religion was always alive and well out there in the real world, so little visited by Death-of-God faddists or by Tom Wolfe. Wolfe is so sloppy he even says things that work against his own ideological drift, as when he includes Marx in the handful of men whose thoughts have influenced history "unaided by any political apparatus."

He is not only wrong to begin with, but cheerfully incorrigible. A piece written before the revelations of CIA and FBI and IRS misdoings mocked the idea that our police might be spying on us in secret. He reprints the piece in 1976, unaware that the laugh is now on him. His proof that we could not have a police state was the fact that "the only major Western country that *allowed* [my emphasis] public showings of *Macbird* - a play that had Lyndon Johnson murdering John F. Kennedy in order to become President - was the United States (Lyndon Johnson, President)." It is hard to know exactly which con that verb "allowed" is trying to work - does he mean to imply that *Macbird* was suppressed in France and England, or that it should have been suppressed here, or both? Those who, like Wolfe and McLuhan and Eric Hoffer, go for the Big Insight, are not allowed to test, alter, or develop any line of thought. The Insights have to be thrown out, formed and disjunct, to lie there, separate pearls, almost all fake, too many new ones arriving for us to search out the few that are genuine.

Wolfe's act, like Eric Hoffer's depends on a spoofing of the experts, on posing as the anti-intellectuals' intellectual. Sometimes Wolfe has to make up a group of intellectuals for the sole purpose of attacking them. He finds that masters of "the conventional Grim Side concepts" are calling his third Great Awakening "fascist." He does not name these Grim Sliders, because he is making the group up out of a few small and antagonistic voices - those of his own allies from the *Commentary* set who called the hippies fascistic, and the very different investigators who are probing the connections of Sun Myung Moon with the Korean CIA.

Why bother with a writer who has been so spectacularly and consistently wrong about American life? For the brio of his performance? I suppose. He benefits from the freak effect of literacy on the right. But there is more to it than that. Wolfe is sometimes right almost by accident. He only sees exotics, but sometimes he sees through them. There was no "new journalism" in any serious way, but Wolfe tried to make his case for putting a new label on old things by remarking that fiction had ceased to play its traditional role of reaching character through exquisitely observed milieu. Ten years after he started saying that, Gore Vidal was proclaiming the sterility of experimental writing in this journal, John Leonard and Wilfrid Sheed were calling fiction a higher gossip, and there was renewed interest in "realistic" novels. They were repeating Wolfe's thesis, without noticing the fact.

Wolfe talked nonsense about McLuhan as a neural recircuiter; but that leads, in this collection, to a brilliant attack on Freud's concept of repression. Don't count Wolfe out, either, in his attack on postwar painting. The howls of reaction to *The Painted Word* resemble the treatment given his comments on fiction in the Sixties. It adds to the enjoyment of the performance that Wolfe's own gifts for observation and reportage are not very good. He boasts that his journalism is more accurate than the conventional kind, even by conventional norms -yet he called me, once, for a set of dates and facts to include in his anthology of journalism, and he got almost every one of the items wrong. In the same way, it is fascinating to watch him attack Pop Art with the comic-book tricks and "Pow!" techniques of a Pop sensibility.

He is a walking clash of style with content, like all capitalist "conservatives" - he is a puritan dandy. Yet dandyism often reflects a moment when self-indulgence reaches a pitch that is almost self-denying; and the right-wing devotion to capitalist goods - to growth and change and expansion - involves a kind of discipline by materialism. You have to use all the gadgets cranked out by the system to prove that the system works, that the "happiness explosion" will reach "every class level" if we just keep feeding it.

We even have to use the bombers. Wolfe's essay on Yalie aristocrats of the air, our aces over Vietnam, is written with the contagious enthusiasm of a Thirties biplane movie. It is absolutely certain that no one who *could* write so lovingly of that air war *would* do so now - no one but Wolfe. Though the Vietnamese never show up in his article, there is a comic Oriental straight out of the Thirties - the aircraft carrier's Filipino steward, who gets things off to a quaint start by waking flyers with his chimes and the cry of "buy borty-bibe" (5:45). The rest is all air heroics, with only one dim glimpse - down through the clouds - of the real enemy, who is not Vietnamese. Just when a transport site has been knocked out, the Vietnamese come up with an even greater weapon against Americans:

> On the third day they massed the bomb strike itself. They tore the place apart. They ripped open its gullet. They put it out of the transport business. It had been a model operation. But the North Vietnamese now are blessed with a weapon that no military device known to America could ever get a lock on. As if by magic. . .in Hanoi. . .appears. . .Harrison Salisbury! Harrison Salisbury - writing in *The New York Times* about the atrocious American bombing of the hardscrabble fold of North Vietnam in the Iron Triangle! If you had real sporting blood in you, you had to hand .it to the North Vietnamese. They were champions at this sort of thing. It was beautiful to watch. To Americans who knew the air war in the north firsthand, it seemed as if the North Vietnamese were playing Mr. Harrison Salisbury of *The New York Times* like an ocarina, as if they were blowing smoke up his pipe and the finger work was just right and the song was coming forth better than they could have played it themselves.

The only other villains of the piece are William Sloane Coffin and Kingman Brewster, whom the Yalies must get back at with their bombs - Mr. Chips never betrayed the boys in the trenches!

Ms. Emerson, in this book of reflections on her experience as a war correspondent, abroad and at home, wants us to look down through the clouds and see Phred's people, bleeding. Unfortunately, every time the clouds part, the first sight we get is of Ms. Emerson. She musters her flock in a matronly way, and quotes the funny English of her favorite, Luong, in a manner that put him dangerously close to Mr. Buy Borty-Bibe. One of the functions of the flock is to give us more sets of eyes through which to see Gloria and her agony:

Long after Tay Ninh, when I was living in Massachusetts, Luong wrote me a letter that put into words what the trouble was, what I had refused to admit. He said that whenever there was time, he and the reporters, the ones I knew and others who came after, would talk about me: "All have this remark about you: you are the only one who cannot overcome your Vietnam experience."

It is all a little too obviously Ms. Emerson's war. Everyone tells us that in the book. When she is insufficiently distressed that a tree is endangered, Richard Goodwin tells her, "You would care if the tree was in Vietnam." Emerson describes an Ellsberg groupie who grabs his nameplate off a symposium table. But Emerson herself shows a groupie tendency for all those connected with the war. Sent, after her return from Vietnam, to cover a livestock auction, she finds she cannot concentrate on the cattlemen because she sees two veterans standing near - and black veterans at that: "One wore the canvas and leather boots, another his Army shirt with the sleeves cut off. I wanted to stay with them." Emerson is a very nun of protest. She seeks community with "other women who knew what I knew," and makes a pilgrimage to Lillian Hellman's home.

I doubt that even someone less self-dramatizing than Emerson could make us care about the Vietnamese. The most evil aspect of the war was that we did not wage it either for or against them. They were not the issue. If they had been, we would have witnessed the deliberately inflamed racism of World War II. The fact that we were supposed to be supporting some Vietnamese made it hard to work up the blatant hatred for "Gooks" that we were obliged to feel for "Japs" and "Krauts." Showing napalmed little girls did not sting the American conscience. The pictures were regarded as unpleasant, and that was held against those who displayed them - much as pictures of aborted fetuses are now. Neither set seems to make converts. After all her spluttering, Emerson must admit that the best thing written about the war preceded America's entry into it - Graham Greene's *The Quiet American*. And that book was not really about Vietnam, but about the divisions within our colonizing West, the clash of Pyle with the narrator. (Ironically, it is Pyle who shows an interest in Vietnamese cultures.)

It is natural that Emerson should succeed a little better in reporting on war protest at home than on the war itself. That was where the battle had its origin. Hawks kept bombing the Vietnamese to get even with Bill Coffin, to show that America could not be wrong, to silence the critics. But Emerson sees malice where there was little, and saintliness where there was little, and has no mind at all for sorting out various kinds of mindlessness on both sides. In the rice fields, her kind of screaming did not affect the bombers. Outside the Pentagon, it may have helped the generals. Where the ironies are not attended to, the tragedy does not reach us. Instead we see a cartoon hermit figure carrying a doomsday placard - but one that does not read, in her case, THE END IS NEAR. Rather, THE END HAS ALREADY OCCURRED.

We do not know, yet, whether the nation learned anything from Vietnam. Public reaction to the Mayaguez incident seems to indicate that it did not. Ms. Emerson and Mr. Wolfe do not so much learn from the Sixties as keep reliving them - Emerson in ineffectual protest, and Wolfe in a brilliance of destructive technique.

Mauve Gloves & Madmen, Clutter & Vine

Reviewed by Ross Feld

From *Saturday Review* 4 (22 January 1977), 39-40. Reprinted with permission of OMNI INTERNATIONAL, LTD.

In the Sixties, Tom Wolfe was fun because he could tag as stylish (and mimic) behavior everyone else assumed was merely weird. But now, in the Seventies, when we have no style but think we're flush, when we're no longer Merry Pranksters or Flak Catchers but just a bunch of folks full of attitudes - now even the zingiest journalist has got a problem. Attitudes give birth to attitudes, which sour as fast as milk, and the sharpshooter either turns curmudgeon (like Malcolm Muggeridge) or fancies himself a satirist.

Muggeridge at least has a faith, a place to withdraw back into. Wolfe, with his popcorn style and tailor's fussiness, has only the world, and it's one he doesn't much care for anymore. We're in the "Me Decade," this collection of essays flappingly asserts; we brim over with silly selfishness and deplorable postures. Wolfe interestingly opposes this idea with a piece on the chivalric gesture and class found in the behavior of F-4 fighter-bombers "jousting" over Vietnam: to hang on the precipice of your mortal soul in a flying hunk of metal is better than crossing Dr. Freud's perilous gulch (the former presumably hasn't too much "me" about it - or much "you" either). The distinction is piquant, I'd say. In his last book and now this one, Wolfe seems to be going after tinsel with an ax. Two or three of the pieces here are still fun, one is fine, but the whole is increasingly no-account and over-fried.

The Mature Wolfe

Nereo Condini

Reprinted with permission of *The New Leader*, January 31, 1977. Copyright © the American Labor Conference on International Affairs, Inc.

This new collection of essays, journalism and fictional sketches (with a title John Berryman would have loved) reveals a different Tom Wolfe. He does not content himself here, as he once did, with mad torrents of words that could be enchanting, but often were gratuitous and cavalier. The old Wolfe was daring and sometimes felicitous in describing a kaleidoscopic world. Jazzy, syncopated rhythms enlivened his dayglo syntactic bravuras, making the page shimmer and tremble. Yet his prose was too much like the tumultuous gush of the acid movement he was chronicling - a theater of the '60s drug scene enacted in all its exuberance and apotheoses, crammed with "screeling screamers, megascope, fooling pooling. . . ."

Mauve Gloves, by contrast, brings to mind one of those ancient Chinese tapestries that at first seems merely a huge multicolored blotch. Upon closer inspection you notice trees, animals, people, then the intricate jewelry the men are wearing, and finally the intimations of immortality in the crevices of their skin. So, too, initially Wolfe's present sensibility appears to identify with the fashions of contemporary life. Soon, though, it becomes apparent that he is mocking, not praising, in this deceptive maze of social analysis, sardonic humor and poignant ironies.

But the best way to describe the mature Wolfe is to present the characters in his latest book. The first, in the title piece, is the semifictional author of *Under Uncle's Thumb.* Instead of his new novel, this famous man of letters is tackling the ridiculous world of necessity he has woven for himself: payment, expensive clothes, cocktail parties (Clutter & Vine is his florist, Mauve Gloves his caterer). It is the same kind of phony beauty that Wolfe will expose more and more often in the sketches that follow, and it is opposed to the one he cherishes: the beauty of real style and elegance, the beauty that uncovers truth, defies death and cares for the immortal Now. Wolfe's writer, however, warns of repression and police brutality - just as the fake futurologists go on about the tragedy of pollution, the disaster-mongers get hysterical over rampant fascism, the New York rich try to upgrade their low-rent accents and crave anything but their real selves.

The hijackers in "The Perfect Crime" symbolize this warped perspective, too. Their false acts of bravery stand in sharp contrast to Wolfe's real heroes, the pilots immortalized in "The Truest Sport: Jousting with Sam and Charlie." Wolfe is furious at those who reviled the American boys in Viet-nam, at the doves who would recommend the exclusive bombing of military targets in Hanoi and expose our flying aces to suicidal missions.

Despite the lousy liberals, though, the pilots stand their ground. On the carrier *Coral Sea*, John Dowd and Garth Flint are knights taking off to go jousting with SAMS (Russian missiles) and Charlies (ground fire) - sticking to the rules, obeying their code of honor, fighting for glory, indifferent to death. Their attitude transcends all fears and links them to, more than anything else, a holy brotherhood held together by an athletic regard for form and sporting combat.

Living with the utmost intensity, Dowd and Flint return to the carrier: "This flight deck - in the movie or the training film the flight deck is a grand piece of gray geometry, perilous, to be sure, but an amazing abstract shape dominating the middle of the ocean as we look down upon it on the screen - and yet, once the newcomer's two feet are on it - geometry - my God, man, this is a. . .skillet! It *heaves*, it moves up and down, as the ship moves up and down into the wind and, therefore, into the waves, and the wind keeps sweeping across, sixty feet up in the air out in the open sea, and there are no railings whatsoever - and no way whatsoever to cry out to another living soul for a helping hand, because on top of everything else the newcomer realizes that his sense of hearing has been *amputated entirely* and his voice is useless."

His two heroes notwithstanding, Wolfe's relentless attacks on mannerism far outweigh his occasional tributes to valor. In "The Intelligent Coed's Guide to America," "The Perfect Crime," "Pornoviolence," "The Me Decade," and "Funky Chic" he lambasts the people who used to criticize LBJ for being tough on the Reds, and now love to feel persecuted and oppressed by the dire forces of fascism lurking in the country. Voicing an indignation they do not really feel, they behave like their cronies in Europe during the '60s, who said, "it no longer is necessary to produce literature, it is only necessary to live *la vie intellectuale*."

In place of literature and old-time values, Wolfe observes, we now have violence. We watch blood, earthquakes and floods in our theaters, and read about them in the gory headlines of our newspapers. We are victims of a nouveau vulgarity - parvenu manners and bad taste glorified. What is more, the populace wants new pleasures, more leisure, all the kicks money can buy.

To circumvent the boredom that the soup of fists and ketchup will inevitably bring on, Wolfe puts forth a modest proposal: "In the latter days of the Roman Empire, the Emperor Commodus became jealous of the celebrity of the great gladiators. He took to the arena himself, with his sword, and began dispatching suitable screened cripples and hobbled fighters. Audience participation became so popular that soon various *illuminati* of the Commodus set, various boys and girls of the year, were out there, suited up, gaily cutting a sequence of dwarfs and feebles to short ribs." Why, Wolfe asks, can't we do the same?

He suggests that the mess of pornoviolence started, in part, with that crazy Doktor's legacy of libido, the sticky heirloom that sways the men and women of today and warns that if you don't have sex regularly, you contribute to the moral ruination of the country. Because of Freud's hangups, we are doused with prescribed therapeutic spasms, with "heaving, groaning, biting, sticking, jamming, nuzzling guzzling, skotophilia, rut-boar grunting. . . ." "The Me Decade," the glorification of the self, has ignited a fiery mysticism unquenched by the modernistic, rational efforts of the Protestant and Catholic churches.

While Wolfe's view is a bleak one, on the whole he tries not to let the sour satirist get the better of him. In "Funky Chic" and "Honks and Wonks," though, his humor turns biting, his irony savage. He is fascinated with fashion and appearances: Things are put on and off, he says, according to changing tides and values. In the '60s it was fashionable to be ostentatiously rich, but today the debutante heroine wears blue jeans, *loves* little black children, and even *learns* from them. Manners reveal the man in his age, and pronunciation tells whether you come from Beacon Hill or Newark. Indeed, "no one is able to resist that delicious itch to reveal his own picture of himself through fashion."

In Wolfe's cosmology, "honks" are the true artistocrats, the Kennedys with their nasal knighthood, the Gucci-Pucci old girls; "wonks" are the poor, the blacks, the blue collars, the chicanos, and the phonies. By opening their mouths, these people lay bare their hidden aspirations, their defeats, their frustrations. The attentive listener sees how some try to lose their accents, others correct them, and still others flaunt them.

Wolfe's sympathy lies with the last - "Dis is da way I tawk and dis is da way I'm *gonna* talk, an you betta lissen." And despite his allegiance to the "honk" world of style and beauty, a pervasive nostalgia for the mud always brings him back to the other camp: "Laiiike, nyew nyeoow, man, ai mean, Fisha's island is a groove and a gas comcompaaaiiihed. . . ."

But most of the time the new Tom Wolfe tries to keep his distance. Writing with all the vitality of the old, he makes every effort to be, at the same time, cool, firm and dignified. This, added to Wolfe's wit and a lyrical quality that every now and then breaks through, makes *Mauve Gloves* an invigorating experience.

Mauve Gloves & Madmen, Clutter & Vine

Reviewed by Gerard Reedy

From *America* 136 (5 February, 1977), 113,115. Reprinted with permission of America Press, Inc., 106 W. 56th Street, New York, NY 10019. © 1968, 1973, 1975, 1977, 1983 and 1988. All rights reserved.

This book collects Tom Wolfe's researches in the 1970's: the joys of mini-computers, summerwear on Martha's Vineyard, the inside of an aircraft carrier off North Vietnam, male cosmetics commercials, college lecturers, skyjacking, sensitivity, porn, Freud, denim, private-school accents, getting a cab in New York City and much, much more. Wolfe so richly details his facts and trends that one wonders whether he has had time to do anything else but take notes and write since the decade began. In his energetic accumulation of detail and in his clever way of isolating cultural metonyms, Wolfe is a marvel, a phenomenon for any writer to admire.

Although Wolfe is anti-fad and anti-elite throughout, the exact moral or philosophical position from which he satirizes his subjects is not always clear. He scorns the "me-decade" of self-indulgent self-knowledge, but we do not learn how he feels about the unexamined life. He derides the Cassandras of the college-lecture circuit, yet we cannot believe, from other essays in this book, that he altogether disagrees with them. He writes an apparently unironic essay, detailed to the point of asphyxiation, on the pilots who bombed North Vietnam, and the gadgets they treasured; in this case, because of a surfeit of popular negatives, perhaps Wolfe is exactly right to suppress the obvious point of view.

The structure of "The Commercial" shows that Wolfe is at times nervous about point of view. First one narrator, then a second, tells the same incidents; at the end, a third, omniscient narrator assures us that both previous narrators live happily ever after. Also, in the first sketch, the title piece, the satirist's values scarcely rise above those of the subject satirized.

Writing such satire of contemporary mores - especially of contemporary intellectuals - involves a special kind of boldness and sense of personal identity. Somewhere out in the heartland, where *New York* magazine is not Revelation, there are plenty of fundamentalists preaching Wolfe's sermons from moral texts much more clearly defined than his own. Wolfe distances himself from these social critics by the hipness of his style and the superiority and clarity of his perceptions. Still, I feel an unresolved tension here between old values and new forms, between the desire to be taken seriously and the need to be popular.

Wolfe includes a number of his willowy, very funny drawings. His writing style is chummy but avoids vulgarity. His paragraphing sometimes seems to be made up of prefabricated blocks. Because Wolfe's topics are so contemporary, I would have appreciated a listing of exactly where and when these sketches first appeared, statistics that are no small part of Wolfe's meaning.

Lastly, Wolfe's impudence delighted me at least 80 percent of the time. What other commentator would wonder whether, if Freud had taken cold showers instead of analyzing himself, "the tenor of life today. . .might be radically different"? How curious and nice to find such an old-fashioned moralist who, at the same time, knows intimately the way we live now.

Mauve Gloves & Madmen, Clutter & Vine

Reviewed by Everette E. Dennis

Originally published in *Journalism Quarterly* 54, 2 (Summer 1977), 408-409. Reprinted by permission of *Journalism Quarterly*.

Often criticized by his detractors for not delivering on books he has promised for years, Tom Wolfe provides a partial answer with occasional collections of shorter pieces, some of which have appeared in magazines before. This book is one of those compilations. Most of the 12 stories and essays assembled here are of recent origin, though a couple go back to the mid-and late 1960s.

For the journalist it is a particularly instructive collection that demonstrates once again Wolfe's extraordinary abilities as an observer of American manners and morals. Whether he is the Balzac of our times remains to be seen, but surely he offers the reader insights and playful analysis, a quite revealing perception of the passing show. Who else looks with such Edwardian disdain on a world of pocket calculators and leisure suits? Who else observes consciousness-raising sessions, meditation and self-help programs and declares that we have become the "Me Generation?" Who else can size up a pretentious party on Martha's Vineyard and declare that it is a class-conscious coalescing of two subsets of American elites - the "New York Media & Lit. people" and the "Boston People." As he puts it:

"Until the Media & Lit. people began going there about 10 years before, Martha's Vineyard had always been a Boston resort, 'Boston' in the most proper sense of the word. There wasn't much the Boston people could do about the New York people except not associate with them."

Of course there is no one quite like Wolfe writing in America today. He is our most perceptive observer of the nuances of American life. His considerable knowledge of sociology and his sensitivity to social class, clearly as an elitist observer, make the results of his "investigations" both dazzling and infuriating.

Wolfe in his 1970s writing is less the saturation reporter and more the critic. In this collection his pieces on "Mauve Gloves & Madmen, Clutter & Vine" (a slice-of-life story of a west side sweller in New York who is tallying up his life expenses on a pocket calculator from which the title is taken) and "The Me Decade and the Third Great Awakening" (an explanation of the self-indulgent and inner-directed life style of the 1970s) stand in marked contrast to a delightfully funny item from the 1960s also included here: "Pornoviolence." In "Pornoviolence," which originally appeared in *Esquire* 10 or so years ago, a detached Wolfe has stringers for the *National Enquirer* meeting each other at a bash in a

New York hotel. Wolfe's new work is more analytical, though sometimes in subtle ways. And the writing style is more controlled, less given to the adjectival barrage of the 1960s.

Still Wolfe is at his best when he describes furniture and fashion. With a scholar's sense of organization, he takes on those phenomena of popular culture that most scholars, indeed, most serious writers and journalists, find taboo. So he takes us to Yale where sartorial eloquence was once the rule and finds instead that:

"The unvarying style at Yale today is best described as Late Army Surplus. Broadway Army and Navy enters heaven! Sons in Levi's break through that line! that is the sign we hail! Visible at Elm and York are more olivegreen ponchos, clodhoppers, and parachute boots, more leaky-dye blue turtle-necks, pea jackets, ski hats, long-distance trucker warms, sheepherders' coats, fishermen's slickers, down-home tenant-farmer bib overalls, coal-stoker strap undershirts, fringed cowpoke jerkins, strike-hall blue workshirts, lumberjack plaids, forest-ranger mackintoshes, Cong sandals, bike leathers, and more jeans, jeans, jeans, jeans, jeans, more prole gear of every description than you ever saw or read in a hundred novels by Jack London, Jack Conroy, Maxim Gorky, Clara Weatherwax, and any who came before or after."

Thus Wolfe helps us understand the movement from "Radical Chic" to "Funky Chic."

There is a dynamic quality to Tom Wolfe's writing for he sees things as others do not see them. His piece on "the Perfect Crime," for example explains why the taking of hostages is the perfect crime for the 1970s. By assaulting the system the terrorist, hijacker or hostage-taker can deal with more traditional frustrations involving class, love and money, Wolfe says. Interesting that this essay should have appeared two months before the kidnapping of Patty Hearst.

This collection is replete with bright, fun-to-read articles, ranging from "Honks and Wonks," which deals with accents and social class, to "The Intelligent Coed's Guide to America," a look at the intelligentsia and the college lecture circuit. On top of this is the usual visual treat of Wolfe's own drawings that illustrate in an outrageous way his equally outrageous essays. Or are they so outrageous? Are they perhaps demonstrating how nonfiction writing can involve, excite and recreate reality? It may be that Wolfe is America's most creative journalism teacher with continuous demonstrations in his own work that give clues about the revitalization of print.

The Lives of Writers

Thomas Powers

From *Commonweal* 105 (3 March, 1978), 142-43, 147-48. Reprinted with permission of *Commonweal*. © *Commonweal* .

No crueler writer ever lived. If he were a lepidopterist (and he is, in his way) he wouldn't find his pleasure in the chase, out there in the fields with his net and his handbook, creeping up on a butterfly as it rested on a twig, its beautiful wings breathing in and out. He'd like that well enough - the wonderful moment when you know you're going to get it - but the real pleasure would come later, as he shook it gently into his choloroform bottle, careful not to disturb the dust on its gorgeous wings, and later still, back in his study, when he took a plain steel pin, the kind tailors use, and skewered the plump little dead body to the mat board in his display case. A perfect specimen of it type. *Nailed.*

Tom Wolfe is not a generous writer. He's gifted in almost heroic proportion, not only with the writer's ear for irresistible words (a common enough talent, in truth), but with independence of mind, an amiable manner which persuades people to tell him things, and a genius for effortless self-promotion. He's not just good at what he does; he's a figure as well, somebody in particular, a presence, unique. People instinctively see his work as a whole; each new article enlarges our perception of who he is. It's hard to say what he'll add up to in the end, but he has certainly burst the cocoon of anonymity, and his ability gives him a fair shot at being the sort of writer people call great. But no one ever called Tom Wolfe generous.

His peculiar gift is for satire, but it is satire of an odd sort. He is not like Juvenal, angry and excoriating, animated by fierce passion. Far from it. His portraits are pitiless enough, but he seems to speak from a great distance, as if none of this mattered very greatly to him. Occasionally he speaks of himself as "the man in the white suit," amused and remote, a visitor at the carnival taking in the sideshows. His targets are ordinary humbug, inflated self-esteem, cant, childish preoccupation with style, confused and timid sensibilities. His world is a pampered place, filled with the rich, sometimes pugnacious follies of the over-protected. But Wolfe is not trying to reform us; the silliness amuses him, just as it might have amused him at the court of Louis XIV. He might have written a fine piece about the Duc de Saint Simon, who would strut and preen for a month in the afterglow of an amiable remark by the King. Unlike Juvenal, Wolfe does not long for a braver age. There is no Puritan or Republican fire in him. He is amused in the manner of a man convinced that human nature is immutable, and it is his strength to see that our age is as sunk in vanity and folly as all the rest.

Take his portrait of the "well-known American Writer" X in *Mauve Gloves &*
Madmen, Clutter & Vine, author of *Under Uncle's Thumb* and about to embark
on a new work. X is sitting in his study in his seven-room apartment on Manhattan's Upper West Side. A pile of bills is on the desk in front of him. He unzips
the cover of his pocket calculator and begins to add up what it costs him to live
for a year - $1,000 a month for the maintenance and mortgage on his apartment,
nearly $7,000 for private schools for his two children, another $7,000 for the
place on Martha's Vineyard. And that doesn't even count the ordinary bills, the
$800 owing for a cocktail party last month, the $500 for library stairs specially
made in Hong Kong, the $248 for a pair of boots made in England. X is adding it
all up - *chuck! chuck! chuck!* - as he taps the keys on his little calculator.

But really he is only putting off the moment of work, mulling over the way he
lives now. (Not brooding; it is clear Wolfe doesn't think X has the depth for
honest brooding over anything much larger than a fancied slight to his dignity.)
He is thinking about the Vineyard - an absolute necessity! it isn't *fair* to keep the
kids in the city all summer - and the people that he has been meeting there,
important people, *big* people, the kind whose intimacy can help to make him big
too.

And he's thinking about those $248 boots, caked with mud in the back of his
closet. He wore them to his father's funeral on a rainy day in Chicago, but somehow, he just couldn't wipe the mud off those boots. His father had been an
immigrant from Russia, a tailor throughout the Depression, a self-educated man
who could quote Goethe and Dante in his heavy accent. And somehow, thinking
of his father's life and his own life, X couldn't wipe the mud off those boots.
When he got home he tossed them into the back of his closet where they lie still,
curling and cracking.

Another writer might have done something else with those boots. He might
have inverted the story, turning it inside out like a sock, and made them the point
rather than merely an episode. Those boots are telling X his life is hollow and
empty; they speak to whatever is honest in him. But not Wolfe; he's tougher than
that. Never give an inch. X treasures those boots because they prove his sensibility. He's almost proud of them. If people only *knew*. . .

Besides, Wolfe has got another point in mind, and he isn't about to let it slip
away. X has already been nailed with his own pretense and tender self-regard,
but there is one detail more in Wolfe's portrait of the well-known American
writer. X puts away his calculator and daydreams. He rolls a clean sheet of paper
into his typewriter, and taps out the working title of his new book:

Recession and Repression
Police State America
And the Spirit of '76

It would be unfair, if it weren't true. There are writers like this. Wolfe artfully
declines to name his victim, but anyone who regularly reads the political journal-

ism which comes out of New York editorial offices can think of half a dozen candidates off the top of his head. The writers with agents like sharks and gold American Express cards who would turn murderous if Elaine ever put them in the back room. The kind of writers who snickered about the Nixons in private, and sneered in print. Slick champions of Democracy, Justice and Freedom, their own lives are as filled with poisonous intrigue as a Florentine court. Self-appointed defenders of the poor and oppressed, they can burn their way through enough money in a year to support a woman with six children on welfare for a decade. Their work is a crisp catalog of public sin and corruption, but they melt in the company of the great, toads slipping their way through crowds of people with drinks in their hands, trying to get *close.* . .

New York writers, and a lot of their cousins elsewhere, are indeed cursed with a kind of mandarin attitude towards the world. Their animosity towards business in all its forms has about it a touch of 19th-century disdain for trade. The people who mattered had incomes, not jobs. It is not much different now. No one in his right mind would go into *business.* Advertisingmen are whores, corporate executives all thieves, public officials corrupt, ordinary people with ordinary jobs objects of pity. Mandarin writers are hypocritically, even willfully blind to the realities of economic life. Someone has to support *them* after all; someone has to build and run those businesses which sustain the government with its billions in taxes, and put the ads in the magazines which run the mandarins work. But the new mandarins brush all that aside with the same wave of contempt; America is all hustle and ticky-tacky.

It is the same with almost every other aspect of national life: a willful blindness to the sheer complexity of the world, a reduction of genuine dilemmas to cheap moral certitude. How are we to end the arms race? How are we to free the banished classes or poor from their awful dependence on cold institutions? How are we to sustain our economy as we slide down toward the bottleneck of diminishing resources? How are we to keep the generators running without strip-mining, nuclear plants and imported oil? Such questions pose no problems for the new mandarins. In their snug minds there is an answer to everything, and it is only accident their answers never threaten *them* with war, unemployment lines, schools that don't teach, cold houses, or the loss of those precious two months on the Vineyard.

Wolfe's "well-known American writer" is out there all right. He is probably snickering over something in the Sunday *Times* right now, thinking of stirring himself for a late brunch at One/Fifth, eyeing his wife across the breakfast table and wondering how he can engineer a free moment to phone that girl he met at a party the night before, the one who said she just *loves* writers.

So why do I call Wolfe the least generous of writers? Well, his choice of subjects seems so odd and arbitrary. If the mandarins exist, paid too much for too little, and not so much made as destroyed by their good fortune, nevertheless they are few in number. There may be a grotesque disparity between their satiny lives and their public *personae* of gritty iconoclasm, but they are very far from being representative of the lives of writers as they are more generally lived. The truth of the matter is that no profession is so ill-paid as writing. Everybody involved in the production of a book - from the editor on down to the stockroom boy - makes a living of *some* sort, with one exception: the author. He, more often than not, is working for free. The major trade publishers issue perhaps 12,000-15,000 new titles a year - it depends on what you're willing to call a book - but I should be very much surprised if as many as two hundred of their authors were actually living on what they earned from writing.

How do they live then? Partly by writing for magazines, exhausting work which pays badly - as little as $50 or $75 for a book review, rarely more than $1,500 for a major article. More often by teaching on the side (from $800 to $1,500 a semester, depending on the school), or by doing free-lance editorial work, or on grants (for which you pay in spiritual coin ten times over), or by depending on a wife or husband with a regular job, or by living on savings. Most of them don't last long. You see their names for a year or two, and then they break and disappear. Their credit cards are withdrawn, their savings gone, their agents sorry to report that the best offer for a book was $5,000. Some few manage to handle a job as well as freelancing on the side, perhaps even managing a book or two, always hoping for the freedom which might come with a big paperback contract. Disappointment is the air they breathe. It is not that their work is second-rate (although financial desperation will kill a talent quicker than anything else), but that there is not much demand for it. It seems there are a lot of magazines when you try to read them all, but there aren't so many really, and most of them are poor too. Writers do not work for free from choice, but from necessity. It is not often the world will pay a man a living wage simply to hear what he's got on his mind. Read George Gissing's *New Grub Street;* it hasn't changed one whit.

Wolfe's "well-known American writer" was settling down to a book on recession and repression, an ambiguous exercise for one so free from both. But there *was* a recession, and it was not so long ago that repression was very much the mood of Washington. Who wrote about the hardship and the danger? It certainly wasn't Wolfe, who was writing about "The Girl of the Year" during Vietnam, and the ballooning pretensions of modern painting during Watergate. His choice of subjects is his business - and I would certainly rather have him write about ephemeral peacocks, than not to write at all - but it doesn't sit well for him to speak with such scorn of those with a shade broader interests.

He could say in his defense - although he is certainly not a man given to defending himself - that his target is the "well-known American writer" who makes such a good thing out of bad things, but it is not the mandarins who write about war, injustice and threats to freedom in any important way. They borrow attitudes which have already won the day. The people who have gone before are a motlier crew, armed with nothing but their own passion and conscience, publishing in small magazines, living as they can, trying to hold out against the world's indifference. Not many of them last; all are heroes in their way.

They have their failings - intolerance, perhaps, or a tendency to exaggerated alarm - but superciliousness is not one of them. They remind me of Samuel Johnson and Richard Savage, wandering the streets of London all night for want of the price of a bed. They were "not at all depressed by their situation," Johnson later told Joshua Reynolds, "but in high spirits and brimful of patriotism, traversed the square for several hours, inveighed against the minister, and 're-solved they would *stand by their country.*' "

The "well-known American writer," meanwhile, is wondering how to squeeze a clause on advertising into his contract, and Wolfe is going through his check stubs, with a smile of distant amusement.

The Right Stuff

Orbital Chic

Ted Morgan

From *Saturday Review* (15 September, 1979), 35-38. Reprinted with permission of OMNI INTERNATIONAL, LTD.

Does anyone out there remember the New Journalism? In the Sixties and early Seventies, a bunch of writers started doing outrageous things with nonfiction to get away from the "the pale beige tone" of orthodox journalism. The idea was that the reporter could write journalism that would read like a novel. He could use all the techniques of fiction, the entire literary arsenal of the great novelists - pages of dialogue, streams of consciousness, shifting points of view - but he would apply them to real people and real situations, and it would all be accurate because he had acquired a depth of information that had not before been demanded in newspaper work. He had glued himself to his subjects, sometimes for months, until he was able to reconstruct entire scenes, and write as though he knew the workings of their minds.

In 1973, the New Journalism gained the status of a movement with the publication of an anthology of the work of 23 of its practitioners with a long introduction by its editor, Tom Wolfe, the movement's generalissimo and chief theoretician. . .Tom Wolfe, the Che Guevara of the New Journalism!

Wolfe was not at all shy about broadcasting the group's achievements. The New Journalism, he said, was "causing a panic, dethroning the novel as the number-one literary genre, starting the first new direction in American literature in half a century."

Well, one doesn't hear a great deal these days about the New Journalism, which seems to have joined other fads of the Sixties in the dustbin of history. One trouble with the New Journalism was that it wasn't new, as Wolfe himself acknowledged. Boswell tried it, prodding Dr. Johnson into situations he could then describe. So did Mark Twain in *Innocents Abroad*, Chekhov in *A Journey to Sakhalin*, and Orwell in *Down and Out in Paris and London*. Lytton Strachey, a "New Journalist" in *Eminent Victorians*, used inner monologues, and in his famous passage on the death of Queen Victoria got inside her head, with not a single critic daring to ask what he was doing there. The New Journalism was not an invention of the Sixties or a new departure of any kind; it had a long tradition and involved techniques that many good writers have been using for centuries.

Nor was there much to the claim that the New Journalism read like fiction because most of the time it didn't, and when it did, it was the Arthur Hailey kind of fiction: "I am going to tell you more than you need to know about a movie studio." The best of the New Journalism consisted of set pieces and, with rare exception, did not explore character or reach a satisfying resolution. The New

Journalists were at their most effective dealing with highly dramatic subjects - the Hell's Angels, mass murder, the Vietnam War - or celebrities such as Ken Kesey, Joshua Logan, and Leonard Bernstein. Chekhov once said that most people don't have extraordinary things happen to them, they go to the office and eat cabbage soup. A good short-story writer or novelist could find his material in that humdrum multitude, but the New Journalists were confined to the unusual.

In retrospect, the New Journalism was not much more than nonfiction written by a handful of very good writers - among them novelists as different in style as Norman Mailer, Truman Capote, Joan Didion, Terry Southern, and John Gregory Dunne, as well as those two masters of overstatement, Tom Wolfe and Hunter S. Thompson. A lot of lesser writers rode their coattails, and the movement had a brief flowering.

Wolfe also claimed that he had invented a literary style. He talked about "my style," which everyone loved to parody. "Even hostile parodies admit from the start that the target has a distinct voice." But Wolfe's writing was reminiscent of that of the great French writer Louis-Ferdinand Céline. Wolfe's description of his own style was also an exact description of Céline's: "the lavish use of dots, dashes, exclamation points, italics . . .and of interjections, shouts, nonsense words, onomatopoeia, mimesis, pleonasms, the continued use of the historical present, and so on." Compare a page of Wolfe with a page from *Death on the Installment Plan*, and note a certain . . .kinship.

Of course Wolfe made the style his own. He naturalized it, and shaped it like the hand-tailored suits he favors so that it did not look like a hand-me-down from a distant cousin. He brought to the style a sheer verbal inventiveness, a comic zest, an ear for the American vernacular that few writers in any genre could match; and there was enough energy in his prose to light up Lincoln Center. He became, along with Hunter S. Thompson, one of the two writers of nonfiction whose style achieved instant recognition - read one paragraph and you knew whose it was.

Some of those who admired the style said that Wolfe was limited to minor subjects, to flaky crews like Ken Kesey and his Merry Pranksters, to cultural footnotes like the birth of radical chic. Would he ever let go of marginal events to grapple with something big, like a presidential election or the history of the great media empires? Perhaps to show that he could handle a major theme, Tom Wolfe wrote *The Right Stuff*, which is nothing less than a history of the manned space program as seen through the minds of the astronauts and other participants.

The first Americans to make orbital flights, the Project Mercury astronauts., are shown here, warts and all. As astronauts, the Original Seven found themselves at the apex of the Brotherhood of the Right Stuff, which is the mystique of all fighter pilots, who consider themselves a privileged order because they have the courage to take risks and the skills to survive. "The right stuff was not bravery in the simple sense of being willing to risk your life. . . .Any fool could do that. . . .No, the idea (as all pilots understood) was that a man should have the ability to go up in a hurtling piece of machinery and put his hide on the line and have the moxie, the reflexes, the experience, the coolness, to pull it back at the last yawning moment."

The manned space program was developed at a time when the nation was in a phase of intense patriotism inflamed by the Cold War. The program dramatized the rivalry between the United States and the Soviet Union, the strength of the national will. John McCormack rose in the House of Representatives to say that the United States faced "national extinction" if we did not overtake the Russians in outer space. Lyndon Johnson, in 1957, told a congressman who complained that the space program cost too much: "I, for one, don't want to go to bed by the light of a Communist moon."

In this fevered climate, the astronauts found themselves clasped to the nation's bosom as instant heroes. But NASA owned them now, and NASA was a reincarnation of the old studio system with its stars under contract. The Original Seven were dragged to press conferences where they had to talk about their religious beliefs and their perfect home lives and otherwise portray themselves as Mr. Cleans. The public assumed that they were the greatest pilots and the bravest men precisely because of their wholesome backgrounds: small towns, Protestant values, and strong family ties. The studio stars had to be presented to their millions of fans with their teeth capped and their faces lifted. They went on publicity tours, and spent a lot of time on platforms. Any congressman up for reelection could borrow an astronaut for the day, since NASA depended on congressional appropriations.

Behind the cosmetics, as Wolfe shows, the astronauts were out getting drunk, cheating on their wives, and otherwise cutting up. Only John Glenn, the "Mr. Presbyterian" of the seven, lived up to the image. He wanted desperately to be the first American in space, but after two years of training, Alan Shepard was picked, with Glenn and Gus Grissom as backups. Glenn was stunned, although the backup spot turned out to be the best, since the first two flights were suborbital, and he was the first astronaut to make an orbital flight.

Throughout Project Mercury the Russians stayed ahead, but at least the astronauts had put America in the race with Shepard's flight on May 5, 1961, a month after Yuri Gagarin had taken Vostok I in orbit around the earth. Though part of the astronauts' image was that going into space was a tremendous feat of flying, in reality they were glorified flight attendants, guinea pigs who could do very little manually. After all, an ape had made the first orbital flight. In training like that of the Original Seven, the apes underwent behavior modification (electric shocks on the soles of their feet) so that they would learn to throw the right switch.

Some of Wolfe's funniest pages have to do with the training program. During a stress test, a psychologist handed Pete Conrad a blank sheet of paper and asked him to study it and tell him what he saw, "and Conrad stares at the piece of paper and then looks up at the man and says in a weary tone, as if he fears a trick: 'But it's upside down.' This so startles the man, he actually leans across the table and looks at this absolutely blank sheet of paper to see if it's true. . . .This was *not* the way to produce the Halo Effect." Sure enough, Conrad was dropped.

The great moment came when John Glenn made an orbital flight. The sailors on the ship that brought his capsule in painted white lines around his footsteps on the deck. He went to the White House, received a medal from the President, and addressed a special joint session of Congress, whose ranks he would one day join. In New York, a great welcome was given to the Original Seven: "Perhaps that was what New York was for, to celebrate those who *had it*, whatever it was, and there was nothing like the right stuff, for all responded to it, and all wanted to be near it and to feel the sizzle and to blink in the light."

The risk was real. Gus Grissom lost his capsule and almost drowned. Scott Carpenter failed to listen to the control center, almost ran out of fuel, and nearly missed his reentry. Sometimes the astronauts waited for hours inside the capsule before lift-off, cramped and sweating and wondering whether it was worth it. But it never occurred to any of them to resign. These were men who would much rather have died in outer space, burned to a crisp during reentry in the atmosphere, than be left out of the drama. Besides, they got what Wolfe calls the *goodies*, the most obvious of which was an exclusive contract with *Life* magazine for their story. They could afford to buy new houses in nice neighborhoods.

One day, while he was a guest aboard the presidential yacht, Glenn got into a conversation with Kennedy about the arrangement with *Life*. A soldier ran just as great a risk in battle, Kennedy said, and did not expect compensation from *Life*. Yes, said Glenn, but suppose the press was camped on that soldier's doorstep, watching his family's every move. The *Life* contract was saved.

By 1962, the astronauts were up to six-orbit flights. As he flew over Latin America, Wally Schirra said, "Buenos dias, you all." In May 1963, Gordon Cooper made the final flight in the Mercury series, completing 22 orbits (the Russians had 48). By this time, NASA had shifted to the moon program, and the Next Nine, who included Neil Armstrong and Frank Borman, had succeeded the Original Seven.

Wolfe handles this complicated story with his usual brio. The technical and historical material slows him down a bit but most of the time he is at full throttle.

The Right Stuff is a splendid adventure story, an updating of *The Seven Samurai*, but it is more than that. It shows our propensity to manufacture heroes, and, just as quickly, to forget them; it shows how a scientific program was exploited for political advantage; it provides a revealing character study of seven exceptional Americans; and it proves conclusively that there is laughter in outer space.

Skywriting with Gus and Deke

R. Z. Sheppard

May 5, 1961: the day Alan Shepard scratched his back on the edge of space an America entered the manned space race. At last. Since 1957 there had been all those Sputniks - *Mechtas* and *Vostoks* - beeping overhead, clockwork reminders that the heavens were in the hands of the godless Bolshevik. The script had gone awry. A nation only 40 years from feudalism was secretly lobbing what looked like customized samovars at the free world while priapic Vanguards and Jupiters wilted on their pads or exploded prematurely for all the world to see. Democracy could be embarrassing.

The oaken voice of Walter Cronkite echoes in the memory of America's entry into the competition. There were resonant suspense at lift-offs and tremolos of pride at splashdowns: America still had the right stuff, Wolfe's buzz word for the indefinable attributes of the astronauts. His long awaited book about test pilots and the Mercury flights recalls those years through the eyes and nerve endings of the first astronauts, their wives and even the conditioned chimpanzees who rode prototype capsules downrange from Cape Canaveral: The chimp's "heart rate shot up as he strained against the force, but he didn't panic for a moment. He had been through this same sensation many times on the centrifuge. As long as he just took it and didn't struggle, they wouldn't zap all those goddamned blue bolts into the soles of his feet. There were a lot worse things in this world than g-forces. . . .The main thing was to keep ahead of those blue bolts in the feet!. . . .He started pushing the buttons and throwing the switches like the greatest electric Wurlitzer organist who ever lived. . ."

The jazzy mix of facts and fictional technique, Céline's ellipses, the gadzooks delivery and a presumptuous ape's-eye view that would have curled Henry James' worsteds - these are unmistakable parts of Wolfe's style. It is still called the New Journalism, although the form is as old as the Beatles and the author is now 48. Like the Beatles, Wolfe has had a revolutionary impact on his field. His imitators have spread like dandelion fluff and his work still stirs furious debate.

Yet even the creakiest practitioner of the inverted-pyramid style of journalism will have to agree that behind the mannered realism of *The Right Stuff* thumps the heart of a traditionalist. The organizing principle of the book is an old-fashioned fascination with, and admiration for, the test pilots and fighter jocks of the U.S.'s first astronaut team: Scott Carpenter, Gordon Cooper, John Glenn, Gus Grissom, Wally Schirra, Alan Shepard and Deke Slayton. In addition, the book has a superhero, Chuck Yeager, a World War II combat veteran who broke the sound barrier in 1947 and rewrote aviation history in experimental rocket-powered planes of the '50s and early '60s.

Yeager dips out of Wolfe's pages as the undisputed king of the right stuff, the man whose no-sweat, West Virginia drawl sounds like the archetype for modern airlinese ("We've got a little ol' red light up here on the control panel that's tryin' to tell us that the *lan*din' gears're not. . .uh. . *lock*in' into position"). He is also the book's main foil, a member of a vanishing breed of hot-rock pilots in an age of increasingly automated flight.

The astronauts were sensitive about their missions' being controlled by earth-bound technicians. The chosen seven had pulled out of enough tight corners and survived enough glitches to rise to the top of what Wolfe, in a seizure of cliché avoidance, calls "the ziggurat." As a reminder that he was there too, Yeager told reporters he did not want to be an astronaut because they did no real flying. He then rubbed it in by saying that "a monkey's gonna make the first flight." Shepard, Glenn and company bucked back, demanding and getting concessions like an override control stick and windows in the capsule. The men had been selected for their experience, superb physical conditioning and ability to stand psychological stress. What the groundlings had not anticipated was commensurate egos.

John Glenn, for example: Wolfe sketches him as a bit of a prig, a jogging, straitlaced Presbyterian driving an underpowered Peugeot, who scolded his colleagues for their after-hours whoopee. The current Senator from Ohio, Wolfe suggests, may have gone to NASA officials in an effort to replace Shepard on the first flight. Others, too, according to Wolfe, would act in ways that demonstrated that "feeling of superiority, appropriate to him and to his kind." Gus Grissom almost certainly blew the hatch too soon, flooding and sinking his capsule, and then stubbornly maintained that the machine "malfunctioned." Scott Carpenter, a man who could hold his breath for 171 seconds, ignored warnings about wasting hydrogen peroxide fuel and nearly skipped off the earth's atmosphere during re-entry.

Six years in the research and writing, Wolfe's most ambitious work is crammed with inside poop and racy incident that 19 years ago was ignored by what he terms the "proper Victorian Gents" of the press. The fast cars, booze, astro groupies, the envies and injuries of the military caste system were not part of what Americans would have considered the right stuff. Wolfe lays it all out in brilliantly staged Op Lit scenes: the tacky cocktail lounges of Cocoa Beach where one could hear the *Horst Wessel Song* sung by ex-rocket scientists of the Third Reich; Vice President Lyndon Johnson furiously cooling his heels outside the Glenn house because Annie Glenn would not let him in during her husband's countdown; Alan Shepard losing a struggle with his full bladder moments before lift-off; the overeager press terrifying Ham the chimp after his proficient flight; the astronauts surrounded by thousands of cheering Texans waving hunks of rare meat during an honorary barbecue in the Houston Coliseum.

Although Wolfe touches on spacerace politics and the psychology of courage, his views are neither unconventional nor meant to be. As our finest verbal illustrator of trends and fashions, he is interested in the truths that lie on surfaces. These truths are not superficial, though they are frequently overlooked in an age partial to overexplanations and psychic temperature taking. A 19th century novelist of manners would have understood perfectly. Readers in the 21st century will too, when they turn to Wolfe to find out the kind of stuff their grandparents were made of.

* * * *

Nearly 15 years ago, a vanilla tornado named Tom Wolfe whirled out of *Esquire* and the New York *Herald Tribune's* Sunday magazine supplement to announce the coming of the pop-rock culture. Readers accustomed to spending their weekends with articles like "Brazil: Colossus of the South" were suddenly snapping awake to such Wolfean fare as "Oh, Rotten Gotham - Sliding Down Into the Behavioral Sink," "Natalie Wood and the Shockkkkkk of Recognition" and "Muvva Earth and Codpiece Pants." The prose itself rollicked with words like "lollygagging" and "infarcted," embedded in pages that were covered with a confetti of punctuation marks.

The writer was equally eye-catching: a tall, pale, boyish figure whose trademark was a gleaming white suit. He looked like a collegian out of Hell's Angels, or a swell in Evelyn Waugh's *Vile Bodies*. Raised in Richmond, Va., Wolfe spoke softly and courteously, exuding an air of the right stuff. But he wrote like a hit man. "Tiny Mummies! The True Story of the ruler of 43rd Street's Land of the Walking Dead!" was a surprise attack on the genteel *New Yorker* magazine and its shy, venerated editor, William Shawn. A shocked cultural establishment struck back. An outraged Joseph Alsop and E. B. White called Wolfe's piece brutal, misleading and irresponsible. Richard Goodwin sent a bolt from the White House. "I didn't think I'd survive," says Wolfe, "but it taught me a lesson. You can be denounced from the heavens, and it only makes people interested."

He put that lesson to use again in 1970 when he discovered an invitation on a colleague's desk announcing a cocktail party honoring the Black Panthers. The event was to be held at the Manhattan home of Maestro Leonard Bernstein. Wolfe attended, steno pad and ball point ready. The result was *Radical Chic*, another heretical howler that captured the well-intentioned banalities of "limousine liberals." A few years later, in *The Painted Word*, Wolfe took on the New York art establishment, setting forth the impish thesis that a few powerful critics controlled what was painted and sold.

Wolfe is certainly a man who would rather lead than follow. *The Right Stuff* grew out of his "curiosity about what made men shoot dice with death." What he discovered in thousands of miles and more than 100 interviews was that pilots lived "in a world where there are no honorable alternatives." Wolfe has already done all the research on Gemini, Apollo and Skylab, and plans to write about them as well. Why did the current book take six years? "It was a structural problem," he says. "There are no surprises in the plot and a great many characters."

While waiting for his muse, the author took on other writing assignments, including a 20,000-word introduction to a book about the New Journalism. He also was married, 16 months ago, to Sheila Berger, the art director of *Harper's* magazine. The couple live in a town-house apartment at the heart of Bloomingdale country in Manhattan's East 60s. Wolfe, in fact, is the flaneur of Third Avenue, who enjoys few things more than window shopping and observing his fellow Eastsiders in their varying plumage. He himself owns nine $600 white suits, a style he says sadly has been debased by *The Great Gatsby* and *Saturday Night Fever* knockoffs. He recently went to yellow silk, but notes that the suit is so loud "dogs skulk away."

Wolfe's unchanging style of expensive elegance is clearly a harmless form of aggression and a splendiferous advertisement for his individuality. The game requires a lot of reverse spin and body English but it boils down to antichic chic. Exclaims Wolfe proudly: "I own no summer house, no car, I wear tank tops when I swim, long white pants when I plan tennis, and I'm probably the last man in America to still do the Royal Canadian Air Force exercises."

The Right Stuff

Reviewed by C. Michael Curtis

From *The Atlantic* 244 (October 1979), 107. Reprinted with permission of *The Atlantic*.

Tom Wolfe's long awaited astronaut book has finally been delivered, ten years late and right on time. On time because NASA's space program may now be antique enough to be considered with detachment, and on time because we seem always in need of a reminder that national vanity and organizational imperatives are no substitute for the simple dignity of human life.

Wolfe is respectful of the achievements of the space program, but he is wonderfully frank about the human frailties they exposed. The physical, engineering, and other technical skills of the astronauts are well known, and justly admired, but little has been written about the internal rivalries that infected the program, about the marital stresses that had to be papered over for public relations purposes, about the extramarital rompings that provoked John Glenn to a private (and bitterly resented) scolding of his colleagues, about clashes between Glenn and NASA administrator James E. Webb, and other matters.

That Wolfe can weave together these ragged strands of the astronaut story without minimizing the extraordinary courage, the sometimes incredible technical virtuosity, of these hand-picked space explorers (and of some of their less publicized predecessors and successors), is a tribute to his skill as a journalist and his sensibility as a student of humanistic values. *The Right Stuff* is Tom Wolfe's most ambitious book, and his best.

The Magnificent Seven

James Bishop

From *The Illustrated London News* 268 (January 1980), 65. Reprinted with permission of the author.

In the early 1960s seven young Americans were chosen as astronauts for the Mercury programme to launch men into space. They instantly became a focus of public attention, packaged heroes of the New Frontier, symbols of American determination to win the space race, and recipients of some of the most remarkable experiments that modern medical and scientific invention could devise. They also became, for a time, rather rich.

The right stuff of the titles was what an older generation would probably have called *sang-froid*. It was an essential element, apparently, in all American fighter pilots, and of the astronauts, though as a quality it was never defined, nor was it talked about in any way. A young man going into flight training might think he was entering some sort of technical school to acquire a certain set of skills. Instead he found himself in a fraternity divided between those who had it and those who did not. "It", the right stuff, clearly involved bravery, but it was no bravery in the simple sense of being willing to risk your life. Any fool could do that, notes Mr. Wolfe. "No, the idea here (in the all-enclosing fraternity) seemed to be that a man should have the ability to go up in a hurtling piece of machinery and put his hide on the line and then have the moxie, the reflexes, the experience, the coolness, to pull it back in the last yawning moment - and then go up again *the next day*, and the next day, and every next day, even if the series should prove infinite. . . .A career in flying was like climbing one of those ancient Babylonian pyramids made up of a dizzy progression of steps and ledges, a ziggurat, a pyramid extraordinarily high and steep: and the idea was to prove at every foot of the way up that pyramid that you were one of the elected and anointed ones who had *the right stuff* and could move higher and higher and even - ultimately, God willing, one - that you might be able to join that special few at the very top, the elite who had the capacity to bring tears to men's eyes, the very Brotherhood of the Right Stuff itself."

The selection of the astronauts created a new elite in this brotherhood, though this was not at first appreciated by those who volunteered. There were doubts about the system - it was not really flying, after all, and the agonies on this score were intensified when it was learnt that the first flight was in fact to be made by a monkey. But the intensity of public interest, the extraordinary tests that the candidates were forced to go through before selection, and the eventual dramas of the space flights themselves, ensured that they became a new group of the Brotherhood, to be superseded later by the even more elite band who went to the moon.

From the detail provided by Mr. Wolfe there can be no doubt that each of the seven Mercury men - John Glenn, Alan Shepard, Scott Carpenter, Gordon Cooper, Walter Schirra, Gus Grissom and Deke Slayton - earned their brief terms at the summit of the pyramid of all-American heroes. Not only did they have to go through the ordeals of space flight and the training it involved, and with knowledge that at that time they were following in the wake of the Russians, but they and their families were subjected to the remorseless interest of the American and the world's Press and television, and they were themselves scrutinized almost to breaking point by the space programme doctors and psychiatrists. In this cause they were required, the author tells us, to give themselves enemas, to produce regular stool specimens, to masturbate into tubes so that their sperm counts could be measured, to describe (to shrinks with notebooks) what they saw on a blank sheet of paper. Those who said "a blank sheet of paper" were evidently marked as having "inhibited imaginative capacity": the candidate who said "But it's upside down" would get cheers from most of us, particularly when the psychiatrist looked down at the paper to see if it was true, but he did not make it to become one of the magnificent seven.

As will have become evident, Mr. Wolfe's book describes the lives of the Mercury astronauts in great detail, and if the reader ultimately concludes, like the young reviewer of a book on another subject, that *The Right Stuff* tells us more about the astronauts than we really want to know, there is no denying its excitement and readability. Mr. Wolfe writes like an American journalist, which he is, and paces his book with the skill of a novelist, which he also is. At times we may wonder which attribute predominates, but so powerful is the narrative that we do not pause long enough to worry about it.

The Legend on the License

John Hersey

Copyright © 1986 by John Hersey; published in *The Yale Review* (Winter, 1986), 289-314.

The imminent death of the novel is announced from time to time, but the very repetitiousness of the bulletins testifies to stubborn vital signs. I bring other news from the hospital. Journalism is on a sickbed and is in a very bad way.

The trouble did not begin but came out into the open with the appallingly harmful phrase Truman Capote used in 1965 to categorize *In Cold Blood*. It was, he said, a "nonfiction novel." The blurring of fiction and journalism sanctioned by that phrase is now widely practiced and widely condoned. This has not been particularly good for fiction; it may be mortal to journalism.

In fiction that *is* fiction, no holds need be barred. Novelists may introduce or disguise real people and real events as they choose. Tolstoy disguised all but the generals. Dreiser's *An American Tragedy* was suggested by an actual crime, but he did not feel the need to call his creation "a true-life novel." Malraux, who had an enormous influence on some of the novelists of my generation (e.g., Ralph Ellison), often depicted originals - among others, Chiang Kai-shek in all the splendid irony of his left-wing youth. E.L. Doctorow has had harmless fun with Morgan, Ford, and others. And so on.

The only caution in all this is the one so acutely perceived by Flannery O'Connor (in *Mystery and Manners*): "It's always wrong of course to say that you can't do this or you can't do that in fiction. You can do anything you can get away with, but nobody has ever gotten away with much." In other words, there are tests. A test, for one thing, of quality; of art. Or, to put it more brutally for authors, a test of gifts. But the point is that always, in fiction, there is the saving notice on the license: THIS WAS MADE UP.

As to journalism, we may as well grant right away that there is no such thing as absolute objectivity. It is impossible to present in words "*the* truth" or "the whole story." The minute a writer offers nine hundred ninety-nine out of one thousand facts, the worm of bias has begun to wriggle. The vision of each witness is particular. Tolstoy pointed out that immediately after a battle there are as many remembered versions of it as there have been participants.

Still and all, I will assert that there is one sacred rule of journalism. The writer must not invent. The legend on the license must read: NONE OF THIS WAS MADE UP. The ethics of journalism, if we can be allowed such a boon, must be based on the simple truth that every journalist knows the difference between the distortion that comes from subtracting observed data and the distortion that comes from adding invented data.

The threat to journalism's life by the denial of this difference can be realized if we look at it from the reader's point of view. The reader assumes the subtraction as a given of journalism and instinctively hunts for the bias; the moment the reader suspects additions, the earth begins to skid underfoot, for the idea that there is no way of knowing what is real and what is not real is terrifying. Even more terrifying is the notion that lies are truths. Or at least these things used to be terrifying; the dulling of the terror that has come about through repeated exposure tells us how far this whole thing has gone.

Let me now drive my own stakes in the ground. I have always believed that the *devices* of fiction could serve journalism well and might even help it to aspire now and then to the level of art. But I have tried to honor the distinction between the two forms. To claim that a work is both fiction and journalism, or to assert, as Doctorow recently did, that "there is no longer any such thing as fiction or nonfiction; there is only narrative" - these are, in my view, serious crimes against the public. In a backward look in *The New Journalism* Tom Wolfe, citing a piece of mine from 1944, remarked, "Here we start getting into the ancestry of the New Journalism." The word "ancestry" makes me feel a bit like the Peking Man, and in laying claim to authority in this field I prefer to think of myself as nothing more remote than a grandfather.

Now. After reading three recent publications - Tom Wolfe's *The Right Stuff*, an entertaining book, Wolfe's best so far; Norman Mailer's *The Executioner's Song*, a powerful work that unquestionably enhances Mailer's claim to the kind of literary top billing he has always so tiresomely shined after; and Truman Capote's "Handcarved Coffins," a gobbet of commercial trash by this once brilliant writer in his new collection, *Music for Chameleons* - I am one worried grandpa. These three hybrids clinch it. The time has come to redraw the line between journalism and fiction.

1

"Handcarved Coffins," which Capote calls both "nonfiction" and "a short novel," belongs here, in the company of the Wolfe and Mailer books, only because of Capote's place in the line of parentage of the hybrid form; it can be dealt with briefly. The story must represent to its author a nostalgic yearning for the remembered powers of *In Cold Blood,* the fine, shapely, hard-fibered novel (as novel) that appears to have been the model Norman Mailer wanted to knock off its pedestal, but couldn't quite, with *The Executioner's Song*. Vivid as *In Cold Blood* was as a novel, it had serious flaws on the nonfiction side, arising from the fact that its actions and dialogue had been reconstructed long after the described events, yet were presented in the book with all assurance as being exactly what had happened; the dialogue, rebuilt from a great distance, stood within the authenticating marks of direct quotation. Besides suffering from troubles like these, which are intrinsic to a genre that claims to be both fiction and not, "Handcarved Coffins" groans under others far more grievous.

For one thing, the tale does something that journalism simply must not do: it strains credulity well beyond the breaking point. There is a much-too-muchness about it, which convinces one that the fictionist has decidedly had the upper hand over the journalist. The story is told in interview form, through a series of dialogues between Capote and a number of characters, the most prominent being a detective from a certain State Bureau of Investigation, who is trying to solve a succession of ghastly murders that have been announced beforehand to the victims, in all cases but one, by the arrival in their hands of beautiful miniature coffins, carved from "light balsam wood" and containing candid photographs of the doomed persons. The murderer has dispatched two of his victims, an elderly pair, by insinuating into their parked car, to await their return to it, nine rattlesnakes that have been "injected with amphetamine." Perhaps we can swallow that one. But try this: A recipient of one of the little coffins, driving along a lonely road in "an eccentric vehicle of his own invention" with no top and no windshield, is cleanly decapitated by "a strong steel wire sharpened thin as a razor" and stretched across the road between a tree and a telephone pole at exactly the right height to catch him just under the chin; the wire "slice[s] off his head as easily as a girl picking petal off a daisy." And so on, murder after murder, until we have been taken far beyond the last shore of belief. (We will come back in due course to this crucial matter of belief.)

An even worse fault of this creaky tale is that it is told as if in a game of blindman's buff. It is the reader who is blindfolded. He has no idea where he is. The story takes place in an invisible place: a nameless town in an unspecified state. The characters are *there*, but they are unseeable as real people. Their names have been changed. Capote says he "had to omit a few identifying things" (*The New York Times*, January 7, 1979) - which implies his having substituted other made-up ones. (The principal suspect "had long simian-like arms; the hands dangled at his knees, and the fingers were long, capable, oddly aristocratic." Altogether, the ace among rules of reliable reporting - that the facts should be "hard" - is here repeatedly and fatally broken.

2

Tom Wolfe's *The Right Stuff* is a vivid book, a tainted book. It gives an account of the Mercury phase of the United States space program, and its thesis is that test pilots of rocket aircraft, genuinely, and the seven Mercury astronauts, more ambiguously, shared an ineffable quality compounded of spiffy courage, arrogant recklessness, dry-palmed sass, and super-jock male potency (on earth they indiscriminately balled "juicy little girls," and in the sky they whipped around in Pynchonesque flying phalluses), to all of which Wolfe gives the catchy tag "the right stuff." Wolfe's style-machine has never run more smoothly than in this book. The writing is at times wonderfully funny. Some of the passages on flying are classy. A quick and easy read. Then why tainted? Because Wolfe is the paradigm of the would-be journalist who cannot resist the itch to improve on the material he digs up. The tricks of fiction he uses dissolve now and then into its very es-

sence: fabrication. The notice on the license reads: THIS WAS NOT MADE UP
EXCEPT FOR THE PARTS THAT WERE MADE UP.

The source of the taint is the pair of pieces Wolfe wrote in 1965 for the
Herald-Tribune Sunday magazine about *The New Yorker*. We must recall them at
some length, because in them one finds in gross form the fundamental defect
that has persisted ever since in Wolfe's writing, and that is to be found in the
works of many of the "new journalists," and also indeed in that of many "nonfiction novelists" - namely, the notion that mere facts don't matter.

In the introduction to *The New Journalism* Wolfe tried to laugh off his *New
Yorker* pieces. He called them "some lighthearted fun.... A very droll *sportif* performance, you understand." They were nothing of the kind. They made up a
vicious, slashing lampoon. Begging the question whether *The New Yorker* may at
some point have deserved a serious critique, there seems to be no way to explain
the stunningly irresponsible street cruelty of Wolfe's exercise except by guessing
that he could not bear to face it that "his" New Journalism would have to be
measured sooner or later against the meticulously accurate and vivid reporting of
such *New Yorker* writers as A.J. Liebling and Daniel Lang, and against the vivid
devices used by the wonderful Joseph Mitchell or, let's say, by Lillian Ross and
Truman Capote; who in turn were writing in an honorable tradition, not New at
all, reaching back to George Orwell, Henry Mayhew, James Boswell. . .

Wolfe called his first piece "Tiny Mummies! The True Story of the Ruler of
43rd Street's Land of the Walking Dead." This "true" story was a collage of
shameless inventions. Not satisfied with making up lots of little decorative details, such as imaginary colors and types of paper used at *The New Yorker* for
memos and manuscripts, Wolfe reached farther into the territory of fiction to
devise blunt weapons with which to assault William Shawn, the magazine's editor. He dreamed up a Shawn memorandum which was supposed to have warned
the staff against talking to him; he gave a description of the magazine's editorial
process which according to an analysis of Wolfe's pieces by Renata Adler and
Gerald Jones, was erroneous "in every particular, large and small"; and he gave
a picture of Shawn's role that "was not a little untrue, not half true, but totally,
stupefyingly false."

Shawn's "retiring" nature, Wolfe asserted, could be accounted for by "what
the records show, actually, in the Cook County (Chicago) Criminal Court" - that
Leopold's and Loeb's original intended victim in their famous murder had been
"a small and therefore manageable teenage boy from the Harvard School,"
whose first name was William ("the court records do not give the last name"),
and that the two had decided not to kill William Shawn "only because they had a
personal grudge against him and somebody might remember that." Shawn's
trauma is totally a Wolfe fantasy. The court records *do* give the last name of the
intended victim, and the first as well. It was not a teen-aged William Shawn. It
was a nine-and-a-half-year-old boy named John O. Levinson, who testified at the
trial.

The coda of the second piece, the climax of the whole charade, is a perfect example of a Wolfe fantasy flying out of control. Wolfe has been building a (false) picture of Shawn slavishly attached to the formulas of the founder of the magazine, Harold Ross. In this scene we see Shawn sitting alone at home, on the very evening when down at the St. Regis the staff is celebrating the magazine's fortieth anniversary. According to Wolfe, Shawn is listening to "that wonderful light zinc plumbing sound" of Bix Beiderbecke's recording of "I Can't Get Started": "(those other trumpet players, like Harry James, they never played the real 'I Can't Get Started')." At the end of the recording "Bix hits that incredible high one he died on, popping a vessel in his temporal fossa, bleeding into his squash, drowning on the bandstand. . . . *That* was the music of Harold Ross's lifetime. . . . Here, on that phonograph, those days are *preserved*. . ."

Adler and Jonas:

> The facts are, of course, that "*That*" was not "the music of Harold Ross's lifetime." Or anybody else's. The facts are that "Bix" did not die playing, nor did his death have anything to do with his "temporal fossa." He died in bed, of pneumonia. Nor did Beiderbecke make a recording of "the real 'I Can't Get Started.' " In fact, he never played it - with or without "that incredible high one." It would have been difficult for him to play it. "I Can't Get Started with You" was written in 1935, four years after Beiderbecke's death.

When Wolfe wrote his advertisements for himself in *The New Journalism*, nine years later, he still couldn't suppress his snickers at the reaction to his *New Yorker* caper, and to the subsequent new wave of nonfiction, on the part of "countless journalists and literary intellectuals," who, he said, were screaming, "*The bastards are making it up!* I'm telling you, Ump, that's a spitball he's throwing. . . ." But his laughter had an edge of nerves; altogether too many folks in the stands had seen and called attention to his applying a little greasy stuff to the pellet.

In the seven years since then, two things have happened: Wolfe has grown quite a bit more careful (and hard-working), and the public has become increasingly inured, or maybe the word is numb, to the blurring of fiction and journalism. *The Right Stuff* has been accepted as fairly accurate by people in the know. I talked with a number of journalists who had covered the space program, and while one complained of "outright lies" in the book, all the others seemed to think that Wolfe had "made an effort to be as accurate as he could be," that he had "done his homework," that he had made mistakes, but those had been errors of judgement and value that any conventional journalist might have made. Most of them thought he had been too kind to Scott Carpenter and too hard on John Glenn. The official National Aeronautics and Space Administration view was also favorable. Christopher Kraft, in charge of the Johnson Space Center in Houston, declined to talk about the book, but his public relations chief, John MacLeish, said after consultation with others that despite a number of technical errors there was "a high degree of accuracy" in the book. The two astronauts I talked with, John Glenn and Deke Slayton, said, respectively, that Wolfe was "accurate on the details of my flight" and "mostly pretty accurate."

Taint, then? Well, alas, yes. Some questions remain. Enough to add up. Enough so that, in the end, one cannot help wondering whether even these interested parties, in their numbed acceptance of the premise that there is no difference between fiction and nonfiction, between real life and a skillfully drawn image of a dream of it, haven't been to some extent taken in. I give you the example of the way in which Senator Glenn, in speaking to me, paid tribute to the hypnotic ambiguity of Wolfe's prose. Glenn is pictured in the book as an insufferable prig, a prude, a killjoy, yet he said to me, "I came out pretty good in the book, so I can't complain." NASA seemed to think it had come out pretty well, too. Did it?

Wolf's fiction-aping journalism, he wrote in 1973, "enjoys an advantage [over fiction] so obvious, so built in, one almost forgets what a power it has: the simple fact that the reader knows *all this actually happened*. . . .The writer is one step closer to the absolute involvement of the reader that Henry James and James Joyce dreamed of and never achieved. . . ." Whew. That *is* a big advantage. But let's focus for a moment on much smaller things, such as that little word "all."

In defining the New Journalism, Wolfe wrote that a journalist need use just four devices of fiction to bring this amazing power to the page: scene-by-scene construction, dialogue, point of view, and what he called "status details." But the resources of fiction are by no means so barren as all that. One essential requisite and delight of fiction, for example is the absolute particularity it can give to every individual, every character. Wolfe has apparently ruled this out; he is a generalizer. Let him find a vivid or funny trait in more than one member of a class, then without exception the whole class has it. Thirty-six military pilots show up at the Pentagon to apply for the space program; without exception they wear "Robert Hall clothes that cost about a fourth as much as their watches." "They had many names, these rockets, Atlas, Navajo, Little Joe, Jupiter, but they all blew up." All test pilots talked something he calls Army Creole. All seven astronauts went in for Flying and Drinking, Drinking and Driving, Driving and Balling. All Russian space vehicles were launched "by the Soviet's mighty and mysterious Integral" - though, as Wolfe knows, Integral was not a person or a state organ but a space ship in Evgeny Zamyatin's novel, *We*. "Every wife. . ." "Every young fighter jock. . . " "Everyone. . ." "Invariably. . ." "All these people. . ." "All. . ." ("*All this actually happened. . .*")

Another big advantage over other writers that Wolfe apparently feels he has is that since he is using fictional modes, he is, even though dealing with nonfictional matter, freed from the boring job of checking verifiable details. If something turns out to have been dead wrong - well, that was just the free play of fancy. Some of the many details Wolfe should have checked but obviously did not are: The kind of car John Glenn drove. Whether Slayton, pictured as an active partisan at the meeting Wolfe calls the Konokai Seance, was even present.

What operant conditioning means. The Latin name for the chimpanzee. What jodhpurs are. What cilia means. When the compass was invented. . . .

But there are disadvantages in the method, too, at least for the reader. One is the frequent juxtaposition of passages that are wholly made up with others that are only partly made up or, beyond the use of one of the four devices, not made up at all. Side by side, for example, are a long parody of an airline pilot's voice reassuring the passengers on the last leg of a flight from Phoenix to New York when the landing gear won't lock, and an account of how the test pilot Chuck Yaeger gets drunk, breaks two ribs falling off a horse on a moonlight gallop, doesn't tell the base doctor, and two days later goes up in an X-1 and buffets through the sound barrier, hurting so badly his right arm is useless. (Right stuff.) Both passages are funny, wildly hyperbolic, interchangeable in voice and tone. It is not hard to tell which of these is mostly made up (or is it wholly made up?). But what becomes not so easy, after many such oscillations, is to perceive exactly where the line between reporting and invention in any "real-life" episode actually lies.

This difficulty is immensely reinforced by the way Wolfe uses his third fictional device: point of view. At will, he enters the consciousness of his characters. We have the stream (or in Wolfe's case one has to say river) of consciousness of wives of astronauts, waiting out re-entry. We find ourselves in each astronaut's mind as he barrels across the sky. For an awful moment we become Lyndon Johnson. We may be dismayed to find ourselves suddenly trapped in a chimpanzee's head. Finally (James and Joyce certainly never gave us *this* pleasure) we are right there in God's mind, out of patience with John Glenn and barking at him, "Try the automatic, you ninny." Beyond the dicey issue of freely inventive re-creation of thoughts and dialogue, long after their transaction, a further trouble is that Wolfe never makes the slightest attempt, which any novelist would make as a matter of course, to vary the voice to fit each character. What we hear throughout, ringing in every mind, is the excited shout of Tom Wolfe. Each astronaut in turn *becomes* Tom Wolfe. Without even a little jiggle of lexical sex-change each astronaut's wife becomes Tom Wolfe. Right Stuffers who are alleged to speak nothing but Army Creole are garlanded with elegant tidbits like *esprit, joie de combat, mas alla!* The chimp talks pure Wolfe. God help us, God becomes Tom Wolfe and with His sweet ear chooses the Wolfeish "ninny."

"Class has always been Tom Wolfe's subject," John Gregory Dunne has written (*The New York Review of Books,* November 8, 1979). Dunne see Wolfe as exposing the unmentionable in a purportedly egalitarian society: the existence of class. Wolfe is always on the side of the outsider, the underdog. Low Rent is good. He declares himself a literary lumpenprole, one of "the Low Rent rabble at the door," of "the Kentucky Colonels of Journalism and Literature." Placing such great emphasis on status seems to have affected Wolfe's decibel range. Whispering, as any outsider knows, is genteel. Understatement is upper class. A consequence of such understandings is the central disaster of this gifted writer's voice: He never abandons a resolute tone of screaming. The test of every sentence is : Will its sound waves shatter a wine glass at twenty feet? It is not surprising that he writes so beautifully about the rupture of the sound barrier.

While he has largely cooled his typographical excesses in this book (there are only three exclamation points, and no italicized words at all, on the first page), the aural and psychological overamplification is still very much there. The voice of every character, even that of a quiet woman like Glenn's wife, is Jovian. One can say that the charm in Wolfe is his enthusiasm. On nearly every page, though, this attractive quality sends him floating off the ground. When he is establishing the driving part of Flying and Drinking, Drinking and Driving, Driving and Balling, in which "all" the astronauts indulged, his excitement over their recklessness at the wheel leads him to write, doubtless in a *sportif* spirit: "More fighter pilots died in automobiles than airplanes." No time period. According to Navy statistics which Wolfe himself cites, there was a 23 percent probability that a Navy career pilot would die in an aircraft accident. Did one in four die on the road? In 1952 sixty-two American Air Force pilots died in crashes in thirty-six weeks of flying at Edwards Air Force Base, 1.7 per week. Did two a week die in cars? The point is not that this little example of possibly humorous overkill announces in itself the death of journalism. The point is that this one happened to be readily catchable. How many others are not? Are they on every page? How can we know? How can we ever know?

And so we come through many cumulative small doubts back to the issue of "accuracy." Let us grant that among Wolfe's works, this book is relatively "accurate" (perhaps because relatively much of it is based on written records, notably the NASA official history, *This New Ocean: A History of Project Mercury*). But "relatively 'accurate' " may not be good enough, when we look for the whole meaning of the work.

By now we are thoroughly skeptical, and, remembering John Glenn's having read the abuse he took at Wolfe's hand as praise, we begin to see abysses of ambiguity, of ambivalence, in the book. Wolfe loves what he loathes. The individual words mock and slash and ridicule; the sentences into which they are combined somehow ogle and stroke and admire. As Eric Korn put it (*Times Literary Supplement*, November 30, 1979), "If there's one thing more unlovable than the man of letters showing his contempt for physical valor, it's the man of letters fawning on physical valor. Wolfe contrives to do both at once." Glenn and NASA are both right and awfully wrong to think they come out "pretty good."

Looking back, we see that this double-think has been there, off and on, all through Wolfe's work. His class struggle seems to be in his own heart. The New Journalism was a product of the sixties, and like much of what hit the kids in that decade, Wolfe's struggle seems to have been a generational one. To adopt his voice: Young and new are good, old and old are bad; but O I love you Mummy and Daddy, you bitch and bastard. This lumpenprole affects beautifully tailored white suits and his prose often gives off a donnish perfume - *prima facie, Beruf,* pick your language. If Tom Wolfe is at all interested in class, it is in a new elite of those few "outsiders" who, at any given moment, are "in." The quasi-fictional method allows Wolfe to be both out and in.

Precisely this ambiguity makes for really zippy entertainment - the dazzle of the magic show. Great fun. But. It leaves us with serious doubts about a mode of journalism that straddles in its ambiguities the natural and obligatory substance of such a book: the horrendous issues of the space program, its cost, philosophy, technological priorities, and impact on national jingoism and machismo in a cold-war atmosphere which, as we saw in the winter of 1979-1980, could so easily be brought to dangerous warmth.

I believe that the double-think flaw is intrinsic to Wolfe's method. One who gets the habit of having it both ways in attitude and substance. The legend on the license really does matter.

As to deeper and subtler forms of social harm that this journalism also may cause, more later. . . .*

---

* This article continues to discuss Norman Mailer's *The Executioner's Song*, and is edited at this point with the author's permission.

From Bauhaus
to Our House

Tom Wolfe vs. Modern Architecture

Hilton Kramer

From *Saturday Review* 8 (October 1981), 65-66. Reprinted with the permission of OMNI INTERNATIONAL, LTD.

Six years ago, Tom Wolfe wrote a very short book called *The Painted Word*. It purported to give us the lowdown on the contemporary art scene. It wasn't the art itself that mainly concerned him, however. He did not, as a matter of fact, seem to know much about it. What really interested him was that people with money and social pretensions bought this art, often at very high prices, and people with brains - intellectuals - took it seriously enough to write long critical essays explaining it. He found much to ridicule in the activities of both groups, and nothing to admire. The whole art scene was, for him, little more than a farce foisted upon the public by a cabal of critics and millionaires seeking influence and status.

Now Wolfe has written another short book about art and its public. This time the art in question is modern architecture, which - to no one's surprise - he doesn't much like. Because he doesn't like it, he naturally assumes that other people of taste and intelligence agree with him. After all, what is there to like in this monstrous display of glass walls and poured concrete? Yet the undeniable success of modernism in architecture - the sheer number of buildings that have been built, and the vast sums of money lavished on their design and construction and maintenance by people with brains, money, and influence - must somehow be accounted for. The purpose of *From Bauhaus to Our House* is therefore to explain how we came to be hoodwinked into accepting an art that, in Wolfe's opinion, we actually loathe.

It turns out that the principal cause of our aesthetic misfortune has been our supine surrender to European influence. Several generations back, it seems, we made a terrible mistake in allowing crackpot foreigners like Walter Gropius, Mies van der Rohe, and Le Corbusier to lead us astray. The wicked European avante-garde corrupted us! Wolfe doesn't come right out and say that these European malefactors sapped our vital juices, but that is clearly what we are expected to believe.

Once upon a time, according to this scenario, America could boast of a healthy native culture that had nothing - well, almost nothing - to do with Europe. Exactly what it consisted of remains, alas, a little vague. Frank Lloyd Wright was apparently part of it. There was jazz, of course. And the realistic novel. There was also, earlier on, the tendency of the American rich to commission buildings that looked like French chateaux and English manor houses. Did this, perhaps, reflect some European influence? Well, yes. But it was all right because it wasn't avant-garde. And anyway, it was somehow appropriate to American power.

But starting in the 1920s or thereabouts, the baleful influence of European modernism began to make itself felt. The road to ruin began at the Bauhaus in Germany after World War I. It was there that Gropius, Mies, and others launched their noxious ideas on the unsuspecting world. "It was more than a school," Wolfe correctly observes of the Bauhaus; "it was a commune, a spiritual movement, a radical approach to art in all its forms, a philosophical center comparable to the Garden of Epicurus." This "radical approach to art" might have had some meaning for a Europe that had been devastated by the war - Wolfe is not too clear about that - but it was definitely alien to the untroubled spirit of American culture. About *that* our author is remarkable confident.

Yet, contrary to all reason and expectation, this alien movement managed to acquire some enthusiastic disciples in the United States. The principal offenders were the people in charge of the Museum of Modern Art, which - in Wolfe's fanciful history - seems to have been founded in 1929 for the express purpose of subverting our native culture. Never mind that the museum showed Charles Burchfield before it showed Picasso, or that it bought an Edward Hopper before it bought Matisse. A writer with a hot thesis must be allowed certain liberties.

The most fateful of the museum's many acts of aesthetic turpitude, however, was its mounting of a show called "Modern Architecture: International Exhibition" in 1932. This show introduced the work of Gropius, Mies, Le Corbusier, and other modern architects - more than 50 in all, including many outstanding Americans-to the New York museum public. Out of this event came the term, "The International Style," used in the catalogue to describe the work of a handful of European modernists. It was a term that stuck, and many years later came to be all but synonymous with the term "modern architecture."

About this even Wolfe writes: "The show and the catalogue created a terrific stir in the American architectural community, chiefly because of the status of the museum itself. The Museum of Modern Art was the colonial complex inflated to prodigious dimensions." And on the next page he writes: "In 1929 the museum opened, and European modernism in painting and sculpture was established, *institutionalized*, overnight, in the most overwhelming way, as the new standard for the arts in America. The International Style exhibition was designed to do the same thing for European modernism in architecture."

This is an interesting example of Wolfe's hyperventilated method. Overlooked in the hyperbole is the fact that the "terrific stir" alleged to have been created in 1932 did not actually lead to much in the way of new building until some 20 or more years later. As for the "prodigious dimensions" of the museum's "colonial complex," the truth is that in its early years the Modern was so hesitant about showing the radical modernist art of Europe that it was often under attack by American modernists for being backward and reactionary. In painting, the museum tended to favor realist, regional, and neo-romantic styles. The claim that it achieved an "overnight" success in establishing modernism "in the most overwhelming way" is nonsense. Its work in acquainting the public with what had been created in European art and design was, in fact, a slow and painstaking process. There was nothing "overnight" or "overwhelming" about it.

The "Modern Architecture" exhibition of 1932 certainly had an influence on architectural thought in this country - which meant, at most, an influence on a couple of dozen people. Yet when the time came to put up new buildings in the decades following World War II, a strict commitment to modernist orthodoxy remained the exception rather than the rule. The rule was to compromise - to produce moderately "modern" buildings with vaguely "traditional" features. (See Lincoln Center in New York for abundant examples.) You would never guess it from a reading of *From Bauhaus to Our House*, but the reason why there are so few superlative buildings of modernist design in this country is that there have been few opportunities to create them. Most of what passes for "modern architecture" is commercial hack work tricked up with a modern look.

Still, in rare cases where buildings of great distinction have been created - in Lever House, for example, or the Seagram Building - Wolfe can be counted on to mock them. He simply doesn't know the difference between a great design and a failed or foolish or vulgar one. There is, indeed, very little about modern architecture that he does understand. What really interests him is the world of money and manners - a rich subject, to be sure, about which he has written brilliantly elsewhere. But neither art nor aesthetic thought has any reality for him apart from its role in that world of money and manners. He is helpless when it comes to dealing with the artistic issues that lie at the heart of this book.

For this reason, too, the so-called "death" of modern architecture and the whole phenomenon of "post-modern" architecture remain a mystery to him - as, indeed, they must remain to anyone who, like Wolfe, sees nothing in the life of culture but a succession of fashions and fads. The truth is far more complicated, of course. The great appeal of the modern movement in architecture derived from its lofty attempt to integrate the interest of aestheticism, the needs of society, and the methods of industrial production in a coherent and realizable vision of the good life. That it conspicuously failed to achieve this lofty objective has long been recognized.

But the inquiry into the reasons for that failure is not well served by a writer on the lookout for comic scapegoats. Modern architecture was not, after all, a foreign plot to take over America - and there is something repugnant, in any case, in the idea that all of modernist culture represents some sort of alien threat to the purity of American life. In the end, that is the idea that governs *From Bauhaus to Our House*.

Prose and Prejudice

Garry Wills

From Universal Press Syndicate. Reprinted by permission of Garry Wills.

Tom Wolfe, the stylish literary brawler who keeps a punching bag by his typewriter, is at it again. In his new book, *From Bauhaus To Our House*, he takes on the architectural establishment.

Even if you disagree with Mr. Wolfe, you have to admire his outspoken assault on entrenched nonsense. He says "the Bauhaus atmosphere," which gave us modern architecture, is a more proper subject for "group psychologists" than for architectural historians. He tells us Le Corbusier's work "progresses shortly from special pleading to false witness."

His final judgement on modernism? "In the jet age these ideas of the 1920s began to wear a very quaint and half-timbered look. This, of course, made it easier for some feeble intellects to 'adopt the modern style,' and we are all familiar with the dandified figures in the drafty and obsolescent sport cars who practice modern architecture as if it were a finished period style. . ."

You can't beat Wolfe for vigor of style, can you? But, I've not been quoting Wolfe at all. I've been quoting an article written in 1955. It appeared in *Architectural Review*, and was written by the esteemed critic Reyner Banham. Bauhaus pretensions were punctured a quarter of a century ago. Mr. Wolfe does not know that. The list of things Mr. Wolfe does not know is astonishing. Take this sentence from his new book: "There were no manifestos in the world of art prior to the 20th century."

If we go back only two centuries, we find manifestos setting the program for many artists - Burke on The Sublime, Gilpin on The Classical, Reynold on The Grand Style, Diderot on Sentiment, Ruskin on Pre-Raphaelitism, Pugin on Gothic. Like most reactionaries, Wolfe yearns for the past without knowing much about it.

The burden of his new work is that Americans should have denied intellectual visas to the Bauhaus architects, so a genuine American style could arise. This ban on suspicious foreigners amounts to setting up a House Committee on Un-American Houses. The "socialism" of Gropius and Le Corbusier made dupes of us all. In this book, in other words, Mr. Wolfe is once again joining his fellow dandy, William Buckley, in giving elegant verbal poses to nativist prejudice.

Mr. Wolfe's politics are unintentionally comic - modernism was no more "leftist" than some of the things it displaced and Mr. Wolfe praises (e.g., social realism). But commie hunters' ability to identify their prey is in inverse proportion to their ardor for the task.

More important, the idea that an American style can be bred by banning foreign influence is at odds with all our experience. American style did not grow by isolation, but by cross-fertilization. Even such pungently American products as Benjamin Franklin's "Poor Richard" and Mark Twain's "Colonel Sellers" had foreign models - respectively, Swift's "Isaac Bickerstaff" and Dickens' "Wilkens Micawber."

Who was more American than Franklin? Yet the best student of his vocabulary, L.M. MacLaurin, found that he deliberately avoided Americanisms. For that matter, Noah Webster's American dictionary has been falsely described as nationalistic in its emphases. Webster repeatedly said that America's language is the same as England's and "it is desirable to perpetuate that sameness."

But the traffic was never one way. Franklin gave to the old world, after taking from it. His "Poor Richard" appeared in France as "Bonhomme Richard" and supplied Europe with more than the name for a boat. American architects, as well, had already helped form the International Style before it came back to these shores for praise and ridicule.

Sealing borders to keep out un-American thoughts is a sign of intellectual poverty, not strength. It is the kind of thing the Russians do. The real effect of our reactionaries is always to make us imitate the enemy they fear most.

Tom Wolfe Behind the Facade of Modernism

Benjamin Forgey

From *Book World* 11 (15 November, 1981) 10. © 1970, 1982, 1987 *The Washington Post*. Reprinted with permission.

The failures of modern architecture have by now been so thoroughly catalogued that one turns to Tom Wolfe's slim volume, *From Bauhaus to Our House,* with a grudging respect for his presumptuousness in picking yet again at the theme. What is it, one wonders, that Wolfe has to add to the by now nearly unanimous vote of no confidence in the modern movement? Wolfe has a way with words and he tells a mean story, but does he actually have anything new to say?

The answer is a very lower-case yes. Basically, the book is a case of crying Wolfe one more time. *Bauhaus* is distinguished by the same total loathing of modern culture that motivated *The Painted Word*, Wolfe's book about modern painting. But Wolfe is on somewhat solider ground when dealing with the world of architecture. His cultivated feel for the social surfaces of contemporary American life, and especially for the strategies, tactics and gestures of power, is somehow more in tune, perhaps simply because the game is bigger.

In *Bauhaus*, he scores his best points when describing the affectations of his targets, as in a wildly satirical version of a daily life of fresh vegetable mush and intellectual presumption at the Bauhaus in Desau, Germany, during the 1920s. He is funny, and on the mark, in pointing out how the sense of mission and style filtered down to American architecture students during the 1950s: "The place [a student apartment] would be lit by clamp-on heat lamps with half-globe aluminum reflectors and ordinary bulbs replacing the heat bulbs. At one end of the [sisal] rug, there it would be. . .*the Barcelona chair*."

Wolfe's outrage at the posings of the rich and fashionable at New York parties, as always, serves him well. In *Bauhaus*, he tells of an encounter that may even have planted the seed for the book in the mind of the still-fledgling writer. Contrary to the reigning dogma of New York's modernist tastemakers, Wolfe admired the buildings of Eero Saarinen, and in a magazine article he had mentioned this. "I ran into one of New York's best-known architectural writers at a party," Wolfe recalls, "and he took me aside for some fatherly advice. 'I enjoyed your piece,' he said, 'and I agreed with your point, in principle. But I have to tell you that you are only hurting your own cause if you use Saarinen as an example. People just won't take you seriously. I mean, Saarinen. . .' "

Wolfe's point here is that the world of modern architecture was a cult. To depart from the dogma as Saarinen did in his dramatic, expressive buildings, was to become an apostate and to suffer expulsion. It is a serious point, though hardly a new one. The degree to which important decisions were made, big money spent and buildings built in far-flung places based upon the received opinions of people who talked only to themselves in New York, Chicago, Boston and other outposts was an astonishing, widespread flaw of the modernist movement.

It is to be expected that he credits none of the achievements of modern architecture - hardly anyone will do that any more - but it is a bit surprising that Wolfe refuses to acknowledge that things have changed at all. To Wolfe, "postmodern" architecture is the same old shell game. I suppose to admit things have changed, and to credit writers such as Jane Jacobs, Robert Venturi, Christopher Jencks and Peter Blake with having helped effect these changes, would ruin the story Wolfe set out to tell.

But it would have been true. Whether good or bad, the signs of a serious, difficult debate about the challenges and prospects for architecture are everywhere. *From Bauhaus to Our House* contributes nothing to this discussion.

Wolfe: Tilting His Lance at the Glass Box

Peter Grier

From *The Christian Science Monitor* 74 (14 December 1981), B3. Reprinted by permission from *The Christian Science Monitor* © 1981 The Christian Science Publishing Society. All rights reserved.

For the most part, architects should not be let near a typewriter. Their prose often ends up with an adjective to verb ratio of about 37 to 1, saying things such as "the articulation of the perimeter of the perceived structures and its dialogue with the surrounding landscape." (Which, reportedly, prompted a Harvard logician to ask "What did the landscape have to say?") As Tom Wolfe's "The Painted Word" picked at the absurdities of modern painting, so "From Bauhaus to Our House" attacks the literary underpinnings of modern architecture, those theories of modernism by which buildings have been judged since Walter Gropius, The "Silver Prince" of the Bauhaus.

Wolfe's point in this splendidly witty little book is that modern architects design in code. A structure may be so beautiful it causes eyes to water and autos to stall: it may be so wonderfully functional people love to work or live in it, but if it wasn't designed according to an intellectual theory, well, how can we be expected to take it seriously? So beach houses sprout steel spaghetti intended to express "inner structure," skyscrapers are paneled with acres of glass as an expression of purity, and "decoration" becomes a dirty word.

The granddaddy of all codes, of course, is the famous "form is function." Hones material. Flat roofs. Clean right angles. As Wolfe points out, the Bauhaus theorists first began practicing their "functional" dictum in northern Europe.

"At this swath of the globe, with enough snow and rain to stop an army, as history has shown more than once, there was no such thing as a functional flat roof."

Actually, claims Wolfe, function and form have little to do with it. Instead, the codes are just a mad race to be avant-garde, to be out front with this month's Ultimate Theory. "The main thing was not to be caught designing something someone could point to, with a devastating sneer: 'How very bourgeois.' " Thus was born the Avenging Architect, with a vision so pure clients must not be allowed to muddy it.

"The client no longer counted for anything except the funding. If he were cooperative, not too much of a boor, it was acceptable to let him benefit from your new vision."

There is no denying that Wolfe has landed a sitting duck target. One need only look at the World Trade Center in New York City or at Boston's Prudential Center to see how the glass box got out of hand. And the "postmodern" building now rising - the most famous being Philip Johnson's AT&T building in New York, which looks like a giant Chippendale highboy - often use decoration and for ironic, not aesthetic, purposes. After a few decades, the joke of a monstrous piece of furniture may wear thin.

It is easy to dismiss a host of modern homes as "insecticide refineries." But Wolfe, while zapping architects for their literary silliness, never admits that some of their designs are at least interesting to look at. I.M. Pei's Hancock Tower in Boston is a marvelous piece of sculpture, when its windows aren't blowing out.

And if Philip Johnson and his buddies wanted to start some really good guerrilla warfare, they could argue that Tom Wolfe *writes* by theory. As a pioneer of the much-abused term "new journalism," Wolfe has pasted fictional techniques onto reporting, a synthesis that would cause many city desk editors to punch out their computer screens. He is also entering something of a postmodern phase himself, moving from decorative prose to cleaner, more functional sentences - who today would title a book, as Wolfe did in 1965, "The Kandy-Kolored Tangerine-Flake Streamline Baby?"

Lords of Glass, Steel and Concrete

Blake Morrison

First published in *Times Literary Supplement* (26 March, 1982), 337. Reprinted with the permission of Blake Morrison..

A fair index of a writer's attitude to modern architecture is the degree of pleasure he takes in making the almost statutory reference to the demolition of the Pruitt-Igoe apartments, St. Louis in 1972. This award-winning housing project, designed by Minoru Yamasake, architect of the World Trade Centre, completed in 1955, and having a mere seventeen years' life-span, was the first and most famous example of what has since become a trend among local authorities, in Britain as well as in the United States, to destroy buildings commissioned by them only a short time before.

In the case of Pruitt-Igoe, a largely migrant population from the flatlands of the rural south found the Corbusian high life (fourteen-storey blocks, covered aerial walkways, green lawns below) turning into a vandalized wasteland, and they persuaded the city to seek a remedy. As Tom Wolfe describes it in *From Bauhaus to Our House* - and the relish in the description is representative of his book's general hostility towards modern architecture - here was a "historic moment", for two reasons:

> One, for the first time in the fifty-year history of worker housing, someone had finally asked the client for his two cents' worth. Two, the chant. The chant began immediately: "Blow it. . *up!* Blow it. . *up!* Blow it . . *up!* Blow it. . *up!* Blow it. . *up!*" The next day the task force thought it over. The poor buggers were right. It was the only solution. In July of 1972, the city blew up the three central blocks of Pruitt-Igoe with dynamite.

The demolition of high-rise buildings may yet become the great spectator sport *de nos jours*, filing the gap once occupied by public hangings. Already, over the last few years, footage of the latest toppling tower-block being cheered through its descent by an enthusiastic crowd of onlookers has become a recurrent feature of the television news. "WATCH IT COME DOWN" is the gleeful slogan on demolition lorries: the men in hard hats never lack for an audience. No doubt some deep apocalyptic yearning is satisfied by the spectacle: it is possible to feel, as Hardy did in his poem about the sinking of the Titanic, that here is human overreaching being undone by the Immanent Will. (The same superstition was felt when a small plane flew into the side of the Empire State Building in 1945, and when Ronan Point collapsed in 1968: man had come too close to God and been punished for it.)

On another level, though, the satisfaction surely derives from a philistinism which can't decently be expiated elsewhere: the same civilized people who express outrage at the story of Hitler's burning of paintings and books are prepared to admit that they find the sight of a falling building one of the most exhilarating in the world. The reason may lie in the nature of architecture itself. It is the most overweening of the arts, and the one that least lets us alone. A gallery we can't walk out of, a book we can't close, and art we can't even turn our backs on because it is there facing us on the other side of the street as well - little wonder that people should want, if only occasionally, some obliterating revenge. Painters and writers can talk grandly of how they "live for" their art and of how their art in turn provides a model for us to "live by". Architects have no need of such special pleading: theirs is an art we must live in. Gropius presumably had this in mind, though his etymology isn't entirely to be trusted, when he suggested that "architect" was "a name signifying *Lord of Art*".

Like all lords, though, architects find that their power carries a burden of responsibility. Novelists and artists, when their touch fails, suffer little more than indifferent sales or bad reviews. But the audience of architects is a trapped one - a tenantry, even - and the price they must pay when they fail to give that audience what it wants is to find themselves and their buildings being wished to hell. A variation on this punishment was proposed recently by a television critic of *The Times,* when he suggested "that the planners and architects who occupied positions of municipal power in the Sixties should be put in the stocks, and that when all the available rotten eggs have been thrown they should be made to live out their miserable lives in the concrete hells they have created."

Vehemence such as this can derive from quite respectable motives: the belief, for example, that the coming of the new in architecture has too often meant the destruction of the old. Architecture is more willfully self-consuming than the other arts. The arrival of Picasso didn't necessitate the destruction of paintings by Rembrandt, nor the coming of Stravinsky and Joyce the elimination of Handel and Fielding. But Modernism in architecture has been more costly: as conservationists repeatedly remind us, many beautiful buildings have perished in order to make way for the glass and steel and concrete of the present day. This might matter less if Modernism in architecture could claim the range and diversity of Modernism in other arts. But it is open to the charge of having adopted but a single strand of Modernism - the one we associate with the Cubist, the minimal, the gridlike, the straight, flat and rectangular. The spirit of Brancusi, Mondrian, Becket, and Cage is there but not, it seems, that of Gaudier-Brzeska, Moore, Matisse, Pound, Diaghilev, Pirandello and the rest. Reyner Banham and Charles Jencks have tried to show that this is a false charge (Jencks even goes so far as to identify six separate movements in Modernist architecture), but for most people the "International Style" that reigned between the wars and the "New Brutalism" that came after constitute the main current of modern architecture, and all the other "-isms" are diversions of no consequence. A typically confident pronouncement is that of Paul Johnson: "All sensible and sensitive people know that modern architecture is bad and horrible." Even Johnson might not dare to be so sweeping about modern art.

But perhaps the main grudges against modern architecture concern its functionalism, or lack of it. On the one hand Modernist architects are reputed to have designed buildings of severe rationalism which cater, albeit monotonously, for a mass society. The notion of a new "Machine Age" recurs frequently in their theoretical discourse, though in appearance and principle their buildings look even further forward to the computer. Their crime is utilitarianism and impersonality. On the other hand, they are said to be no more constrained by utilitarian motives than were their contemporaries in other arts: they uphold self-expression and "imaginative freedom" - creation unfettered by thought for the consumer - every bit as defiantly as did the Romantic and Symbolist poets. This is evident in their famously fanciful projects, some unrealized (Frank Lloyd Wright's one-mile high tower for Chicago, the clouds round its upper storeys making it look like some Transylvanian castle), some regrettably fulfilled (Conrads' and Sperlich's *Fantastic Architecture* provides many candidates for this category). It is also evident in their manifestos, which were issued more regularly than even those of the Dadaists and Vorticists. Hans Poelsig in 1919 put a typical view: "The artist is concerned only with the means whereby he can plant this earth with creations of his imagination. . .only as an afterthought does he attempt to reduce his creations to the level on which life today is conducted." To the detractor, such a view will seem a dire fulfillment of Ruskin's wish that the profession of the architect might be united with that of the sculptor rather than of the engineer: modern buildings are not machines for living in but sculptures, that happen to house people.

The tension, so pronounced that modern architecture can be vilified equally for drab pragmatism and wild Utopianism, is exemplified in the work of its three undisputed European masters, Gropius, Le Corbusier and Mies, all of whom feature prominently in *From Bauhaus to Our House*. Gropius wanted his buildings to be "objective objects which serve specific purposes" yet he also spoke of the need to "build in fantasy without regard for technical difficulties. To have the gift of imagination is more important than all technology." Le Corbusier took on the mantle of a rigorous technician who wanted to "establish the elements of the house on a mass-production basis", but he wasted much of his life on unsolicited, unremunerative and utterly implausible plans to reconstruct Paris. Mies allied himself with a "secular" age ("we do not respect flights of the spirit so much as we value reason and realism") and with the "trend of our time towards anonymity": but, as Lewis Munford pointed out, he gave little thought to the "site, climate, insulation, function or internal activity" of his building (the tenants of all that glass and steel found themselves with huge heating bills) and his secularity did not prevent him from claiming a spiritual quality for his work: "God is in the details". All three architects could be characterized as formalists rather than functionalists, stylists more than social engineers. Their masterpieces leaked.

They spoke a language not of "need" and "living space" but of rhyme, rhythm, balance, proportion and "the vernacular."

In the hands of those hostile to modern architecture, these contradictions all too easily turn into charges: that modern architects arrogantly ignore the wishes of those who commission their building and those who inhabit them; that their first priority has always been to impress their colleagues, not to serve the public; that designs have more reality for them than buildings (hence their hostility to the suburbs - too sprawling to accommodate the drawing-board: and that the "functional" is not, after all, either practical or efficient. These are among the accusations Tom Wolfe makes in his new book, a study of architecture (mainly American) between 1919 and the present.

For those who know Wolfe only through his early work of the late 1960s - *The Kandy-Kolored Tangerine-Flake Streamline Baby, The Electric Kool-Aid Acid Test, The Pump House Gang, Radical Chic and Mau-Mauing the Flak-Catchers* - it may come as a surprise to find him writing about modern architecture at all, let alone with such hostility. For Wolfe first made his mark as a journalist, or rather New Journalist, who specialized in articles about alternative sub-cultures - California *Surfer-kinder* gangs of Hell's Angels, London nightliters, Ken Kesey and the Pranksters, Marshall McLuhan and Allen Ginsberg - and whose exuberant style suggested a receptivity to the shock of the new. The style, however, was deceptive: for all the dots, asterisks, italics, exclamation marks, ampersands, capitalizations, bizarre headings and comic strip vrooooms and aaaarghs, Wolfe's stance was essentially that of a man who thinks, speaks and has a sense of history when all around him pursue an amnesiac, inarticulate hedonism. In this sense he was hardly a New Journalist at all: he had neither the hyped-up subjectivity nor the manic involvement which were the hallmarks of the genre and which could be found in the work of Hunter S. Thompson. Had Wolfe been living in England in the 1960s he would have been writing for the *Spectator* not *Oz*: he was always more of a Christopher Booker than a Richard Neville. In recent books he has emerged clearly as a right-wing satirist - or "mandarin moralist", as he was once called - whose targets range from Abstract Art (vigorously attacked in *The Painted Word*) to the rivalries and inefficiencies of the American space programme (affectionately sent up in *The Right Stuff*). His interest is no longer in those who lack or avoid power, but in those who seek and abuse it. All of which makes modern architecture, involving as it does questions of aesthetic imperiousness, bureaucratic misdirection and financial wastefulness, an obvious subject for Wolfe to treat at book length.

The argument as one would expect of him, is desperately simple, the tone that of a man who has discovered some wonderfully obvious truth overlooked by everyone else. In the years after the First World War a number of young American architects flocked to Gropius's Bauhaus, believing that (as Malcolm Crowley put it) "they do things better in Europe". Gropius's aesthetic, the equivalent of a vegetarian diet, was severe and simple: he talked of "starting from zero" and of the need to serve the proletariat. Until 1922 he thought this meant celebrating the artsy-craftsy and hand-made. But when Theo van Doesburg "took one look at Gropius's Honest Toilers and Expressionist curves and sneered and said: *How very bourgeois*", he changed his slogan to "Art and Technology" and celebrated the machine-made. This was typical of what was happening throughout Europe: architects competed to be as "nonbourgeois" as possible making different decrees about the acceptability of colours, cornices, lintels, architraves, sloping roofs and so on. They also formed themselves into what Wolfe calls "art compounds," enclaves through which they were able to free themselves from their patrons and dictate their own terms. Remarkably, they succeeded: the much despised bourgeoisie came cap in hand to the compound asking for designs. This was the inspiring vision which the American boys took home with them in the 1920s.

The first signs of the arrival in America of the International Style came, Wolfe claims, in 1932, when Henry-Russell Hitchcock and Phillip Johnson wrote a catalogue for a show at the Museum of Modern Art which distinguished between true architecture and mere building (Wolfe fails to point out that Ruskin had made the same distinction in 1854), celebrated the work of Le Corbusier, Mies, Gropius and Oud, and deprecated the Americans and their skyscrapers. The catalogue hit home hardest among the Rockefellers and other rich patrons of the arts who, "baffled but impressed", urged American architects to follow the European lead. When Mies, Gropius and other refugees arrived in the States in the late 1930s, they found themselves being worshipped as "white gods"; and "within three years the course of American architecture had changed, utterly." (Wolfe's is a cheapskate version of history, where all changes are "utter" or "overnight" or "all at once".) Frank Lloyd Wright, having only recently won recognition, was swiftly demoted and "treated as a species of dead man". The vogue was now to build only one kind of building - the meagerly proportioned "glass box". Thus it came about that at the period of its greatest exuberance, or what Wolfe calls its "full-blooded, go-to-hell, belly-rubbing, wahoo-yahoo youthful rampage," America was saddled with buildings of the utmost mean-spiritedness. What had begun as worker housing for a depressed, poverty-stricken Europe in the "rubble" after the First World War had ended as the reigning architectural style of the richest nation on earth.

Wolfe deals sympathetically with the "apostates" who sought a way out of the grim consensus of the glass box - Edward Durrell Stone, Eero Saarinen, Morris Lapidus, John Portman, above all Frank Lloyd Wright. For him they are true parochials like Andrew Wyeth (and therefore not parochial), men of "rude animal vigour" who express something of "the hog-stomping Baroque exuberance of American civilization." In academic circles, though, they have met with "anathematism" - a shrug, a snigger and "that look". For to announce a departure from the reigning style one has to play the game right, as Robert Venturi did in his *Complexity and Contradiction in Modern Architecture*, which pretends to attack the compound mentality while preserving its tenets.

Wolfe gives excessive space to Venturi, as he does in his last two chapters to arguments between rival American schools like Venturi's Pop movement, the Rats (Rationalists), the Whites, the Grays and the Structuralists. This makes his book oddly imbalanced: after the irreverent treatment of Le Corbusier ("*Corbu!* the way Greta Garbo was *Garbo!*"), Gropius ("the Silver Prince") and Mies ("he looked rather like a Ruhr industrialist"), there's something insular about his respectful attention to American architectural debates of the last five years. But the existence of these arguments, and the energy invested in them, back up Wolfe's claim that architecture is no less a matter of building than of writing and drawing, its proper medium not brick but paper. (As Frank Lloyd Wright said of Le Corbusier: "Well, now he's finished one building he'll go write four books about it"). A feeling exists that there is "something sordid about doing a lot of building". We are back again to the argument of *The Painted Word*: modern architecture, like modern art, is dominated by that "Holy Tornado" Theory.

But Wolfe tries at least to end on a triumphant note, with Philip Johnson's AT&T building in New York. This surrey with the fringe on the top - an arch and rectangle at the bottom rising through a Rolls-Royce radiator grille to end in the flourish of a Chippendale highboy - must be the most famous uncompleted building in the world. Whether Wolfe likes it is not entirely clear; what he does like is that its designer, Philip Johnson, a former "miesling", should have leap-frogged all the prevailing fashions - "Look! I have established a more avant-garde position. . .way out here" - and got away with it. It is a hopeful of apostasy in an era sapped by timidly-followed trends.

It will be apparent that much of what Wolfe says has been said before, and not only by himself in *The Painted Word*. The view that the Bauhaus architects fled from totalitarianism in Europe only to impose it in the United States was expressed long ago, and more succinctly, by Frank Lloyd Wright. And there is nothing new either in the complaint against the monotony of current architecture - it was voiced in the nineteenth century as well as in ours. When, for example, Wolfe writes of a Mies campus that "The main classroom building looked like a shoe factory. The chapel looked like a power plant. The school of architecture [looked like] a Los Angeles carwash", or claims that today "every child goes to school in a building that looks like a duplicating machine replacement-parts wholesale distribution warehouse", he is echoing Dickens in *Hard Times* on the "severely workful" aspect of Coketown: "The jail might have been the infirmary, the infirmary might have been the jail, the townhall might have been either, or both, or anything else." There are also the mistakes and false emphases, which even the amateur of modern architecture can't help but notice: Simon Rodia (the architect of the Towers of Watts) instead of Simone Rodilla, or the roman- tic notion of American exuberance which leads Wolfe not only to exaggerate European influence in America (there was already much in the indigenous sky- scraper tradition to prepare the way for glass boxes and curtain walls), but to celebrate structures, like the florid lobby of John Portman's Regency O'Hare Hotel in Chicago, which is of no great architectural distinction.

Yet as always with Wolfe the false premises are bound up with vigorous and often hilarious descriptive passages. His claim that the only people occupying worker housing today are the bourgeoisie and those on welfare, the workers having fled to the suburbs, is highly suspect. Equally dubious is his model of what Gropius once called the "egocentric *prima donna* architect who forces his personal fancy on an intimidated client" - nowadays both parties are likely to be faceless committees. But these are suggestive myths and they provide the book's liveliest and most sympathetic passages, in which Wolfe takes the side of the little man against corporate bureaucracy. In Wolfe's world, occupants tired of waking at five on summer mornings defy the ban against curtains instituted by architects to maintain the purity of their building's facade; they resist the regulation whiteness and bareness of their rooms by scattering brightly-coloured silk cushions about the place; office workers shove "filing cabinets, desks, wastepaper baskets, potted plants, up against the floor-to-ceiling sheets of glass, anything to build a barrier against the panicked feeling that they were about to pitch headlong into the streets below." Such passages are not only humorous but show Wolfe's heart to be in the right place: what he dislikes about modern architecture is its arrogance of power, its totalitarian policing of the impulses of those who live in it.

But in the end, even by its own modest journalistic standards (a *Harper's* essay made into a book), *From Bauhaus to Our House* is too philistine to carry any real conviction. Partly this is to do with Wolfe taking up a position on Modernism somewhat to the right of Evelyn Waugh and Kingsley Amis. But it is also that he seems to have no real sensitivity to buildings in themselves, only to the controversies surrounding them: he makes fun but doesn't take pleasure. This shows up especially in his treatment of the Seagram building, which he apparently sees as just another glass box and which he gives little more that a sneering caption review. The Seagram, though, is a building which can make even the hardest sceptic see the point of Modernist architecture. Where Ruskin in his century thought shade crucial to buildings because it expresses "a kind of human sympathy, by measure of darkness as great as there is in human life," Mies and others have sought to transcend human frailty and doubt, erecting neo-Platonist structures which restore through their glittering surfaces the space and air they steel from the street. It is not a humane architecture but nor are its aspirations - grace, order, harmony - unknown to the human spirit. Though Wolfe may have a point in defending the yahoos his book is the poorer for failing to see any virtue in the houyhnhnms.

Crying Wolfe

Stephen Mullin

From *The New Statesman* 103 (26 March, 1982), 20-21. Reprinted with the permission of New Statesman and Society and the author.

'Architecture,' says the blurb, 'is a subject Tom Wolfe feels passionately about.' That, apparently, is sufficient basis for rewriting the entire history of the Modern Movement in 132 small, wide-margined, double-spaced large typeface pages. Once, some historical knowledge would have been felt useful. The New Journalism, however, dispenses with such fuddy-duddy conventions, inventing facts instead to suit a felicitous turn of phrase.

Thus, Thirties workers 'complained ' about 'worker housing ' (untrue); there is 'no such thing as a functional flat roof ' (untrue), and Le Corbusier called his houses 'machines for living' (still untrue, even if it is the most persistently quoted mistranslation in the canon). Rhetoric rules, with every page a minefield of italics, exclamation marks and one-word conversation stoppers. And, if all else fails, lack of content can always be disguised with pen portraits of the main protagonists: 'Le Corbusier was a thin, sallow, nearsighted man who went about on a white bicycle'. Louis Kahn 'was not too much to look at either. He was short. He had wispy reddish-white hair that stuck out this way and that.' Well, we wouldn't want to have much to do with that sort of person, would we?

What a shame. Because, tucked away in the last pages of this slim volume, is a genuinely funny, acute and revealing set of observations on elite architecture in the United States, which could have formed the foundation for two or three thumping good essays. The impenetrable waffle of the Structuralists, the giggling camp of Charles Moore and the Repro stylists, and the paternalist populism of Venturi, all get memorable put-downs on a par with Joan Littlewood's immortal torpedo - 'piping Beethoven down the pits' - that sank Arnold Wesker with all hands. And Wolfe's bitchy invective races at last into full gear when he sights the ultimate exponents of 'meaningful' architecture - the rarefied conceptualists who have finally abandoned construction for the unsullied purity of the exhibition drawing.

Then - nothing. Or, rather, an oddly meandering attempt to pull the whole thing together by suggesting that, whatever their labels, American architects have conspired since the Thirties to keep their clients firmly under their thumbs, taking what they're given 'like a man.' Not like the good old days when 'we used to give them Norman country manors with everything but the pile of manure in the yard.' And the villains of the piece? Why, those nasty, socialistic foreigners who came over before the war and seduced the credulous, open-hearted Americans with their talk of 'worker housing'. Not for nothing does Wolfe call Walter Gropius the Silver Prince; the memory of the impoverished European aristocrats who snitched all the heiresses at the turn of the century still lives on.

And the lost leader? Frank Lloyd Wright, without a doubt, who might, Wolfe implies, have created a truly American architecture for the American century. But the American century turned out to last a scant 25 years, and Wright - himself no slouch at ordering clients around - never got Broadacre City off the drawing board. 'We wuz robbed': the Jeffersonian cry of anger against the huddled masses who swamped the agrarian dream a hundred years ago rings out sharper than ever in puzzled, isolationist, resentful America.

But, of course, the polyglot radicalism of the immigrants eventually washed away in the American melting pot, and Gropius himself lost his cutting edge in the monumental flab of the Architects' Collaborative. As Wolfe observes, American students are 'unable to sit still for ideology', and this is both 'a saving grace' and 'an intellectual weakness'. Alien ideas can be rendered harmless, but, in the absence of ideology, what is one to put in their place?

There are clues. Buckminster Fuller, who rates a paragraph from Wolfe, has spent his life anticipating an ideology-free technological revolution which still always seems to be just around the next corner. And, for more detailed discussion of this American Grail, and its relationship to the muddled and often absurd theorising of the Modern Movement, Wolfe could usefully have studied Reyner Banham's two classics *Theory and Design in the First Machine Age* and *The Architecture of the Well-Tempered Environment*. But then, Banham is an Englishman who has made his home in America, and has had the temerity to lecture its clients on their own culture. Which may explain why Wolfe cannot bring himself to mention him. It's not just Europeans, apparently, who allow ideology to drive out rational discussion.

From Our House To Las Vegas

Richard Guy Wilson

From *Virginia Quarterly Review* 58 (Summer 1982), 533-36. Reprinted with permission of *Virginia Quarterly Review*.

The inspection of one's navel or the defining of what is American about America is a national preoccupation. This introspection began with the rise of nationalism in the Western world and has continued undiminished throughout the 20th century. More than any other people, Americans have produced a vast corpus of commentary that ranges back and forth over the turf of "What is American?" in art, literature, and architecture.

These thoughts are provoked by a flood of recent books on American architecture and particularly the three under review, which give three very different interpretations of "What is American architecture?" One is academic history, the second is essentially a picture book, and the third is a raging polemic. Whiffen and Koepper's *American Architecture, 1607-1976* covers the development of American architecture from the first white settlement to the very recent past. The book is eminently serious and respectable, rather boring and dull, and certainly destined to become a book in architectural history courses. Illustrations are in general good, and a significant number are plans. However, these cover only about a third of the buildings mentioned in the text, and only a few interiors are shown, almost all of them public or religious buildings. The research is in general up-to-date, and the book strives for a neutral noncritical stance, though some of the authors' favorites come through: for Whiffen, who writes the section from 1607 to 1860, it is the early colonialists: and for Koeper, who writes the later section, it is Mies van der Rohe. But the authors do include material on many architects who have long been neglected in standard histories, especially those who stood apart from the modernist mainstream of the 20th century.

American architecture for Whiffen and Koeper means anything produced within the 48 states (not Alaska, Hawaii, or our overseas embassies - many by eminent Americans - or our imperial possessions). In a brief three-page forward, they assert that American architecture has always been very acquisitive, dependent upon foreign inspiration. Rather gingerly they claim possibly an American sensibility for clear-cut clarity of form, enlargement of scale, free-flowing space, and a pragmatic "make-do" attitude. Architecture for them is a capital "A," meaning buildings designed by architects (the colonial period, when there were few if any architects in the sense we know them today, is naturally excepted) and certainly not native Indian structures or the more ephemeral factories, gas stations, and the suburban house.

Nothing could be more different than *The End of the Road: Vanishing High-way Architecture in America*, which is essentially composed of excellent photographs by Mr. Margolies, accompanied by a 12-page introduction. The book is not academic history but rather a paean to "America's definitive contribution to the art of design in the twentieth century." Margolies covers the development of roadside architecture: gas stations, diners, and signs, which parallel the American involvement and love affair with the automobile. Frankly, the history is simplistic and the writing unmemorable, but the images are striking: giant oranges, Chinese pagoda gas stations, huge milk bottles, and "linger longer motor inn" cabins. Margolies represents a burgeoning group of "popular architecture" enthusiasts who are attempting to reassess the neglected aspects of our environment.

Sloppy though Margolies is, he does bring up an important issue. Architecture is a form of communication, and the image it presents, whether flat-roofed glass skyscrapers or high-pitched roofed, half-timbered houses, communicates a meaning. The American acceptance of modernism in the 20th century, especially the extremely reductivist abstract machine image style, born in Europe and imported here in the late 1920's and the 1930's, and the dominant image until very recently of most capital "A" architecture is the theme of Tom Wolfe's *From Bauhaus to Our House*. The Wolfe book has caused a considerable furor in architectural circles for this reason: Wolfe castigates almost all of the "stars" of the architectural establishment as either dupes or scoundrels engaged in a conspiracy to foist upon the American public an alien architecture full of intellectual pretension but with little comfort or visual appeal. Tom Wolfe can be easily dismissed. He is neither an architect nor a serious architectural critic or historian; rather he is a "pop" journalist, fun to read as he punctures pretensions, fun, that is, as long as he doesn't step too close to you with his pin. Nevertheless, Wolfe is an intelligent man with impeccable scholarly credentials, and there is a certain truth, though overstated, in what he says. The "colonial complex" of Americans led to the adoption of European architectural images created by Mies van der Rohe, Walter Gropius, and Le Corbusier in the 1920's as a response to specific social, political, and aesthetic conditions. The result was the submergence of a rich American strain and the simplification of architecture to clean, spartan surfaces. American excess, the "Christmas-tree ornaments" on top of the Empire State and Chrysler buildings in New York became passé, condemned as of no value. Frank Lloyd Wright, who is perhaps the only truly great and original American architect, and who paradoxically influenced some of the Europeans, was never accepted by pretentious American intellectual architects. Along with Wright, there were other American originals: Edward Durell Stone, Eero Saarinen, Bruce Goff, and Herb Greene who "actually catered to the Hog-stomping Baroque exuberance of American civilization." Wolfe overstates the actual facts; all of these men were eminently successful and certainly much admired at one time, though they have remained outside the intellectually controlled "compound."

The current group of younger architects, who have been called "post-Modernist," meaning they are questioning some of the reductivist thinking of their fathers and attempting to reassert a visual language of history, excess, and ornament offer little hope to Wolfe; Robert Venturi's *Complexity and Contradiction*, first published in 1966 and seen by many as a significant break with orthodox modernism, engaged in the same intellectual pretensions as Gropius or Le Corbusier back in the 1920's. And again Wolfe has a point. The only way to make a reputation, to be heard, is to be outrageous, and back in 1960 Venturi's "Main Street Is Almost All Right". . . or "Learning from Las Vegas" was extreme. Yet the change has occurred: The Bauhaus is dead, Long live Las Vegas.

The question of what is really American preoccupies all three of these books, and unfortunately, the only one who really makes a strong claim for an answer is Mr. Margolies. Wolfe clearly doesn't present any solution. Whiffen and Koeper just record what has been done; they accept it all. Architecture can inspire: it can mean more than simple function; it can be an art. The question is, especially for one writing from Mr. Jefferson's University, what has the last 50 years of American architecture meant? What is the American consciousness as expressed in the most public of all the arts? And the answer can be very depressing.

From Bauhaus to Our House

Reviewed by Albert Bergesen

From *American Journal of Sociology* 89 (November 1983), 739-41. Reprinted with permission of Albert Bergeson.

When Leland Stanford, Jr., died in 1884, Leland, Sr., wanted to build a memorial and enlisted the services of famed landscape architect Frederick Law Olmsted, who had designed New York's Central Park and the Berkeley campus. Leland, Sr., wanted a campus of his own in Palo Alto. Olmsted wanted something like Berkeley, with buildings interwoven among trees, streams, and rolling hills. He wanted Stanford further up in the foothills. Leland, Sr., wanted his memorial university on flatland to better realize its essence as a monument to his son. The client wanted a memorial. The architect wanted a naturalistic park. The client got his way. Stanford University was built on flatland, complete with a large triumphal arch, Memorial Arch, and a Memorial Court, a Memorial Church, and a monumental symmetrical courtyard, Inner Quad. I do not know for sure, but it would seem that Olmsted got his way on at least one thing; the Mausoleum is off among the trees, to the right, as you drive up Palm Drive.

For Tom Wolfe in *From Bauhaus to Our House* that is the way client-architect relations should be: tell them what you want. You are paying; you decide. He suggests, however, that things have changed. Today there would be an international competition, a panel of judges composed of a lot of university architecture professors, and a winning design. Some sort of glass box or austere modern building would be built. Think of William James Hall at Harvard. This might not be so bad if most clients did not hate the austere box that became known as the International Style. For Wolfe, both the modern style and the relative independence of the architect began with the post-World War I European architects who formed autonomous "art compounds" like the Bauhaus or the Dutch group De Stijl and were committed to producing, as he puts it, "worker-housing cubes" and a no-frills "nonbourgeois architecture." Thus, they used no ornaments, no facades, no columns, no pitched roofs, no color, no luxurious materials like granite, marble, limestone, or red brick, but only the bare essentials: concrete, wood, steel, glass, or stucco buildings with flat roofs, sheer facades, thin walls, and colored white, beige, and grey, with an occasional spot of black for accent. "The inner structure, the machine-made parts, the mechanical rectangles, the modern *soul* of the building, completely free of applied decoration" (p. 26). Form follows function. Modern architecture. The glass box. Walk downtown. It is omnipresent.

As if that were not bad enough, says Wolfe, the leaders of this movement emigrated to the United States and dominated American architecture. What began as worker housing in Germany and Holland became the predominant form of corporate American architecture. Worker housing as the New York skyline. Ironic. They not only arrived, argues Wolfe, but became ensconced at the leading universities: Gropius was made head of the Harvard School of Architecture; Moholy-Nagy started the New Bauhaus, later the Chicago Institute of Design; Josef Albers started a rural Bauhaus at Black Mountain College and, in 1950, moved to Yale as head of fine arts instruction; and Mies van der Rohe became dean of architecture at the Armour Institute of Chicago, which merged with the Lewis Institute to become the Illinois Institute of Technology. From Wolfe's point of view, they arrived and conquered. The International Style, as austere modern architecture came to be called, became the standard, and deviation was treated as just that: deviance. There remains a general disdain for nonmodern architecture, although there seems to be some tiring of the glass-box syndrome. There are murmurings of a postmodern architecture. This, however, seems more rhetorical than real, bound up with the writings of Robert Venturi and a lot of talk about the naturalness of Las Vegas or McDonald's golden arches. In short, there seems to be no alternative movement on the horizon other than a pinch of ornamentation here and there under the somewhat inflated label of postmodernism.

For Wolfe the biggest problem was that these Europeans had intimidated Americans - our "colonial complex," he calls it - and given us an architecture unfitting the boisterous imperial position of America at the height of its capitalist glory. We do not need austere, functional worker housing but something more dramatic, decorative, and triumphal to mirror America's place as the hegemonic - or declining hegemonic - state. He contends further that the workers do not even like this kind of functional housing. The only ones who benefit from all this are the architects in their isolated compounds, expounding this and that theory of the ideal architecture.

Then there is the question, What are we to make of Wolfe himself? John Gregory Dunne recently called Wolfe an anthropologist, and I think he was partly right. Some used to say that Goffman was something of a great social observer, watching and reporting all that interaction. But Goffman was really more the theorist perhaps the American contributor to substantive theory, as opposed to the writings about others which often pass as theory. Maybe social archaeologist is a better label for Wolfe since he digs up and uncovers social dynamics we do not want brought to consciousness. Wolfe informs us, through sarcasm and with values that often run counter to our liberalism. But, to focus on his conservatism and reactionary nationalism and miss the ironies and contradictions he unveils is a serious mistake.

Wolfe always raises interesting questions. We may not like his answers, or even his questions, but there are things that need to be explained. Why is modern art getting more abstract, or why did the glass-box paradigm take hold in architecture, or how could a socially conscious architectural community concerned with humanitarian values generate such a cold, austere vision of modern housing? You can always tell that his questions have struck some kind of nerve by the inevitable intellectual stonewalling by his reviewers. For such a purportedly lightweight critic, who always misunderstands art, architecture, or Manhattan parties, there is certainly a lot of huffing and puffing in those reviews. So what does the sociologist get from Wolfe? Many things, obviously. But at the heart of what Wolfe knows intuitively are the ironies and contradictions of modern life, whether they are seen in the appearance of members of the Black Panther party at a chic Manhattan cocktail party or in a socialist dream of proletarian housing becoming the totem of 20th-century capitalism.

There are aspects of lived life, dealt with more often in literature than in sociology but real nonetheless, that Wolfe, in his heavy-handed way, brings to our attention. We seem so inept at dealing with human realities dramatized in literature that maybe the slapstick humor of Wolfe is about all we can digest. I fear that if he wrote more subtly there would be little chance we could pick up what he was saying; we have enough trouble with the belly laughter in which he encases his observation now, without his packaging them in a more refined format.

The Purple Decades:
A Reader

The Best Right Stuff

Paul Fussell

From *New York Times Book Review* 87 (10 October, 1982), 3. Copyright © by Paul Fussell, 1982. Reprinted with permission of the author.

Here's almost 20 years of Tom Wolfe's electric prose, 20 classic pieces, including "The Pump House Gang" (California surfers and their culture), "The Last American Hero" (Junior Johnson, Southern moonshine delivery driver turned stock car racer), "On the Bus" (Ken Kesey and the Merry Pranksters' cross-country LSD bus trip), "These Radical Chic Evenings" (Leonard Bernstein's trendiness), "Mau-Mauing the Flak-Catchers" (the fun of extorting poverty-program cash from whitey in the 60's) and memorable hunks of both "The Right Stuff" and "From Bauhaus to Our House." Nothing new, but a sampling rich enough to prompt a close look at Wolfe. Who is he and what is he up to?

"Only a language experience." That's what Walt Whitman once called "Leaves of Grass," and that could also suggest Mr. Wolfe's distinctive American-ness and hint at one valuable part of his achievement. What he conveys is excitement or shock in the face of anomaly, and he does so by deploying various devices of verbal intensity and oddness. He will repeat a tag and repeat it and finally work it to life: "the right stuff," "burned beyond recognition," "the good old boys," "just like that." He likes shock assonance, as in "rat shacks," "rot bog," "black gas," "an utter shuck," "wavy gravy," "the pick of the litter" and of course "flak-catcher." He will weasel himself into the reader's own intimate space with expletives and street-corner familiarities: "Hell, yes!" "Fat chance, sahib," "Is that irony or isn't it?"

His outpouring of italics and exclamation points signals an American actuality so bizarre that only the most incredulous tone is appropriate. His management of *outré* diction suggests that he's spent as many evenings reading the poems of Gerard Manley Hopkins ("scum slicks, dead dodder vines" decorate the outbacks of the naval air stations where the fliers crash) as listening to teen-agers talking about "goop-heads" and "glop." If most of our current poets knew as much language and cared for it as much as this "journalist," we'd be on the brink of a poetic renaissance or at least a new Romantic Movement.

But Mr. Wolfe doesn't spatter out these wonderful words for their own sake. He exhibits them because they're the right medium for his satiric and moral vision. It's the moralist and humanist in Mr. Wolfe, not the comic, who stigmatizes people busy turning themselves into objects, consumers or mechanical vessels for chemical highs. Or people who try to simplify experience until it accords with a sentimental romantic primitivism ("Yes! Oh my God, those raw-vital proles!"). "Me-Decade" egotism is one of his favorite targets, as well as fake artistic sophistication, the pathetic American quest for purchasable prestige, the obsession with "image" among the high-profit classes, and the vanity and stupidity of the let-it-all-hang-out movement. Mr. Wolfe's writings, says Joe David Bellamy in his introduction, "Show how political power and orthodoxy and fashion-mongering have often run roughshod over originality, virtue, fair play, exuberance, and panache." Mr. Wolfe's moral, he concludes, "would seem to be that those who succumb to the temptation to aspire to the merely fashionable, who thus sacrifice the noble impulse toward individual vision, may end up 'succeeding,' " and that's bad.

What Mr. Bellamy is saying is that for all the comedy he generates in his prose, Mr. Wolfe is a serious admonitor of contemporary folly, and in another age he might be a minister or a prophet or an outright moral philosopher, instead of an "entertainer." Not just Ecclesiastes and Jeremiah and Isaiah, but Veblen and Mencken are his ancestors, although his very contemporary sense that life resembles show business is like the psychologist Erving Goffman's.

Just as Mr. Wolfe hates human vices and follies, he loves their opposites - manifestations of competence, courage and skill - "it," in his treatment of Naval carrier pilots, "the right stuff" of the original astronauts. He is a celebrator of honest self-sufficiency wherever it shows itself, even among the self-propelled elderly magically tooling around America in their silver, bullet-shaped Airstream trailers, independent, curious, questing "people. . .who actually moved off dead center and went out into the world and *rolled*." If Mr. Wolfe is a dread scourge of insincerity and fraud, if he declines to be awed by the Gothic architecture at Yale or hoodwinked by euphemisms or impressed by the self-righteousness of both those on the New Left and those Born Again, he is careful to notice real merit and quick to respond to real emotional need, even among his urban jerks and hoods. "Even schlock has its classics," he says of the old *Confidential* magazine; and the good-looking sillies devoting their lives to surfing elicit his sympathy despite his satire of them, for they are destined for destruction by old age and feebleness, a fate their poor uneducated imaginations haven't in the least prepared them for.

It is Mr. Wolfe's sense of tradition and his command of norms that invite him to notice anomalies, like the ironic contrast between the men's club comfort of the wardroom of the Vietnam War carrier Coral Sea and the appalling vulnerability of the combat pilots who lay down their breakfast napkins every morning and go out to face SAM missiles and antiaircraft fire. Mr. Wolfe's reliance on tradition for his moral and satiric insights may suggest that he's a reactionary, and in "From Bauhaus to Our House" there are occasional whiffs of something very like stuffiness. Reactionary he may be, but I prefer to see him as a skeptic, at his best instinctively distrustful of novel and dramatic solutions to age-old dilemmas. Reading him is exhilarating not because he makes us hopeful of the human future but because he makes us share the enthusiasm with which he perceives the actual. "Golly," he's always saying, "just *look!*"

For old Wolfe fans, this collection will take them back to the heady days when wearing beads and coming clean were going to redeem a corrupt world. For newcomers, here's a fine showcase of goodies to stimulate the appetite and point them toward the original books. But not everything Mr. Wolfe does is perfect. There's no reason to expect a good writer to be a good cartoonist too, and Mr. Wolfe's half-dozen drawings in this book are embarrassingly amateur, the sort of thing best shown to friends at home. He should restrict himself to writing. At that he's splendid, and currently there's no one producing readable essays about American social reality who has not learned from him.

Tom Wolfe and His Dissecting Pen

Jonathan Yardley

From *Book World* 12 (November 7, 1982), 3. ©1970, 1982, 1987, *The Washington Post*. Reprinted with permission.

Tom Wolfe pauses now, after the publication of 10 books, to present his readers with a mid-career anthology. We should be grateful, no doubt, but not to excess. The production of a large, assertive volume such as this as a declaration of one's own stature - all the more so when the writer acquires, as Wolfe has, a pet professor to formulate, complete with footnotes, a rhapsody in one's honor that climaxes in sheer ecstasy: "No other writer of our time has aspired to capture the fabled Spirit of the Age so fully and has succeeded so well." Thus speaks Joe David Bellamy of St. Lawrence University in his introduction; the evidence, predictably, indicates that he exaggerates.

The selections herein gathered were chosen by Wolfe himself, as well as the numerous cartoons and sketches from his own hand that provide malicious and delicious illustration. Therefore *The Purple Decades* is the authorized version, Wolfe's greatest hits as ordained by the master himself. What *The Purple Decades* tells us, then, is that Wolfe sees himself as a chronicler of three broad subjects: the vulgarity, pretension and cynicism of life during the period that he has penetratingly characterized as "the Me Decade"; the con game played on the public by the high priests and priestesses of modern art and architecture; the daring deed of those few remaining souls - stock-car drivers, combat pilots, test pilots, astronauts - who undertake acts of individual courage during an age of collective timidity. His marks in the first category are startlingly high, but rather lower in the second and third; and too often his feats of social observation are gravely diminished by his showy, self-declarative prose.

Certain of the pieces are classics, if minor ones: "These Radical Chic Evenings" and "Mau-Mauing the Flak Catchers," in which Wolfe explores the bizarre encounters between white liberal guilt and black urban radicalism; "The Me Decade and the Third Great Awakening," the definitive examination of the culture of self; "The Intelligent Coed's Guide to America" and "Mauve Gloves & Madmen, Clutter & Vine," in which Wolfe annihilates the cozy little world where the literati and the collegiati reside. These are exercises in social commentary written by a master of the craft, a satirist whose perceptive eye is matched by the exuberant cruelty with which he describes what he sees:

"This teacher was a white woman. She was one of those Peter, Paul and Mary-type intellectuals. She didn't wear nylons, she didn't wear makeup, she had bangs and long straight brown hair down to below her shoulders. You see a lot of middle-class white intellectual women like that in California. They have a look that is sort of Pioneer Hip or Salt of the Earth Hip, with flat-heeled shoes and big Honest Calves."

Or there is the description of a member of America's "native intelligentsia":

"Did he want to analyze the world systematically? Did he want to add to the store of human knowledge?. . . . Did he even want to change the world? Not particularly; it was much more elegant to back exotic, impossible causes such as the Black Panthers. Moral indignation was the main thing; that, and a certain pattern of consumption. In fact, by the 1960s it was no longer necessary to produce literature, scholarship or art - or even to be involved in such matters, except as a consumer - in order to qualify as an intellectual. It was only necessary to live *la vie intellectuelle*. A little brown bread in the bread box, a lapsed pledge card to CORE, a stereo and a record rack full of Coltrane and all the Beatles albums from 'Revolver' on, white walls, a huge *Dracenaena marginata* plant, which is there because all the furniture is so clean-lined and spare that without this piece of frondose tropical Victoriana the room looks empty, a stack of unread *New York Review of Books* rising up in a surly mound of subscription guilt, the conviction that America is materialistic, repressive, bloated and deadened by its Silent Majority, which resides in the heartland, three grocery boxes full of pop bottles wedged in behind the refrigerator and destined (one of these days) for the recycling center, a small, uncomfortable European car - that pretty well got the job done."

How true, and how devastating in its observed detail. Wolfe is a positive glutton for the minutiae of style: the nuances and signals, the designer labels and brand names, through which we attempt to tell the world who we are, or who we think we are, or who we would like to be. So long as he keeps from rattling off into exclamation points and ellipses and capital letters - so long as he refrains from the excesses of a prose style that is capable of saying, "Look at me," with as much self-absorption as any Me Decade encounter-group faddist - he is a penetrating, funny, devastating social critic.

He is less effective as a critic of art and architecture because his chief instruments of attack are ridicule and bile; though more often than not I find myself agreeing with him on specific artists, art gurus and works of art, and though his depiction of modern art as fulfilling the needs of "social chic" strikes me as entirely accurate, he seems nonetheless when dealing with these matters to be less informed than merely prejudiced. As for his pieces about his own brand of heroes - Junior Johnson, Pete Conrad, Chuck Yeager - these are fine pieces of reporting, but they simply don't amount to as much as his social commentary, and the decidedly worshipful tone in which they are couched is rather incongruous coming from one so flamboyantly dandified as is Wolfe himself; no doubt the psychiatrists could have a field day with his obsession with these earthily charismatic figures, but I would not wish that on him.

In all these pieces Wolfe displays himself as father of the "new" journalism. As is invariably the case, the father is vastly more expert that the countless children who have sprung up in imitation. Though he is given to stylistic excess, he rarely permits himself forays into the minds of his subjects that are not substantiated by the evidence he has accumulated; by comparison with all the crypto-Wolfes, he is the very model of restraint. He is also a terrific reporter, and it is unfortunate that Bellamy attempts to elevate him into the higher preserve of literature. Why is it that Wolfe, who so detests pretense, has himself taken on a professor in order to give himself airs? Oh, well: Wolfe's craft, which is substantial, will survive Bellamy's exegesis and Wolfe's own implicit endorsement of it.

The Purple Decades: A Reader

Reviewed by T. Patrick Hill

From *America* 148 (12 March, 1983), 195-97. Reprinted with permission of America Press, Inc., 106 W. 56th Street, New York, NY 10019. © 1968, 1973, 1975, 1977, 1983 and 1988. All rights reserved.

It takes very little, upon calling to mind the 1970's, to be overwhelmed by pessimism. The reasons are everywhere, even for the most obtuse. As Peter N. Carroll, formerly a teacher at the University of Illinois, reminds us, there was the military violence of Vietnam and the pseudo-military violence of Kent State. Domestically, there was an ominous fragmentation among black political forces as some, emphasizing black power, advocated policies of confrontation with the white establishment. Similarly among whites, confrontation, on occasion violent, was the order of the day as radical conservatives rallied to the flag and the President while liberals mounted their antiwar campaign.

Politically, matters were just as bad. The Presidential election of 1972 derided George McGovern's appeal to America "to come home," left the Democratic Party in disarray and set the stage for Richard Nixon's cynical assault on the constitutional foundations of the United States. A greater nightmare, in the form of Watergate, intensified the national trauma and dubious relief came in the person of Gerald Ford. Here was no cathartic knocking at the door, as Shakespeare might have prescribed. The nation had to be content with the pathetic pardon of a disgraced President. This was indeed a paralyzing crisis of political leadership. And there was little to suggest that Jimmy Carter, who succeeded President Ford in 1976, could relieve this crisis. For here was a prophet who eventually was unacceptable everywhere. Moreover, a deteriorating economy, accelerated by the energy crisis, underlined the experience of what the author has called a loss of connection. Ecological problems, unfolding at the same time, suggested disorientation on a cosmic scale. It was, as Dickens had written of an earlier era, "the worst of times."

The question, however, for anyone reading this book must be whether it was also "the best of times," as Carroll seems to suggest. For along with the radical dislocation, there was also in the 1970's a search for positive alternatives. These were movements of social and ideological minorities who pitched their tents beyond the nuclear family to secure other personal identities, and beyond orthodox spiritualities to reach alternative meanings. Carroll judges these efforts as positive and ultimately healing, though why is not made clear. They could, of course, be viewed as instances of fragmentation and so support the conviction that the advocacy of single issues will eventually render America ungovernable. The critical point is that Carroll appears to have no answer to this objection.

Throughout this thinly disguised journalistic essay, he has been content to develop his argument by means of circumstantial evidence. But in using the same evidence, another might conclude with Yeats: "Things fall apart; the center cannot hold;/Mere anarchy is loosed upon the world;/The best lack all conviction, while the worst/Are full of passionate intensity." If nothing else, that seems more plausible.

All the more so when you join Tom Wolfe in his forays beyond the fringe during the 1960's and 1970's. *The Purple Decades* is an anthology containing substantial excerpts from such landmark works as *The Electric Kool-Aid Acid Test*, a superb parody on the promised land to which drugs were said to point, *The Pump House Gang* in which Wolfe delineates counter-cultures, *Radical Chic* in which social elites are observed reflecting, Narcissus-like, their own beauty in the unknown faces of the dispossessed and *From Bauhaus to Our House* which satirizes a persuasion common in America between the two world wars that there was no cultural salvation outside Europe.

In addition to the essays, there is a generous sample of Wolfe's quite brilliant illustrations taken from his book of drawings, *In Our Time*. A useful introduction by Joe David Bellamy, who teaches at St. Lawrence University, adds to the value of this collection.

Wolfe was something of a phenomenon when he burst upon the American literary scene with what is often referred to as the new journalism. It all happened after he got to the Coliseum in New York sometime in the early 1960's to do a routine article on The Hot Rod and Custom Car Show. The article was dissatisfying because it failed to capture some elusive feature of this particular event. Then came the dawning. Here was a subculture, an esoteric enclave quite removed from, but affecting significant changes upon, the mainstream. The farther afield Wolfe looked, the more he saw a society fragmenting under the impact of countercultures like pop art, the hippies, the teen-age cult, the inverted snobbery of all that was considered cool. It was the world according to "proles, peasants and petty burghers." Intellectually far removed from this world, Wolfe has felt its basic pulse and, by means of a highly innovative journalism, given it unmistakable self-consciousness. With an uncanny understanding of the absurd, he saw that "the Me Decade," "Radical Chic" or "The Right Stuff" are their own best parodies. More than any other contemporary social commentator, Tom Wolfe has made this evident.

The Poet Laureate of Pop

Esmond Wright

From *Contemporary Review* 242 (1983), 274. Reprinted with permission of Esmond Wright.

There are twenty-one essays here. Some of them like *Radical Chic*, six from *The Kandy-Kolored Tangerine-Flake Streamline Baby*, and three from *The Pump House Gang* are vintage Wolfe; many are more recent. Tom Wolfe is a man of many parts. Born in Richmond, Virginia and a graduate, as a good gentleman of Virginia might well be, of Washington and Lee in the Valley of Virginia, and of Yale, he has won awards as a writer both for his foreign despatches and for his humour; he has exhibited his drawings in major galleries in New York and conveys something of their quality and impishness here; he is a near-pro ball player as well as a Ph.D. But it is as a writer and journalist that he is best known, for a style that has been described as 'para-journalistic' and 'supercontemporary'; this is the 'poet laureate of pop.' It is a style that relies on slickness, irreverence and the mixing of metaphors, and tries to capture a world (or many worlds) that he clearly recognises as built on organised insanity. It is subjective and emotional; it looks for hidden meanings below appearances; it tries to catch the flavour of 'the whole crazed obscene uproarious Mammon-faced drug-soaked mau-mau lust-oozing sixties.' Even his titles suggest the flavour, as in *The Electric Kool-Aid Acid Test* and in his collected essays *The Kandy-Kolored Tangerine-Flake Stream-line Baby*. ('The Last American Hero' from it is printed here). He himself says that it all started when he covered for *Esquire* the Hot Rod and Custom Car Show at the Coliseum in New York. Here was a new world with its own code; and in the South he discovered that stock-car racing had replaced baseball as the major spectator sport:

> My car is stopped still on Sunday morning in the middle of the biggest traffic jam in the history of the world. It goes for ten miles in every direction. . . . And right there it dawns on me that as far as this situation is concerned anyway, all the conventional notions about the South are confined to. . .the Sunday radio. The South has preaching and shouting, the South has grits, the South has country songs, old mimosa traditions, clay dust, Old Bigots, New Liberals - and all of it, all of that old mental cholesterol, is confined to the Sunday radio. . .We were all in the middle of a wild new thing, the Southern car world. . .

So not having time to complete the article, he typed it out at high speed and gave birth to what he himself calls 'the wowie style.' He found other worlds that were a product of money and invention - rock 'n' roll, or Las Vegas-style neon sculpture dominating supermarkets and hamburger stands in every suburb. What became his forte was analysis of and brilliant descriptions of these American subcultures, with their distinct styles, art forms and status rituals. But as a Ph.D. he can when he wishes write as a scholar and is prepared to do weeks of research; he is as good on architecture as on airmen, on the fashionable world of pop art in New York (as in *The Pump House Gang*); and at his best, in *The Right Stuff*, he can capture a very strange world - in that case the closed world of the Mercury astronauts and space-age pilots - in brilliant fashion, and show not only sparkle but compassion. And he has fathered some phrases that are now part of the language, like 'Radical Chic' and 'the Me Decade'.

As a result, the essays here reprinted are journalism of an inventive quality and a depth that makes it at once comic literature and social anthropology especially of New York City. It is amusing, ironic and splendid reading.

The Bonfire
of the Vanities

Dandy Does Dickens

Christopher Buckley

From *The Wall Street Journal* (29 October 1987), 30. Reprinted with permission of *The Wall Street Journal* © 1991 Dow Jones & Company, Inc. All rights reserved.

It's Literary Event time in the Big City: Tom Wolfe's NEW! Improved! novel of New York has arrived - a damned fat slab of a book, herniating to pick up but impossible to put down. "The Bonfire of the Vanities" first appeared in 29 consecutive installments of *Rolling Stone*, a Dickensian feat of derring-do that won the author more praise for his courage and stamina than for the material itself. Since then he has hunkered down, rolled up his dandyish shirt sleeves and re-written the bejeezus out of it, among other things changing the protagonist from an adulterous writer into an adulterous Wall Street bond trader, and in the end producing a work that may turn out to be the *chef* in his *oeuvre*.

Hard to say; Mr. Wolfe just keeps getting better and better. But "Bonfire" is as delicious as "Radical Chic and Mau Mauing the Flak Catchers," and as gorgeously written as "The Right Stuff" - so - who knows? - this might be it.

Sherman McCoy, conspicuous for his "Yale chin," is pulling down a cool million smackers a year selling bonds for Pierce & Pierce, and living in a $2-point-something-million pad high above Park Avenue. He is a "Master of the Universe" - the financial world quakes beneath his feet, even though he can't seem to explain to his six-year-old daughter what exactly a bond is or, for that matter, why the world needs bond traders. Nonetheless, being a Master of the Universe, he feels entitled to a mistress, and carries on with a jezebel named Maria.

One day on the way to what the *New York Post* would call their "love nest," Sherman misses the turnoff for the Triborough Bridge and ends up lost in the south Bronx jungle. They panic at the sight of all those ferocious-looking poor people and run over a young black man named Henry Lamb, and flee the scene, thereby lighting the match that will eventually ignite the bonfire.

Rich, white defendants are a rarity in the Bronx criminal system. The district attorney is running for re-election, and he plans to use Sherman's lily-white WASP hide as a campaign poster. The instrument of his wrath is his embittered, young assistant DA who lives in a too-small apartment with an infant son and stretch-marked wife.

"Bonfire's" other characters are also a joy to behold: Peter Fallow, the seedy, deadbeat, dipso Brit reporter for The City Light who breaks the story: Thomas Killian, the street-fighting criminal lawyer trying to keep Sherman from the chthonic horrors of Riker's Island: the Rev. Bacon, the black preacher who orchestrates the hatreds of the Bronx mob.

Mark the names: McCoy, Lamb, Fallow, Killian, Bacon - this is a postmodern Dickensian cast, Thackeray, Addison, Steele. Only Tom Wolfe could get away with this, and he's on rock-solid ground. More startling, possibly, is his asseveration that there are no villains in "Bonfire." Good God, the book *teems* with the vain, the greedy, the soulless, the self-important, the envious. It's the Seven Best-Dressed Deadly Sins on parade.

Perhaps more to the point it's us, right down to our $650 New & Lingwood shoes (about which, more anon). Mr. Wolfe isn't looking down, but around, detached, but essentially forgiving. As the Boz of the 1980s, he can't get enough of this human comedy. It is at the same time a harrowingly moral tale that might actually save a socialite soul or two from perdition eternal or secular.

Back when "The Last Tango in Paris" was the rage, Art Buchwald finally put it all in perspective and said that what the movie really was about was the apartment shortage in Paris. "Bonfire" is actually a novel of New York real estate. The protagonist has angered the gods by living in a too-opulent co-op, and his persecutor in the DA's office is *au fond,* a Balzacian wretch who resents having to make his way through a warren of drying female undergarments in the morning to brush his teeth. And who in the end should provide the key piece of evidence that might save Sherman but a scheming, disgruntled landlord.

Randall Jarrell defined the novel as a long stretch of prose that has something wrong with it. Mr. Wolfe's erudite passion for clothing and architecture is fine and dandy, but at times he is incapable of sitting someone down in a chair without making it sound a tad like a caption from Architectural Digest. Wardrobe is even more intrusive. We hear constantly about the $650 New & Lingwood shoes. By page 447, the charm of the clothing leitmotif has worn a hole in its overpriced soles. By page 637, one cries: *"Enough* with the ancient madder neckties, black flannel trousers, and half-brogue shoes!"

The ending, too, is problematic. Mr. Wolfe ties up a dozen loose ends with an epilogue in the form of a news story from the Metro section of the New York Times. It is cleverly parodic, but also pat. The trouble is that by narrative's end one yearns to throw all the characters onto a real bonfire, douse them with Grand Marnier, light a match - or in the present context, a malachite-inlaid Dunhill lighter - and let the flames scorch the empyrean. Instead, their creator lets them escape their just deserts. But this is the way the real human comedy is played out. Everyone gets away! Perhaps Wolfe the journalist is saying, with a wink and a shrug: What do you think this is, fiction?

What The Dickens! Tom Wolfe Has Written a New York Novel

James Andrews

From *The Christian Science Monitor* 79 (3 November 1987), 20. Reprinted by permission from *The Christian Science Monitor* © 1987 The Christian Science Publishing Society. All rights reserved.

To live in '80s New York, Sherman McCoy knows, you have to *insulate*. And few of his contemporaries have done a better job of surrounding themselves with protective cushions than 38-year-old Sherman, son of a famous Manhattan lawyer, educated at Yale, and now one of the top bond traders on Wall Street.

Fifty floors above New York's teeming, dirty streets, Sherman pulls down a cool million a year cutting megabuck deals. He lives in a $3 million Architectural Digest apartment with his social-climbing wife, young daughter, a housekeeper, and a nanny. Weekends are spent in Southampton, evenings at dinner parties of the Rich and Famous or cavorting with a sleek young mistress named Maria. Sherman McCoy's New York is a safe, sound, controlled environment.

Tom Wolfe's New York is less easily held at bay. It's not a melting pot so much as a seething caldron of racial, ethnic, and class resentments. And in the inexorable consequences of an oh, so little mistake, New York - the *real* New York - rushes through a seam in Sherman's insulation.

One night, driving with Maria in his Mercedes sports coupe, Sherman misses an expressway turn and finds himself lost in the hideous streets of the South Bronx. Suddenly they are blocked by a makeshift barricade. When Sherman gets out to remove the debris, he is approached in what seems to be a menacing way by two black youths. In the white couple's haste to get away, one of the teenagers is grazed by the car.

After going to a hospital for treatment of a broken wrist, the boy sinks into a coma. When police trace the car to Sherman, the Bronx district attorney - a publicity-mad Jew running for reelection in a borough dominated by blacks and Puerto Ricans - has what he has ached for: the Great White Defendant.

Prodded by a boozy reporter trying to salvage his career, an aging "movement" lawyer, and a black minister/con artist who finds racial tension helpful in extorting money from liberal charities, the DA sets out with a vengeance to refute community gibes about "white justice" in "Johannesbronx."

Sherman McCoy of Park Avenue and Wall Street, WASP extraordinaire, finds himself caught in the terrifying Dreyfusian vortex where law, politics, and bigotry converge. His case becomes a *cause célèbre* and he a symbol - a symbol whose usefulness requires that he be ground to dust.

Wolfe, a journalist and nonfiction writer best known for his biting social satire and careening prose, is under splendid control throughout this gripping first novel. To be sure, the satire is still there. Wolfe can deftly stage antic scenes, as when haughty waiters in a society restaurant fastidiously step over a heart-attack victim awaiting an ambulance, or a madcap melee in a Bronx courtroom. And the author isn't above naming Wall Street law firms Dunning, Sponget & Leach and Curry, Goad & Pesterall.

But Wolfe never settles for the cheap shot. Even as he skewers the affectations of greedy yuppies and society matrons emaciated by their aerobics, gazes unsentimentally at brutality, self-destructiveness, and self-pity in the underclass, or lays bare the cynicism of prosecutors and defense lawyers who alike feed off the troubles of the hapless "chow" streaming through the criminal courts, he never loses sight of their rounded humanity.

Satire is laid aside altogether when Sherman is yanked into the maw of the criminal-justice system. Stripped of the armor of money and social position that had seemed impregnable, Sherman is vulnerable to previously unimaginable people and forces. No longer an actor but only acted upon, he becomes, he feels, a mere cavity into which others are free to pour the bile of their own fears, hatreds, and schemes. He is a cipher, an emptiness whom detention officers address by first name, the faceless career steppingstone of a young prosecutor drunk on power. "A liberal," Sherman decides, "is a conservative who has been arrested."

Indeed, this book will shake readers who have regarded with unqualified trust the criminal-justice system and the society it mirrors. But the book, if it has political overtones, does not yield banal political conclusions. Wolfe is far too even-handed in his sharp-edged treatment of the characters and their milieus for the novel to be a haven for ideologues.

This book - with its wide canvas, vivid characters who stop just short of being caricatures, stinging humor that betrays the underlying anger of the idealist, and perfect rendering of a specific city in a specific time - invites comparison with Dickens. (The novel was originally serialized, in Dickens fashion, in Rolling Stone.) That may be a reach, but not by much. One has to be grateful to Tom Wolfe for producing a richly textured, contemporary novel whose epicenter is situated in the social concerns that so much of today's minimalist, self-absorbed fiction ignores.

The Bonfire of the Vanities

Reviewed by Thomas Mallon

Originally printed in *The American Spectator* January 1988. Reprinted with permission of *The American Spectator*.

It is Tom Wolfe's triumph in this, his first novel to spend 659 pages on a tale that could be told in three hundred fewer and not only get away with it, but make the reader realize all he's been missing in this age of short-winded and, quite literally, anti-social fiction. *The Bonfire of the Vanities* has a plot, an ingenious one, but plots have never been the main things in novels or lives. They are interesting only when their peripherals are stirred in, repetitive as teletype unless one knows what tax bases support them; what cars people drive to them; what politics and manners give them motive and grammar. All of which is to say that the inner life is nothing - certainly nothing interesting - without the outer life, and that a novel without aspirations toward being an essay is doomed to be just another *modern* novel. The truth, despite Virginia Woolf, is that Mrs. Brown, without Mr. Bennett, is a dull wisp; her facts are, in fact, more intriguing than her thoughts. Tom Wolfe has for the last twenty years been the most stylish essayist in America, the best performer in this country's liveliest genre. Venturing into fiction in mid-career risked being an act of genre-slumming, but has instead turned out to be a kind of mercy mission.

Sherman McCoy, a 38-year-old Master of the Universe, is a million-dollar-a-year bond salesman with a Park Avenue co-op; a fine Protestant chin, an indifferent wife, a lovely little daughter; a Mercedes; and a mistress, a Southern-accented bombshell named Maria, who keeps a little trysting pad for those "moments when the Master of the Universe stripped away the long-faced proprieties of Park Avenue and Wall Street and let his rogue hormones out for a romp!" Sherman's life takes a wrong turn, literally, when one night he picks Maria up at JFK and, on the way home, misses the off-ramp for Manhattan, winding up in the Bronx, where the two of them are, first, the victims of a highway-robbery setup (the tire-thrown-into-traffic scenario) and then, with Maria at the wheel and the two of them trying feverishly to get away, perpetrators of the hit-and-run death of a black kid from the projects named Henry Lamb, who may or may not have been the tire-thrower's accomplice.

Before Henry Lamb dies, and before Sherman and Maria are even sure what's happened, Sherman is exhilarated. Back in his mistress's hideaway, he says: "You're right, Maria. It was like something in the jungle. . . . You know something, Maria? We fought." But poor rich slob that he is, Sherman is about to lose everything, all his WASP birthrights and all his eighties acquisitions, in a chop-licking uproar of trashy politics and tabloid glee.

The Reverend Reginald Bacon, an activist-hustler from Harlem - a "poverty pimp" as the current Mayor of New York used to put it in more verbally confident days -turns Henry Lamb into a symbol of white judicial indifference to black victimization. In fact, the Jewish D.A. of the Bronx is always in *search* of a Great White Defendant, someone whose prosecution will mollify the non-white electorate he'll soon again face, and he eventually manages to find Sherman on the basis of a partially seen license number. Meanwhile, the City Light, a Murdochian daily whose staffers include the alcoholic young Brit, Peter Fallow, turns Henry Lamb into a sacrificial paragon after a phone call to his English teacher at Colonel Jacob Ruppert High School in the Bronx: "At Ruppert," Mr. Rifkind tells Fallow, "we use comparative terms, but *outstanding* isn't one of them. The range runs more from cooperative to life-threatening. . .at Colonel Jacob Ruppert High School, an honor student is somebody who attends class, isn't disruptive, tries to learn, and does all right at reading and arithmetic." From then on, as the ring closes around Sherman, it's always an "HONOR STUDENT" he's mown down in *City Light* headlines (which run to ones like SCALP GRANDMA, THEN ROB HER, and which Wolfe has a gleefully DosPassosian time writing).

New York in the eighties is a single city composed of two worlds, First and Third, poised against each other in a tension alternately dynamic and sickening, and this is Wolfe's real subject, the gulf between White Manhattan, an "offshore boutique," and most of what's north of 96th Street, known to everyone who lives here as the DMA. As *Bonfire's* dyspeptic Jewish mayor rants in one of the frenzied interior monologues that are a specialty of the author's:

Come down from your swell co-ops, you general partners and merger lawyers!. . . . Go visit the frontiers, you gutless wonders! Morningside Heights, St. Nicholas Park, Washington Heights, Fort Tryon - *por que pagar mas!*. . . . Brooklyn - *your* Brooklyn is no more! Brooklyn Heights, Park Slope - little Hong Kongs, that's all! And Queens! Jackson Heights, Elmhurst, Hollis, Jamaica, Ozone Park - whose is it? Do you know? And where does that leave Ridgewood, Bayside, and Forest Hills? Have you ever thought that! And Staten Island! Do you Saturday do-it-yourselfers really think you're snug in your little rug? You don't think the future knows how to cross a *bridge?*

But all is not apocalypse in these 659 pages. Wolfe has time for word-photo essays on changes in upper-East-Side decor between the 1970s and eighties (mirrored walls gave way to lacquer and tile); vignettes of Eurotrash and the bond market; transcripts of the witlessly fake conviviality of the Hive that listlessly parties from Good Building to Good Building. (The only false temporal note Wolfe - or, more precisely, Sherman - strikes, concerns sex: "It was in the air! It was a wave! Everywhere! Inescapable!. . . Sex!. . . There for the taking!" When it's crawled under a latex rock? AIDS makes a brief, and awkwardly obligatory, appearance in a chapter called "The Masque of the Red Death.")

If anything, Wolfe does the Bronx, where Sherman's felony is investigated and tried, better than he does Manhattan. The "chow" arrives each morning at the D.A.'s office, police vans full of those accused of the "same stupid, dismal, pathetic, horrifying crimes. . .committed day in and day out, all the same." Tough little Judge Myron Kovitsky speaks, from the bench, in one of the dozens of idiolects that squawk through the book. "All right, then you know that if you pull any more of that arrant bullshit in this courtroom, you're gonna wish you never laid eyes on Mike Kovitsky!"

What Wolfe really loves is "Tawkin' Irish" (one of the chapter titles), and *Bonfire* is full of Mick-worship:

All the cops turned Irish, the Jewish cops, like Goldberg, but also the Italian cops, the Latin cops, and the black cops. The black cops even: nobody understood the police commissioners, who were usually black, because their skin hid the fact that they had turned Irish. The same was true of assistant district attorneys in the Homicide Bureau. You were supposed to turn Irish. The Irish were disappearing from New York, so far as the general population was concerned. . . . And yet the Irish stamp was on the Police Department and on the Homicide Bureau of the D.A.'s Office, and it would probably be there forever. Irish machismo - that was the dour madness that gripped them all. . . . Irish bravery was not the bravery of the lion but the bravery of the donkey.

Detective Martin has to examine a shooting victim with Assistant D.A. Lawrence Kramer:

Two-thirds of his head was gone. The rear window of the Cadillac looked as if someone had thrown a pizza up against it. The red bib was arterial blood, which had pumped out of the stalk of his head like a fountain. Kramer backed out of the car. "Shit!" he said. "Did you see that? How did they - I mean, *shit!* it's all over the car!" To which Martin had said, "Yeah, musta ruined his whole fucking day."

When Sherman finally fights for his WASP hide, it's not with the Protestant family retainer at his side, but with Tommy ("Whaddaya whaddaya?") Killian, from the Reade Street offices of Dershkin, Bellavita, Fishbein and Schlossel.

But *Bonfire* is no mere ethnic-racial brawl. Wolfe paints a half dozen moral issues in gaudy shades of gray. The Bronx D.A. wants to make it with the voters and Assistant D.A. Kramer, bored with his nice wife and small salary, wants to make it with the gorgeous brown-lipsticked juror he chatted up after the last case he prosecuted. Going after Sherman McCoy is a way to impress both objects of lust. So doubts are shelved, scruples swallowed. They both talk themselves into the nobility of it all ("A highly publicized arrest of this Wall Street investment banker in his apartment - It happened to be a brilliant idea! Demonstrate the evenhandedness of justice in the Bronx - absolutely!"). And the fact is that Sherman McCoy and his girlfriend *did* commit a crime, even if they were high-tailing it away from the Crack King of Evergreen Avenue, whose relationship with "honor student" Henry Lamb is in doubt until far into the book. One of Wolfe's feats is to sicken the reader into ambivalence even as he plies him with hilarity.

In its early chapters *Bonfire* betrays a bit of wedding-night uneasiness between its novelist and essayist, perhaps something left over from the book's origins: Wolfe took his own Dickensian dare for *Rolling Stone* and serialized it over nearly thirty issues of the magazine. Now much changed (Sherman used to be a writer), some of the book's early chapters nonetheless seem too leisurely episodic; scenes don't shift quickly enough until about a third of the way through. But from first to last essayist and novelist collaborate much more than fight. Consider this description of the Bronx D.A.'s press secretary: "Milt Lubell had worked on the old New York *Mirror* back when Walter Winchell still had his column. He had known the great man ever so slightly and had carried his breathless snap-brim way of talking onward into the last days of the twentieth century." To write a paragraph like that, one has to *know* things, and the truth about most of today's novelists is that they don't know much and are interested in less. In the pulseless day of Bret Easton Ellis, Wolfe has decided to be bouncily Victorian, serving up individual chapter titles, even an epilogue. There are some extraordinary set pieces, too: Sherman's arraignment ("A liberal is a conservative who has been arrested"), ludicrously harrowing, the climax of the tragedy of the common millionaire; the death of Maria's piggish old husband, Arthur, at the restaurant *La Boue d'Argent*, a scene Blake Edwards couldn't have staged better.

In the minimalist times Wolfe remains, stylistically, a committed maximalist, a psychedelic Balzac pulling out all his familiar, greased-lightning stops: the exclamation points; the litanies of disbelief ("They're cowards! Parasites! The lice of public life!"); the allegoric categories (women at East Side parties are social X-rays of Lemon Tarts); the onomatopoeia; the lengthily compounded adjectives ("Lit up his face in tones of first-degree-burn pink and cobalt-therapy blue"). Every time the Brit reporter wakes with a hangover the reader has to brace himself: "Fallow opened one eye and saw the telephone lying in a brown Streptolon nest. He was dizzy, and he hadn't even lifted his head. Great curds of eye trash swam in front of his face. The pounding blood was breaking up the mercury yolk into curds, and the curds were coming out of his eye."

All this virtuosity is lavished upon those living and killing in the city conservatives most enjoy hating. But Wolfe is the least biliously scornful of satirists. There is in this immense book, as in all he has written, a kind of bedrock amiability. This is his achievement, not only as a writer, one suspects, but as a man as well. He has gone out in his white suit to stroll the boulevards of glitz and depravity. He has missed nothing and come home whistling.

Golden Crumbs and Mouse Bites:
on a Modern Fable of Manhattan

David Benedictus

From *Punch Magazine* 294 (12 February, 1988), 44-46. Reprinted with permission of the author.

Currently the job losses on Wall Street stand at 18,500. By the end of March they could have doubled. BankAmerica has cut its staff by 23,000 worldwide. Even Merrill Lynch is firing its analysts, which is like Jesus dismissing supernumerary apostles.

You don't notice anything unusual in New York City. They offer you crack on 42nd Street and flesh on 7th Avenue. The salt-beef is just as thick in the sandwiches at Charlie O's, and the skyscraper lights just as brilliant. Should they start to flicker and fade, Manhattan would become invisible from across the river. If you couldn't see it, you might no longer believe it; and since New York, like Wall Street, is founded on faith (that's why they built so high) if no one believed in it, it would vanish, and the land be given back to the Indians.

Sherman McCoy makes a million a year as a bond dealer at Pierce & Pierce. He calls himself a Master of the Universe. What, his young daughter wants to know, is a bond. Sherman is foxed; his wife, Judy, explains: "They're just sort of. . .slices of cake. Golden cake. And Pierce & Pierce collects millions of marvelous golden crumbs." But the trouble is, it's no use being a Master of the Universe unless you live like one, so Sherman has borrowed $1.8 million to buy a Park Avenue apartment, and the loan costs him $252,000 a year, none of it deductible. Then he has a house in Southampton, four servants, why go on? He is *going broke* on a million a year! But he'll survive so long as his Guiscard Scheme (lending money to the French Government) goes through. Ah! The poignancy of "so long as" to people living beyond their means.

An American philosopher recently suggested that we are all characters in a novel being written by God and - which is more worrying - He is about to embark on a second draft. But, on balance I would rather take my chances with the novelist, God, than the novelist Wolfe. For Sherman has every card in the pack stacked against him. One of the cards is a drunken sot of a British journalist (this is a *roman à clef*) working for *City Lights*, a tabloid paper which might well be mistaken for the *New York Post*; another is a dishonest black community leader; another is an ambitious assistant DA; another a Mayor anxious for re-election.

But the most potential of the cards, the Ace of Spades, is Sherman himself, because he has a fatal flaw. Sherman is vain from his full head of sandy-brown hair to his $650 New and Lingwood shoes. And his vanity leads him to try his luck with Maria, who has "creamy flan breasts" and "shimmering shanks insouciantly crossed" and a millionaire Jewish husband who made his millions chartering aircraft to take Muslims to Mecca. Oh, the cards are stacked all right, and the crisis comes when, with Maria in his Merc Roadster, he gets lost in the Bronx. There is a confrontation. A young black is fatally injured. Sherman and Maria are on the run. From now on the city is red in tooth and claw. This critical chapter, "King of the Jungle," is a masterpiece of energetic narrative.

I heard a very clever man talking to Mavis Nicholson the other day about the Holocaust. He said more books have been written about the catastrophe than about any other event in Jewish history. One good, big history was all that was required, he added; everything else that was worth learning could be better learnt from novels.

Yes. And, just as the history of the stock market crash will be written many times over (that's one advantage of being a writer; disasters are bankable) and sociologists will chart the spread of urban decay, so it is from contemporary novels that the next generation will learn how it really was. *The Bonfire of the Vanities* will become a classic. It is plotted with such ambitious cunning that one scarcely notices its length (659 well-packed pages - a rare bargain at £ 12.95). And its scope is so impressive that one can only gasp at the confidence of the detail, the intelligence that informs its style, the sly cynicism of the caricatures. A first novel? Astonishing.

The only problem is that it is such a beastly book. There is a sadistic relish in the way Wolfe humiliates Sherman. When the bond-dealer is in custody, his beautiful clothes are ruined (bad enough) and he is bitten by a mouse. The readers' appetite for his ignominy becomes soured by excess. The writing becomes crude ("Then he sought out Sherman again with his eyes and locked on and then jumped inside the cavity and flailed away, bug-eyed with panic"). Ultimately one begins to wonder whether Wolfe is not flagellating *himself* in the person of Sherman (both are from Yale) for his position of power and privilege and wealth. The Right Stuff. Masters of the Universe.

In *great* novels it is vital that the protagonist has some control over his/her fate. Otherwise one is left with pornography (*Juliette* and *Justine*) or satire (*Candide*). In *The Bonfire of the Vanities* Sherman McCoy is set up merely to be knocked down. A mighty Humpty Dumpty. Brilliant and devastating, but not a pretty sight.

The Far-Right Stuff

George Black

From *The New Statesman* (12 February 1988), 31. Reprinted with permission of New Statesman Society and the author.

Manhattan is an island. Its links to the four outlying boroughs of New York City, unlike the modest, pretty bridges that cross the Thames, are formidable; the great suspension span of the George Washington, the swooping eight-lane race-track of the Triboro, the architectural extravaganza of the 100-year-old Brooklyn Bridge, and the great booming tunnels of steel girders, terrifyingly enclosed, that carry north-bound traffic off Manhattan Island.

There are four outer boroughs in Staten Island, which you can also reach by a ferry that only costs a quarter, there are still rumoured to be working Dutch barns; Queen's, to the east, looks like Wimbledon, but if you superimposed it on the map of London it would reach from Shepherds Bush to Croydon. That leaves Brooklyn, where fancy riverfront terraces give way to the remnants of old Italian and Jewish neighbourhoods and the devastation of the Bedford-Stuyvesant housing project. And, to the north, the Bronx.

Manhattan's relationship to the Bronx is much more a psychological than a physical one. When New Yorkers speak of Manhattan as an island fortress, they're usually thinking of the Bronx. This is the terrain on which Tom Wolfe's new novel is played out. Sherman McCoy, a wealthy 38-year-old, Yale-educated gun-trader picks up his raunchy Southern mistress, Maria, at Kennedy Airport to drive her back to their East Side love-nest. Coming into Manhattan, they lose themselves in a tangle of expressways. It happened to me once when I first came to New York, driving in from upstate, missing an exit sign, then the sudden unnerving sense of heading in completely the wrong direction, ending up in dead-end parking lots in the shadow of monstrous high rises.

For Sherman and Maria, the event is not a petty annoyance but the beginning of a nightmare. Heading up the ramp to yet another expressway, they stop to remove an obstruction from their car. Two black youths appear out of nowhere. A robbery attempt? They don't wait to find out. Maria swerves away, hits one of the youths, drives off. The kid is left with head injuries; the next we hear of him, he is in hospital in a coma.

That basic setup could be taken in a number of directions. Tom Wolfe has the *chutzpah*, to put it generously, to make Sherman the victim of events. So for the next 600 pages he is dragged down into a convoluted series of spider's webs, in which he falls prey successively to (a) the Jewish legal system and political establishment; (b) Irish cops; (c) the demagogic and corrupt leadership of the black community; and (d) the tabloid press, whose villains, since Wolfe has pretty well run out of other racist stereotypes by this point, are English.

It's a set piece for cartoon characters. Wolfe's linguistic fireworks are as wearisome here as they have ever been, turning all his characters into one-line jokes, endlessly repeated. Maria, for example, is a sex-kitten with a Southern accent. Whenever she opens her mouth, Wolfe gives out what she says in plain English, and then in a South Carolina transliteration. She calls McCoy "Shuhmun". *Ad nauseam*. Kramer, the harried Assistant District Attorney out of Columbia Law School has an inferiority complex and views the drama of life as *The Jews Confront the Goyim*. The lower end of the legal bureaucracy is inhabited by types like Killian, the Irish criminal lawyer, whose particular line is to greet McCoy with a cry of "Ayyyyyy, whaddaya, whaddaya" each time he appears in a scene. These verbal ties are funny once, irritating twice, cardboard by the third and subsequent times.

The worst indignities are heaped upon the blacks. Most of them grunt rather than talk, unless they are being coached by Jewish prosecutors to give tainted evidence in exchange for getting off drugs charges. Wolfe tells us the underclass comes in three categories: first, "a round-the-clock shift of Irishmen from Queens and Puerto Ricans from the Bronx" who earn "$200,000 a year to run the elevators." Second, the local religious-political leaders (the book's Jesse Jackson clone is called the Reverend Bacon) whose followers call Jews "Hymie" and belong to organizations with names out of Peter Simple: All People's Solidarity, the Open Gates Employment Coalition and the Third World Anti-Defamation League. Then there's the seething deviant mass that inhabits the Bronx, where each year the cops arrest "forty thousand incompetents, dimwits, alcoholics, psychopaths, knockabouts", for a daily succession of "the same stupid, dismal, pathetic, horrifying crimes."

Wolfe does, I suppose, practise his own kind of misanthropic evenhandedness. He devotes a couple of passages to the inanities of *nouveaux riches* Park Avenue hostesses and their appalling, over-orchestrated dinners parties. Fine; they're a cheap, easy target. And Sherman himself is an ass, with his junk-bond trading and asinine activity. Yet, though he may be a butt of satire, may be socially useless, in Wolfe's cosmology the making of quick Wall Street fortunes is pumped by adrenalin. Sherman is On The Bus, in his own phrase a Master of the Universe, and that puts him, in the end, in the same universe as the pilots and astronauts in *The Right Stuff*.

Sherman's downfall is played as tragedy, a parable for the benefit of prosperous Manhattanites; it confirms and indulges their terrors about the jungle that lies, beyond the Harlem River, and leaves them secure in the belief that the real victims of modern New York are the civilised, beleaguered white upper middle class. Wolfe's Bronx is less a place than a symbol, located outside history and socio-economic change. Just as Park Avenue is, and always has been, white and rich, so the Bronx is, and for all practical purposes always has been, a black, alien presence, full of chaos and menace.

But Wolfe's Bronx won't do as a map to reality. Most of the Bronx's black and hispanic underclass are recent migrants who came looking for work at the wrong time, just as the great urban centers of the North East were ceasing to produce goods and moving towards a service economy, wiping out thousands of unskilled jobs. The old factory days of the Bronx died; the tidal marshes of the South Bronx rotted; the borough was overlaid with more and more concrete spaghetti, the unemployed underclass jammed in between in decaying tenements. The sequel is familiar; imprisoned communities and the sociologist's catalogue from petty crime and drugs, from single parenthood and welfare dependency.

After its quasi-academic rationalisations, like Charles Murray's *Losing Ground*, and its emblematic crimes - Howard Beach and Bernhard Goetz, the "subway vigilante" - 1980s-style racism now has its pulp fiction. *Bonfire of the Vanities* is really an upmarket version of Charles Bronson's *Death Wish* movies. I read most of it on the clattering IRT subway line, traveling to and from my office from Fifth Avenue and 13th Street. One train I use, the slow No. 1 local, starts off deep in the Bronx at Van Cortlandt Park where West Indian teams play cricket in summertime. Another, the No. 2 express, winds under the Bronx to 241 St. and White Plains Road. Four out of five passengers are black or hispanic. You get to recognise some of the faces, especially those of the beggars. There's the Vietnam veteran who moves along the car on a wooden board on castors where he should have legs, and the tall, homeless black man, partially sighted, who stands at the end of the car and makes a little speech. "I know some of you may be alarmed by my appearance," he begins, "and I apologise for that. But I don't mean you no harm." Before he shuffles down the car with a paper cup held out for nickels and dimes, he says, "Thank you all, God bless you, have a safe journey home and a pleasant evening." Reading Tom Wolfe in that setting felt like a contamination. Perhaps on the London Tube, travelling on the Victoria Line between Brixton and King's Cross, it may not seem so bad.

An Icy Dip in the Real World

Paul Baumann

From *Commonweal* 115 (26 February, 1988), 120-22. © Reprinted with permission.

Whaddaya whaddaya? Only one thing stands between thirty-eight-year-old Wall Street whiz Sherman McCoy, once a self-proclaimed Master of the Universe ("There was. . .no limit whatsoever!"), and certain oblivion, and it isn't his aristocratic pedigree, his Yale chin, or his million-dollar income. No, it's the "stone courage," the street smarts, the "donkey" obstinacy of New York City's Irish. Indeed, in Tom Wolfe's novel *The Bonfire of the Vanities*, New York's Irish cops and lawyers, with their deep cynicism and their even deeper, seemingly archaic loyalties, seem to be all that stands between the city's barely realized civil order and anarchy. For among the many things the *Bonfire* is - an ingenious comic extravaganza, a courtroom melodrama, an apocalyptic rumination - it is first and perhaps foremost a 659-page love letter to New York's Irish wiseguys.

Hey, gedoudahere!

But true!

McCoy encounters these fantastic, hardheaded tough guys - Tommy Killian, Bill Martin, Ed Quigley, Bernie Fitzgibbon and a host of others, including the "Jewish Shamrock" Goldberg - when he becomes part of the "chow" fed to New York's criminal justice system. Larry Kramer, the pettifogging assistant district attorney prosecuting McCoy for the hit-and-run injury of an eighteen-year-old black kid from the South Bronx's "Edgar Allan Poe" projects, tells why the Irish are revered. "He knew that something in his (Det. Martin's) eyes would make the boy sense Irish Cop Who Don't Back Off. . .and for the five hundredth time in his career as an assistant district attorney in the Bronx he paid silent homage to that most mysterious and coveted of male attributes, Irish machismo."

Tommy Killian, the fast-tawkin ("This case has nothing to do with justice. This is a war.") criminal lawyer tutoring the wayward bond salesman McCoy on how to survive an "icy dip in the real world," outlines the origins of this singularly Irish urban competence. "Ed Quigley is the best," he says, explaining McCoy's need for a private investigator. "He's your basic hardcore New York Hell's Kitchen Irishman. The kids Ed ran with all became hoodlums or cops. The ones that became cops were the ones that the church got a hook into, the ones that cooked a little bit from guilt. But they all like the same things. They all like to butt heads and loosen people's teeth. The only difference is, if you are a cop, you can do it legally with a priest nodding over you and looking the other way at the same times. Ed was a hell of a cop. He was a fucking reign of terror."

So much for the finer points of casuistry.

As the title proclaims, there is an apocalyptic tone to this, Wolfe's first novel. "Back to blood! Them and us!" New York's Jewish mayor feverishly fantasizes as he is driven from a Harlem stage by a black mob in the opening scene. Thirty-one chapters later, *Bonfire* concludes with a riot in a Bronx courtroom. In between is the hunt for Sherman McCoy, the "Great White Defendant," the answer to Bronx District Attorney Abe Weiss's ("Captain Ahab") most fervent reelection prayers.

For $75,000 Killian and Quigley deflect the press ("The lice of public life!"), the courts, and the politicians, all of whom conspire to lynch McCoy by his prep-school neck. McCoy, shrewd exploiter of a decade of giddy speculation in the bond market, unadulterated Wasp, doyen of Park Avenue, and the blue-blood incarnation of contemporary privilege and status has stumbled into an unrelieved nightmare. While driving his mistress home from the airport, he takes a wrong turn and ends up in the most desolate section of the South Bronx. When two menacing-looking black youths appear, his mistress hits one with the car. An absurd concatenation of events dissolves McCoy's once insulated world.

Wolfe, papa of New Journalism, author of *The Right Stuff*, the sociologist who labeled the 1970s "The Me Generation," and the venomous ventriloquist of *Radical Chic & Mau-Mauing the Flak Catchers,* crams a lifetime of unblinking social observation into *The Bonfire of the Vanities*. Once again we are held in awe by this writer's mastery of point of view, his attention to the subtlest calibration of social status, his lucid exposition, and Rabelaisian humor.

Novelist Wolfe, like journalist Wolfe, is suspicious of sentiment. *Interfaeces et urinam* we are born, and this author seems gleeful about it. Obsessively he mocks the worldly pretensions of his characters by juxtaposing every kind of pride with the crude corruption and folly of the flesh. McCoy must press "the pants of his two-thousand-dollar Savile Row suit [against] the bare toilet seat, his New & Lingwood cap-toed shoes. . .against the china toilet bowl" when reading of his impending doom. And in the novel's most pointed burlesque, the corpse of one sybarite is defenestrated from the ladies' room of a fashionable Manhattan restaurant. He was boorish enough to die over dinner

Bonfire is as ambitious as its operatic title suggests, for it is about nothing less than the self-deluding conceits, the habitual cowardices, and anomie rotting the sills and cracking the foundation of "the greatest city of the twentieth century." Often brilliantly, always extravagantly, Wolfe conjures up the cacophony of voices, the avalanche of lies, the violence, vulgarity, and greed that make New York such an intoxicant. With near perfect pitch, he describes life in and around the besieged Bronx County Building, where a bizarre parade of assistant district attorneys, lawyers, cops, jurists, con men, and thugs puts a face on the abstraction known as the criminal justice system.

However, in the middle of all this Dickensian turmoil, *Bonfire* places the unsatisfactory enigma of Sherman McCoy. McCoy's arrogance, his elitist assumptions, and narrow but towering ambition are readily established. But his obtuse emotional life and bombastic self-pity are too broad a stroke. Despite a welter of details - we know the price of everything he wears, of every piece of furniture in his $3-million-dollar apartment - our protagonist remains something of a socio-logical construct.

Of course, McCoy's fate is emblematic. He's "a Wall Street egalitarian. . .a respecter only of performance," the quintessential Me Generation achiever. He "wants it now." This is also, by a telling coincidence, the code of the street hus-tler and the revolutionary. McCoy and his fellow plutocrats disdain traditional obligations and even prejudices. Money is the only measure of a man, and the display of wealth a necessary social duty. That display is of course a way of re-confirming rank and status, but it amounts to little more than an endless, aimless craving to be admired and amused. In one character's after-dinner excursus on Poe's "Mask of the Red Death," McCoy recognizes his own fatal hubris. "The excitement is so intense and the pleasure is so unbridled and the gowns and the food and the drink and the flesh are so sumptuous - {but} that is all they have. Families, homes, children, the great chain of being, the eternal tide of chromo-somes mean nothing to them any longer. . .they whirl about one another, en-dlessly, particles in a doomed atom."

McCoy's harrowing descent into the maelstrom of the "other" New York brings him up shatteringly against the futility of such an existence. He is aban-doned by business associates, neighbors, and friends. A very Poe-like terror descends. "Remember who you are," his justifiably aggrieved wife scolds him. But when a man dedicated to the atomized whirl is spun off, he discovers that the fall, like his climb to the top, knows no limit. As McCoy explains to Killian, "All these people. . .it's all a thread, Tommy, all these ties that make up your life, and when it breaks. . .that's it. . . .Your self. . .is other people, all the people you're tied to, and it's only a thread."

The pedagogic tone here is jarring, but Wolfe, like all satirists, is at heart a moralist. The disintegration of the self, of which Poe prophetically wrote, is the horror painted in lurid colors across *Bonfire's* huge canvas. Edgar Allan Poe Towers in the South Bronx - Poe, the novel reminds us, lived out his last days in the Bronx - is the most acute manifestation of disconnectedness. Morally, the barbarism of the tenements and jails is the obverse of the social barbarism prac-ticed by the wealthy and so deftly lampooned throughout this novel.

The soullessness is the vanity threatening to consume everything in *Bonfire*. In "The Me Generation and the Third Great Awakening," Wolfe cited deTocque-ville on the insecurity inherent in an egalitarian society. "Not only does democra-cy make each man forget his ancestors, it hides his descendants from him, and divides him from his contemporaries; it continually turns him back into himself, and threatens, at last, to enclose him entirely in the solitude of his own heart." Although Wolfe dismissed such a dire prognosis for America in that essay, clear-ly that is the fate McCoy and his unlikely soulmates among the poor endure. In this sense, Wolfe's admiration for the solidity of New York's working class (ob-viously, they need not be Irish), suggests that only archaic loyalties keep us civi-lized.

This unsentimental report on New York City's ethnic and racial warfare, so eerily echoed in today's headlines, could be wound much tighter. Wolfe is still very much the reporter, and at some gut level these characters are more observed that fully imagined. Still, an exhilarating intelligence animates nearly every scene. And while there is in these pages blarney aplenty - what Irishman won't be gratified as well as astonished to come upon a kind of word for "Irish machismo" at this late date - Wolfe has also given his story a portentousness that would make the master of American Gothic proud.

Eggh, whaddaya?
Whaddaya Want From Me?

Peter A. Quinn

From *America* 158 (2 April, 1988), 363-64. Reprinted with permission of America Press, Inc., 106 W. 56th Street, New York, NY 10019. © 1968, 1973, 1975, 1977, 1983 and 1988. All rights reserved.

Several years ago there was a movie about some people stranded in the desert who escape by building an airplane scavenged from the remains of other machines. In his first attempt at fiction, *The Bonfire of the Vanities*, Tom Wolfe has done something close. He has raided the used parts section of the novelist's machine shop and banged together an array of rusty, dented stereotypes: Rev. Bacon, a high-living, low-dealing black minister with a knack for demagoguery; a coy mistress who sounds and acts like an updated Scarlett O'Hara; a drunken, vainglorious lout of an English newsman named Fallow; a publicity crazed D.A. hell-bent for reelection; an obese, sweating, obnoxious Jewish landlord (complete with Borscht-Belt accent: "We gottuh reel problem."); Irish cops as hard and unyielding as concrete; WASP law firms named Dunning, Sponget & Leach, and Curry, Goad & Pesterall.

Will it fly? Will the father of the New Journalism make a soft landing in the world of fiction? At first it doesn't seem so.

The engines backfire with a black exhaust of exclamation points ("Christ! It's Judy! He'd dialed his own apartment! He's aghast - paralyzed!"). Thumpathumpathumpathumpa - the wheels of the plot pound down hard on the runway as Wolfe creates a backdrop that includes New York City politics and the intricacies of bond trading.

But after rattling and rolling like an old warplane, its wings shaking, *The Bonfire of the Vanities* takes off for a sustained flight. Once aloft, Wolfe looks down his bombsight at a feast of targets: aerobics, interior decorators, Episcopalians, investment bankers, three-star restaurants, maitre d's, funeral homes, television news, tabloids, the rich (new and old alike), politicians, assistant D.A.'s, the courts and criminal justice system, etc.

Bombs away! *Kaboom! Kaboom! Kaboom!* Wolfe rarely misses.

The protagonist of Wolfe's story is Sherman McCoy, a 38-year-old whiz-bang bond trader and self-styled "Master of the Universe" Yale-educated, the son of a grand vizier of one of Wall Street's Anglo-Saxon law firms. McCoy is emblematic of a ruling class that has ceased in any real sense to be interesting in ruling. "These inheritors of the *lux* and the *veritas*" have retired their ancestors' sense of noblesse oblige and have fled the old WASP urge to reform the manners, morals and politics of "the lower orders." Their universe has shrunken to a small wedge of upper Manhattan; their mastery to the making and spending of money on such a scale that a million dollars a year can barely sustain the acquisition and upkeep of the requisite conceits.

The pretensions of this class are the main fuel for *The Bonfire of the Vanities*, a title derived from the quattrocento bauble burning that was inspired by the incendiary preaching of Savanarola. Yet if Wolfe owes the book's name to the Master of San Marco, his account of McCoy's confrontation with the reality beyond Park Avenue is indebted to that other firey son of Florence, Dante.

Driving his mistress back from Kennedy Airport, McCoy, like Dante, discovers himself "in a dark wood/Where the right road was wholly lost and gone." In this case the wood is the South Bronx; the right road, the Bruckner Expressway. Here the gates of hell are marked "EAST GEO. WASH. BRIDGE," and the passage through them heralded by a small barricade and an onomatopoetic bump: *thok*. McCoy's Mercedes-Benz has struck a young black man who may or may not have been a part of an attempt to rob him.

Fleeing the scene of the accident/crime, McCoy inadvertently creates a racial cause célèbre. Thus begins his tortuous journey into New York's netherworld - the crowded, broken-down courts, the demeaning booking process and the sty-like holding pens, all the ordinary indignities of the 40,000 people annually arrested in the Bronx that are made extraordinary because they have finally speared that *rarus piscis*: "The Great White Defendant."

Again like Dante, McCoy would never emerge from this inferno unless he had a wise and experienced guide. Dante's was Virgil; McCoy's, a tough-tawking, street-wise Irishman, Tom Killian, whose rough edges of speech and mind have survived Yale Law School. As Killian puts it, "Yale is terrific for anything you wanna do, as long it don't involve people with sneakers, guns, dope, lust, or sloth."

Killian leads McCoy through the horrors of hell and the terrors of purgatory, instilling in him that most Irish of emotions: deep-seated, inexhaustible resentment. " 'Ayyyyyy,' says Killian to McCoy. 'That's better. Now you're turning. . .Irish. The Irish been living the last twelve hundred years on dreams of revenge. Now you're talking, bro.' "

It is here, however, in McCoy's metamorphosis, that the plot begins to run out of propellant. A callous, greedy and arrogant philanderer who lies to his wife and tries secretly to tape his mistress, Sherman McCoy's emergence as a kick-'em-where-they-kicked-you New Yorker rings as hollow as his new-found pattern of speech (" 'Judge,' said Sherman, 'it don't matter! It don't matter!' "). Even though he trades in his imported English shoes for hiking boots, it's impossible not to see McCoy as a heel.

In *The Bonfire of the Vanities*, Tom Wolfe has not created great and memorable characters, nor has he done for New York what Dante did for heaven and hell, or Dickens for London, or Joyce for Dublin. Few novelists achieve such things, especially on their first try. But he has succeeded in puncturing the pretensions of The Imperial City, the air running out in something between a Bronx cheer and a long, soft *hisssss*. And again and again, he manages to bring the great existential truths of New York down to finely observed details: "egggh, whaddaya? Whaddaya want from me?. . . .It was the age-old New York cry for mercy, unanswerable and undeniable."

Tom Wolfe's first flight as a novelist is a success. Bon voyage.

The Ruling Class

Luther Carpenter

From *Dissent* 35 (Summer 1988), 377-79. Reprinted with permission of *Dissent*.

Many sociologists deny there is a ruling class. Paul Fussell says there is one - but it is "top out of sight." Albert Gore, George Bush, Robert Dole, and Richard Gephardt accused each other of belonging to it but wouldn't be caught dead in it. Donald Trump and Lee Iacocca revel in it. What can a poor boy do?

Two very agitated authors offer to guide us to the truth. Lewis Lapham is a semidelinquent scion of the old elite. He has visited the famed Bohemian Grove and rubs shoulders with those who matter on Manhattan's East Side - yet he is so daring as to edit an old and prestigious magazine. Tom Wolfe's publisher portrays him as "the foremost chronicler of the way we live in America."

Our guides don't give us a systematic description of the ruling class. They even find it hard to name them. Wolfe calls them the "Masters of the Universe" after the children's fantasy figures. Lapham prefers the "equestrian class," which he uses less ironically than Bernard Shaw did in *Heartbreak House*. Shaw's equestrian class lived in Horseback Hall, which "consisted of a prison for horses with an annex for the ladies and gentlemen who rode them, hunted them, talked about them, bought them and sold them, and gave nine-tenths of their lives to them, dividing the other tenth between charity, churchgoing (as a substitute for religion), and conservative electioneering (as a substitute for politics)." Lapham's equestrians aren't really horsemen, but "those who can afford to ride rather than walk and who can buy any or all of the baubles that constitute the proofs of social status."

Both definitions would comfort those who say there isn't a ruling class - Lapham's by its vagueness and Wolfe's by its mockery of pretense. Both however, agree that their subjects *want* to be a separate class. Wolfe's protagonist, Sherman McCoy, struggles to assert class everywhere. He barely restrains himself from waging class warfare when a worker in his garage calls him "Sherm."

The Masters or riders have two attributes - money and maleness. Maleness is a given - there are no important women in either book, just hostesses - and, for Wolfe, a problem. The problem is whether "masculinity" is atrophying in the world of finance. It has no usefulness there, but Wolfe's protagonist still wants it. In Wolfe's scenario, it is necessary to use physical violence against the underclass.

Money leaves the Masters and riders feeling insubstantial. Wolfe's protagonist can't tell his daughter what he does. Sherman doesn't build buildings or print books. He doesn't make anything or have men working under him. His wife woundingly resorts to metaphor: Golden crumbs stick to his hands. Sherman is a bond salesman, but that's not glamorous enough. Lapham describes the same people, those who capture the new money bubbling up in New York.

Wolfe and Lapham are drawn to this new money because its possessors are more colorful, less inhibited than older segments of the ruling classes. Lapham concentrates on them because they are the model presented to all of America to copy; he doesn't ask whether they've really taken power away from industrialists and inherited wealth. These new wealthy have no visible relationship to the means of production and no particular social function. They consume, but are not a leisure class. Sherman McCoy makes millions, but can't leave his desk to go to the bathroom. Above all, the Masters and riders demand. They "want it all" - sex, status, fame. Lapham ultimately sees the basis of their incessant demanding as priestly rather than economic. They are the priests of a civil religion of money.

But they are frustrated by their own civil religion. The things they acquire don't satisfy needs, nor do they confer freedom. If not, why get into this morass of consumption? For both Lapham and Wolfe, the answer is status. But status is intrinsically unsatisfying. It exists in someone else's mind. That someone else is undependable - a rival in status games who grudgingly gives approval while seeking to change the rules and take one's status away. There are no friends here, only "cold. . .lizards" in Lapham's phrase. In his hour of need, no one will help Sherman McCoy. His company drops him; the president of his co-op board wants him out of the building; his mistress runs away with an artist. Even in good times, according to Lapham, "the faithful fall victim to a nameless and stupefying dread."

The chief fear is of losing their status and the money that makes it possible. This fear makes them dangerous. Sherman and his mistress panic and lash out at a boy who intends to rob them. They kill the boy. Here Wolfe and Lapham part company. As Wolfe works out his scenario, the panic is justified. New York City is out to get Sherman - not because of his money, but because he is the "Great White Defendant." "They" - resentful poor blacks, egged on by an evil antipoverty pimp, who leeches off gullible liberals - howl for Sherman's head. Corrupt newspapers, repulsive radicals and feminists, and a D.A. running for reelection all feed the resentment.

Wolfe offers Sherman, and by implication the new moneyed class, a way out. Get rid of your vanities - your belief in the old moneyed class, your desire to join Society, your belief that you can buy immunity - and Fight Back. At the end, Sherman slugs the poverty pimp's assistant. This gives Sherman the same kind of exhilaration he found while selling bonds. It also solves the masculinity problem. It earns the respect of the cops. Sherman has now taken Wolfe's advice, given earlier in the book: Turn "fucking *Irish*. The Irish been living the last twelve hundred years on dreams of revenge."

Lapham erects a different scenario of doom on the same premises of a false god. He likens the riders to Roman senators before the fall of the Republic and to the Ancien Regime in France. That thought makes Lapham pull back. Escape the sterility of the Midas touch; give up the blind faith in money. What is notable about this cry, hidden at the end of the book, is its feebleness. Lapham doesn't really want to change gods. Earlier he has said that he doesn't want to be a prophet, that he finds money truly enjoyable. He has no other god in mind. Maybe an environmental ethic would do, but he has no love for it. So his counsel to the rich is at most a plea for moderation. To take his advice would be to turn back into the colorless WASP elite Lapham can't even bear to write about.

More significantly, think of the advice that neither Lapham nor Wolfe offers to the elite: Carnegie's plea for a Gospel of Wealth, using intelligent charity to buy the masses off and recycle the money; or the Gaullist argument for a welfare state to integrate the workers into the nation and get them to work for its advancement. Neither of these arguments is conceivable to our new moneyed classes. Nor do Lapham and Wolfe exhort the wealthy to perform a service for society, to become competent at ruling. Compare them with the captain of Shaw's *Heartbreak House;* "Learn your business as an Englishman. . . .Navigation. Learn it and live; or leave it and be damned."

These books are revealing, but neither is really worth reading. The humor is mostly one-liners. When Wolfe invents a good line - "A liberal is a conservative who's been arrested" - he can't resist using it twice. Wolfe's book has good observations of cops and courts, punks and fear, but the claim that he's "the foremost chronicler" is a hype. Anthony Lukas's *Common Ground* has much more to say about racial and class antagonism; Robert Parker's early "Spenser" novels come closer to solving the problem of maleness. "Civil religion" is a useful idea (and it doesn't matter that Lapham borrowed a lot from Marx. Old wine in new bottles isn't so bad when the audience would never look at the old bottles). "Civil religion" can account for the self-advertisement of the new wealthy and for the fact that my working-class students feel no hostility to them; it fits the ritualistic nature of American politics.

If these books have some value as observation, major problems come when Wolfe and Lapham try to build on their observations. It might be worthwhile to think about Lapham's fear that the new wealthy are a doomed Ancien Regime - but he offers the idea as an afterthought.

Is Reagan's accumulated deficit really the same as Louis XVI's? One can't just design a new civil religion because there's a need for it; intellectual history is littered with pleas like Lapham's. Similarly, one would be a fool to say that Wolfe's scenario couldn't happen. But there's no need to take Wolfe's advice, to turn New York City into Belfast. Wolfe's scenario has one glaring exaggeration: The power of "Them," Wolfe's black demon and his demonstrators and the supineness of the media and the justice system before them. Whatever one thinks of the Tawana Brawley case, Alton Maddox and Al Sharpton haven't gotten their way.

This exaggeration is matched by another exaggeration. The wealthy are hardly so powerless and ready to drop each other to woo the masses. Look at how the "system" goes on rehabilitating Richard Nixon, Victor Posner, and Ivan Boesky.

Our ruling class has resources that these two authors don't see. They show us the pretenders. These pretenders believe in class intensely. But, as Wolfe and Lapham show, their claims have a precarious base. This new part of the ruling class doesn't rule anything but pieces of paper. They don't manage real things or people; they don't produce or create. The new wealthy have no sense of tomorrow or of the whole of society. All they want to do is to go on making money. That's all they use their power for - to rewrite the rules of the game to give themselves more money, through tax "reforms" and the proliferation of exotic gambling devices such as stock market futures. Since the October 1987 break in the stock market, they have sought to defend themselves against tighter regulation by blackmail; Let us have our way, or we'll cause a depression. They can't create, but they can destroy factories, companies, and cities with their pieces of paper. That makes them dangerous, but we still ought to find ways to cut them down to size.

Works by Tom Wolfe

The Kandy-Kolored Tangerine-Flake Streamline Baby. New York: Farrar, Straus and Giroux, 1965.

"Lost in the Whichy Thicket: *The New Yorker* - II." New York, April 18, 1965, pp. 16-24, 44.

"Tiny Mummies! The True Story of the Ruler of 43rd Street's Land of the Walking Dead!" *New York*, April 11, 1965, pp. 7-9, 24-27.

The Pump House Gang. New York: Farrar, Straus and Giroux, 1968.

"How You Can Be As Well-Informed As Tom Wolfe." *Esquire*, November 1967, pp. 138, 212.

"The Author's Story." *The New York Times Book Review*, August 18, 1968, pp. 2, 40-41.

The Electric Kool-Aid Acid Test. New York: Farrar, Straus and Giroux, 1968.

The Pump House Gang. New York: Farrar, Straus and Giroux, 1968.

Radical Chic & Mau-Mauing the Flak Catchers. New York: Farrar, Straus and Giroux, 1970.

"The Birth of the New Journalism: Eyewitness Report by Tom Wolfe." *New York,* February 14, 1972, pp. 30-45.

"The New Journalism: A la Recherche des Whichy Thickets." *New York,* February 21, 1972, pp. 39-48.

"Why They Aren't Writing the Great American Novel Anymore." *Esquire*, December 1972.

The New Journalism. New York: Harper & Row, 1973. With an anthology edited by Tom Wolfe and E. W. Johnson.

The Painted Word. New York: Farrar, Straus and Giroux, 1975.

Mauve Gloves & Madmen, Clutter & Vine. New York: Farrar, Straus and Giroux, 1976.

The Right Stuff. New York: Farrar, Straus and Giroux, 1979. Bantam Books, 1983.

In Our Time. New York: Farrar, Straus and Giroux, 1980.

From Bauhaus to Our House. New York: Farrar, Straus and Giroux, 1981.

The Purple Decades. New York: Farrar, Straus and Giroux, 1982.

The Bonfire of the Vanities. New York: Farrar, Straus and Giroux, 1987.

"Stalking the Billion-Footed Beast: A Literary Manifesto for the New Social Novel." *Harper's* 279 (November 1989), 49-56.

Additional Readings

Biographical and Critical Reviews

Adams, Phoebe. [Review of *The Electric Kool-Aid Acid Test* and *The Pump House Gang*.] *Atlantic Monthly* 222 (September 1968) 134.

Algeridge, Malcolm. [Review of *Radical Chic & Mau-Mauing the Flak Catchers*.] *Esquire* 75 (April 1971) 76.

Alter, Jonathan. "Two Cheers For Tom Wolfe." *Washington Monthly* 20 (March 1988) 42.

Anderson, Chris. *Style As Argument: Contemporary American Nonfiction.* Carbondale, Ill., and Edwardsville, Ill.: Southern Illinois U. Press, 1987.

Baker, Godfrey. [Review of *From Bauhaus To Our House*.] *Connoisseur* 209 (January 1982) 12.

Ball, Charles. "The Making of a Demigod." *Technology Review* 82 (March/April 1980) 16.

Banham, Reyner. "The Scandalous Story of Architecture in America." *London Review of Books* 4 (May 5, 1982) 8.

Barrett, Marvin. "The Akond Of Swock." *Reporter* 33 (1965) a50.

Bartlett, Joseph W. "The Real Business of *Bonfire*." *Harvard Business Review* 66 (July-August 1988) 16-19.

Baumann, Paul. "An Icy Dip in the Real World." *Commonweal* 115 (February 26, 1988) 120-22.

Berenson, Ruth. "Debunking With Style." *National Review* 27 (August 1, 1975) 843.

Bianco, Anthony. "When Riches Meet Rags: A Timely Wall Street Tale." *Business Week* (November 23, 1987) 18-20.

Blemiller, Lawrence. "Tom Wolfe on the Architecture Schools: O Yale Box! O Harvard Compound!" *Chronicle of Higher Education* 23 (October 28, 1981) 25.

Blue, Adrianne. "The Earthling and the Astronauts." *Washington Post Book World* 9 (September 9, 1979) 1.

Booker, Christopher. "Inside the Bubble." *Encounter* 49 (September 1977) 74.

Bredahl, A. Carl. "An Exploration of Power: Tom Wolfe's Acid Test." *Critique* (Winter 1981-82). Cushman, Robert. "Period Piece." *Spectator* 222 (1969) 585-86.

Broyard, Anatole. [Review of *Mauve Gloves & Madmen, Clutter & Vine*.] *New York Times* 126 (November 26, 1976) c21.

Bryan, C.D.B. "The SAME Day: heeeeeewack!!!" *New York Times Book Review* (August 18, 1968) 1-2, 40

Bryan, C.D.B. "The Sky Is Our Domain." *New York Times Book Review* (September 23, 1979) 1, 34-35.

Buckley, William F., Jr. "Mau-mauing Wolfe." *National Review,* January 12, 1971, p. 51.

_____. "Tom Wolfe and the Painted Word." Southern Educational Associations (1975)

Capouya, Emile. "True Facts and Artifacts." Saturday Review 48 (31 July 1965) 23-24.

Cohen, Ed. "Tom Wolfe and the Truth Monitors: A Historical Fable." *Clio,* 16:1-11 (Fall 1986).

Compton, Neil. "Hijinks Journalism." *Commentary* 47 (February 1969) 76-79.

Conroy, Frank. "Urban Rats in Fashion's Maze." *New York Times Book Review* 92 (November 1, 1987) 1,46.

Coyne, John R., Jr. "Sketchbook Of Snobs." *National Review* 23 (January 26, 1971) 90-91.

Crain, Jane Larkin. "The Old Realism." *Commentary* 56 (October 1973) 84-88.

Davenport, Gary. "Urban Fiction Today." *Sewanee Review* 96 (Fall 1988)695-702.

Davies, Stan Gebler. "Crying Wolfe." *Punch* 282 (March 24, 1982) 497.

Davis, Douglas. "Wolfe Vs. the Bauhaus Boys." *Newsweek* 98 (November 6, 1981) 106.

Dickstein, Morris. "The Working Press, the Literary Culture, and the New Journalism." *Georgia Review,* 30:855-877 (Winter 1976).

Dietz, Lawrence. "Psychic Changes On The Social Landscape." *National Review* 20 (1968) 865-66.

Donaldson, Scott. "The Old Word, The New Journalism, And The Novel." *Sewanee Review* 82 (July 1974) 527.

"Dots." *Book World* 3 (1969) 21.

Dunne, John Gregory. "Hog Heaven." *The New York Review of Books,* November 8, 1979, pp. 9-12.

Eason, David L. "Low Expectations." *New York Review of Books* 35 (February 4, 1988) 8-9.

_____. "New Journalism, Metaphor and Culture." *Journal of Popular Culture* 15 (Spring 1982) 142-49.

_____. "Telling Stories and Making Sense." *Journal of Popular Culture* 15:125-129 (Fall, 1981).

_____. "The Electric Indian." *Partisan Review* 69 (Summer 1969) 535-44.

_____. "Two Exercises in Elegant Minification."*New York Times Book Review (November 29, 1970) 4, 54.*

Edwards, Thomas R. "Low Expectations." *The New York Review of Books.* February 4, 1988, pp. 8-9.

_____. "Two Exercises in Elegant Minification. "*New York Times Book Review* (November 29, 1970) 4, 54.

Eisenberg, Lee. "The Writer in Wolfe's Clothing." *Esquire* (October 1990), 39.

English, John W. "What Professionals Say." *Journal of Popular Culture* 9 (Summer 1975) 233-40.

Epstein, Jason. "Journal du Voyeur." *The New York Review of Books*, December 17, 1970, pp. 3-6.

Epstein, Joseph. "The Party's Over. . ." *Commentary* 51 (March 1971) 98, 100, 102.

Epstein, Joseph. "Tom Wolfe's Vanities." *New Criterion*. 6:5-16 (February 1988).

Fishwick, Marshall, ed. "The New Journalism." *Journal of Popular Culture*, 9:95-249 (Summer 1975).

Gardiner, Stephen. "Faces of the Age: From Garden to Glasscrete." *Encounter* 59 (December 1982) 69.

Gareffa, Peter M., and Mary V. McLeod. "Wolfe, Thomas Kennerly, Jr." *Contemporary Authors*. Mew Revision Series. Detroit, Mich.: Gale Research Company, 1983.

Garrett, George. "Ladies in Boston *Have* their Hats: notes on WASP Humor." *Comic Relief: Humor in contemporary American Literature*. Ed. Sarah Blacher Cohen. Urbana, Ill.: U. of Illinois Press, 1978.

Goldberger, Paul. "An Ear For Buildings." *New York Times Book Review* (October 11, 1981) 1,30-31.

Gorra, Michael. "American Selves." *Hudson Review* 41 (Summer 1988) 401-406.

_____. "Tom Wolfe And The Surfaces Of American Life." *Sewanee Review* 92 (January 1984) 167.

Gray, Paul. "Generation Gaffes." *Time* 108 (December 27, 1976) 62-64.

Grunwald, Lisa. "Tom Wolfe: Aloft in the Status Sphere." *Esquire* (October 1990), 146-152, 154,156,158,160.

Hartshome, Thomas L. "Tom Wolfe on the 1960's." *Midwest Quarterly*, 23:144-163 (1982).

Hellman, John. *Fables of Fact: The New Journalism as New Fiction*. Urbana, Ill,: U. of Illinois Press, 1981.

Hentoff, Margot. "Dr. Pop." *New York Review of Book* 11 (1968) 20-21.

Hess, Thomas B. "The Kamikaze Reporter Settles DownWith His Syntax." *New York Times Book Review* (December 26, 1976) 7, 21.

Hoggart, Richard. "The Dance of the Long-Legged Fly." *Encounter* 27 (1966) 63.

Hollowell, John. *Fact and Fiction: The New Journalism and the Nonfiction Novel*. Chapel Hill, N.C.: U. of North Carolina Press, 1977.

Howe, Irving. "The First Panther She Ever Met." *Harper's Magazine* 242 (February 1971) 104.

Hudson, Christopher. [Review of *Radical Chic & Mau-Mauing the Flak Catchers*.] *Spectator* 227 (October 9, 1971) 518.

Ivester, Stan. "The Latest from the Human Lapsometer," *Chicago Review*, 31:39-45 (Spring 1980).

Johnson, Michael L. *The New Journalism: The Underground Press, the Artists of Nonfiction, and Changes in the Established Media*. Lawrence, Ks.: U. Press of Kansas, 1971.

Kallan, Richard A. "Style and the New Journalism: A Rhetorical Analysis of Tom Wolfe." *Communication Monographs*, 46:52-62 (March 1979).

Kampman, Christina. [Review of *The Right Stuff*.] *Library Journal* 104 (October 15, 1979) 2228.

Kluger, Richard. *The Paper: The Life and Death of the New York "Herald Tribune."* New York: Alfred A. Knopf, 1986.

Lalley, J.M. "Monks of the Acid Theleme." *Modern Age* 13 (Winter 1968-69) 80-83.

Lampton, Michael. [Review of *The Right Stuff.*] *Sky & Telescope* 60 (December 1980) 514-15.

Lehman-Haupt, Christopher. "A Curse on the Theoreticians." *New York Times* 125 (May 27, 1975) 27.

_____. [Review of *The Bonfire Of The Vanities*.] *New York Times* (October 22, 1987) c25.

_____. "The Watershed of Modern Lit?" *New York Times* 122 (1973) 63.

_____. "Tom Wolfe at the Cross-Road." *New York Times* 119 (November 25, 1970) 35.

Lemann, Nicholas. "New York in the Eighties." *The Atlantic Monthly,* December 1987, pp. 104-107. Letters to the Editor. *Harper's,* February 1990, 4-13.

Leonard, John. "Delirious New York." [A review of *The Bonfire Of The Vanities* and *In Search Of New York*.] *Nation* 245 (November 28, 1987) 636-44.

Lewin, Leonard C. "Is Fact Necessary?" *Columbia Journalism Review,* Winter 1966, pp. 29-34.

Lounsberry, Barbara. "Tom Wolfe's Negative Vision." *South Dakota Review* 20:15-31 (Summer 1982).

Lynch, Dennis. [Review of *The Right Stuff*.] *New Republic* 181 (October 20, 1979) 38.

Lynn, Kenneth S. "The Fire This Time." *Commentary* 85 (February 1988)76-79.

Macdonald, Dwight. "Parajournalism, or Tom Wolfe & His Magic Writing Machine." *New York Review of Books* 5 (1965) 3.

_____. "Parajournalism II: Wolfe and The New Yorker." *The New York Review of Books,* February 3, 1966, pp. 18-24.

Mark, Rachel. "Pilots & Astronauts." *Commentary* 69 (February 1980) 85-88.

Michelson, Peter. "Tom Wolfe Overboard." *New Republic* 163 (1970) 17.

Morton, Brian. [Review of *The Bonfire Of The Vanities*.] *Times Educational Supplement* (March 4, 1988) 302.

Posner, Ellen. [Review of *From Bauhaus To Our House*.] *New Republic* 185 (November 18, 1981) 30.

Powers, Thomas." Wolfe in Orbit: Our Mercurial Interest." *Commonweal,* October 12, 1979, pp. 551-552.

Pygge, Edward. [Review of *Mauve Gloves & Madmen, Clutter & Vine*.] *New Statesman* 93 (March 13, 1977) 647.

Quinn, Peter A. "'Eggh, whaddaya? Whaddaya want from me?'"*America* 158 (April 2, 1988) 363-64.

Rabinowitz, Dorothy. "Satire and Beyond." *Commentary* 63 (May 1977) 76,78.

Rafferty, Terrence. "The Man Who Knew Too Much." *New Yorker* 63 (February 1, 1988) 88.

Reese, Thomas J. [Review of *From Bauhaus To Our House*.] *America* 146 (March 27, 1982) 245.

[Review of *From Bauhaus To Our House*.] *Business Week* (November 2, 1981) 20.

[Review of *From Bauhaus To Our House*.] *Commonweal* 108 (December 4, 1981) 696.

[Review of *From Bauhaus To Our House*.] *Library Journal* 106 (November 1, 1981) 2130.

[Review of *From Bauhaus To Our House*.] *New York Times Book Review* 87 (December 5, 1982) 71.

[Review of *From Bauhaus To Our House*.] *Publishers Weekly* 222 (September 11, 1981) 61.

[Review of *Radical Chic & Mau-Mauing the Flak Catchers*.] *Horn Book Magazine* 47 (February 1971) 74.

[Review of *The New Journalism* and *Fear and Loathing*.] *Atlantic* 232 (July 1973) 99.

[Review of *The New Journalism*.] *Choice* 10 (November 1973) 1326.

[Review of *The New Journalism*.] *Horn Book Magazine* 49 (December 1973) 616.

[Review of *The Pump House Gang*.] *America* 119 (1968) 136.

[Review of *The Purple Decades: A Reader*.] *Christian Science Monitor* 75 (February 2, 1983) 15.

[Review of *The Purple Decades: A Reader*.] *Publishers Weekly* 222 (September 24, 1982) 64.

[Review of *The Right Stuff*.] *Atlantic* 244 (October 1979) 107.

[Review of *The Right Stuff*.] *English Journal* 69 (September 1980) 80.

[Review of *The Right Stuff*.] *Horn Book Magazine* 56 (February 1980) 93.

[Review of *The Right Stuff*.] *Publishers Weekly* 210 (August 13, 1979) 54.

[Review of *The Right Stuff*.] *Virginia Quarterly Review* 56 (Winter 1980) 16.

Rich, Frank. "The Right-Wing Stuff." *New Republic* 197 (November 23, 1987) 42, 44-46.

Richardson, Jack. "New Fundamentalist Movement." *The New Republic* 159 (1968) 30, 34-35.

Rose, Barbara. "Wolfeburg." *The New York Review of Books*, June 26, 1975, pp. 26-28.

Ross, Charles S. "The Rhetoric of the Right Stuff." *The Journal of General Education*, 33:113-122 (1981).

Russell, John. [Review of *The Painted Word*.] *New York Times Book Review* (June 15, 1975) 4-5.

Sanoff, Alvin P. "Tom Wolfe's Walk on the Wild Side." *U.S. News & World Report* (November 23, 1987) 57-58.

Scholes, Robert. "Double Perspective on Hysteria." *Saturday Review* 51 (August 24, 1968) 37.

Schraer, Dexter. "Recommended: Tom Wolfe." *English Journal* 70 (December 1981)49-50.

Seelye, John. "The Shotgun Behind the Lens." *New Republic* 168 (August 11, 1973) 22-24.

Sellers, Pat. "*Cosmo* Talks To Tom Wolfe: Savvy Social Seer." *Cosmopolitan* (April 1988).

Shah, Diane K. "It's. . .Guess Who!" *National Observer* 10 (1971) 21.

Shapiro, Karl. "Tom Wolfe: Analyst of the [fill it in] Generation." *Book World* (August 18, 1968) 1.

Sheed, Wilfrid. "A Fun-House Mirror." *The New York Times Book Review,* December 3, 1972, pp. 2, 10-12.

Sheldrick, Michael G. "The First Astronauts: They Had What It Took." *Business Week* (October 15, 1979) 10, 11, 14, 18.

Sheppard, R.Z. "The Haves and the Have-Mores." *Time* 130 (November 9, 1987) 101, 104.

Simonds, C. H. "Popcult Orgy." *National Review* 17 (1965) 989.

Sobran, Joseph. "Case Closed." *National Review* 33 (November 27, 1981) 1426-27.

Sommer, Robert. "Tom And Erving Visited Las Vegas: New Journalism and New Sociology Compared." *Journal of Popular Culture* 9 (Summer 1975) 241-46.

_____. "Tom Wolfe on Modern Architecture: Further Comparison of New Journalism and Social Science." *Journal of Popular Culture* 18 (Fall 1984) 111-15.

Sorkin, Michael. "Wolfe at the Door." *Nation* 233 (October 31, 1981) 445-46.

Stark, Steven D. [Review of *The Painted Word.*] *Progressive* 39 (October 1975) 60.

Stone, Laurie. "Spaced Out." *The Village Voice,* September 10, 1979, pp. 71, 73, 76.

Tanner, Tony. *City of Words: American Fiction 1950-1970.* New York: Harper & Row, 1971.

"Tom Wolfe and His Electric Wordmobiles." *Time* 98 (September 6, 1968) 98-99.

Tuchman, Mitch. "The Writings of Tom Wolfe: The Manchurian Candidate." *The New Republic,* October 25, 1975, pp. 21-24.

Van Dellen, Robert J. "We've Been Had By The New Journalism: A Put Down." *Journal of Popular Culture* 9 (Summer 1975) 218-31.

Vanderbilt, Kermit. "Writers of the Troubled Sixties." *Nation* 217 (1973) 661-65.

Vigilante, Richard. "The Truth About Tom Wolfe." *National Review,* December 18, 1987, pp. 46, 48-49.

Weber, Ronald. ed. *The Reporter as Artist: A Look at the New Journalism Controversy.* New York: Hastings House, 1974.

_____. *The Literature of Fact: Literary Nonfiction in Americn Writings.* Athens, Ohio: U. of Ohio Press, 1980.

_____. "Staying Power." *Virginia Quarterly Review,* 59:548-552 (1983).

_____. "Tom Wolfe's Happiness Explosion." *Journal of Popular Culture* 8 (Summer 1974) 70-79.

Williamson, Chilton Jr. "The Good Stuff." *National Review* 31 (November 9, 1979) 1436, 1438.

_____. "The Intelligent Co-ed's Guide to Tom Wolfe." *National Review* 29 (February 18, 1977) 212, 214-16.

_____. [Review of *From Bauhaus To Our House.*] *Esquire* 96 (December 1981) 19.

Wolcott, James. "Tom Wolfe's Greatest Hits." *New York Review of Books* 29 (November 4, 1982) 21-22.

Weirather, Larry. "Tom Wolfe's Snake River Canyon Jump." *Journal of Popular Culture* 9 (Summer 1975) 211-17.

Williams, David. [Review of *Mauve Gloves & Madmen, Clutter & Vine.*] *Punch* 274 (March 29, 1978) 544.

Wood, Michael. "His Job is to Hide His Opinions." *New York Times Book Review* (July 22, 1973) 20-21.

Yagoda, Ben. "Astronauts and Other Icons of Pop Culture." *Books and Arts,* September 28, 1979, pp. 14-15.

Zalenko, Barbara. [Review of *The New Journalism.*] *Library Journal* 98 (May 1, 1973) 1479.

Zavaradeh, Mas'ud. *The Mythopoetic Reality: The Postwar American Nonfiction Novel.* Urbana, Ill.: U. of Illinois Press, 1976.

Interviews

Bellamy, Joe David. "Tom Wolfe." In *New Fiction: Interviews with Innovative American Writers.* Urbana, Ill.: U. of Illinois Press, 1974, pp. 75-96.

Blue, Adrianne. "The Earthling and the Astronauts." *Washington Post Book World* 9(September 9, 1979) 1. Also above.

Buckley, William F., Jr. "Tom Wolfe and the Painted Word." (An interview taped on *Firing Line* on July 19, 1975). Also above.

Hayman, Ronald. "Tom Wolfe in Interview." *Books and Bookmen.* 25:29-31 (November 1979).

Mewborn, Brant. "Tom Wolfe: Sixties Youth Culture Broke Down the Walls Between People of Different Status." *Rolling Stone* (November 5, 1987).

Monaghan, Charles. "Portrait of a Man Reading." *Washington Post Book World,* September 1, 1968, p. 2.

Sanoff, Alvin P. "Tom Wolfe's Walk on the Wild Side." *U.S. News & World Report* (November 23, 1987) 57-58. Also above.

Scura, Dorothy M., ed. *Conversations with Tom Wolfe.* Jackson, Ms., and London: U. Press of Mississippi, 1990.

Index

About the Editor

DOUG SHOMETTE, a special agent with the United States Department of Veteran Affairs in Dallas, Texas, is enrolled in a Ph.D. program in literature at the University of North Texas. He is working on a similar volume on the critical response to John Gardner.